VOLUME 520

MARCH 1992

THE ANNALS

of The American Academy *of* Political
and Social Science

RICHARD D. LAMBERT, *Editor*
ALAN W. HESTON, *Associate Editor*

WORLD LITERACY IN THE YEAR 2000

Special Editors of this Volume

DANIEL A. WAGNER
LAUREL D. PUCHNER

Literacy Research Center
University of Pennsylvania
Philadelphia

Ⓢ SAGE PUBLICATIONS   *NEWBURY PARK   LONDON   NEW DELHI*

THE ANNALS
© 1991 *by* The American Academy *of* Political *and* Social Science

Editorial Office: 3937 Chestnut Street, Philadelphia, PA 19104.

For information about membership* (individuals only) and subscriptions (institutions), address:

SAGE PUBLICATIONS, INC.
2455 Teller Road
Newbury Park, CA 91320

From India and South Asia,
write to:
SAGE PUBLICATIONS INDIA Pvt. Ltd.
P.O. Box 4215
New Delhi 110 048
INDIA

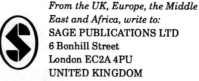

From the UK, Europe, the Middle
East and Africa, write to:
SAGE PUBLICATIONS LTD
6 Bonhill Street
London EC2A 4PU
UNITED KINGDOM

SAGE Production Staff: LINDA GRAY, LIANN LECH, and JANELLE LeMASTER
*Please note that members of The Academy receive THE ANNALS with their membership.
Library of Congress Catalog Card Number 91-61243
International Standard Serial Number ISSN 0002-7162
International Standard Book Number ISBN 0-8039-4479-9 (Vol. 520, 1992 paper)
International Standard Book Number ISBN 0-8039-4478-0 (Vol. 520, 1992 cloth)
Manufactured in the United States of America. First printing, March 1992.

The articles appearing in THE ANNALS are indexed in *Book Review Index, Public Affairs Information Service Bulletin, Social Sciences Index, Current Contents, General Periodicals Index, Academic Index, Pro-Views,* and *Combined Retrospective Index Sets.* They are also abstracted and indexed in *ABC Pol Sci, Historical Abstracts, Human Resources Abstracts, Social Sciences Citation Index, United States Political Science Documents, Social Work Research & Abstracts, Sage Urban Studies Abstracts, International Political Science Abstracts, America: History and Life, Sociological Abstracts, Managing Abstracts, Social Planning/Policy & Development Abstracts, Automatic Subject Citation Alert, Book Review Digest, Work Related Abstracts,* and/or *Family Resources Database,* and are available on microfilm from University Microfilms, Ann Arbor, Michigan.

Information about membership rates, institutional subscriptions, and back issue prices may be found on the facing page.

Advertising. Current rates and specifications may be obtained by writing to THE ANNALS Advertising and Promotion Manager at the Newbury Park office (address above).

Claims. Claims for undelivered copies must be made no later than three months following month of publication. The publisher will supply missing copies when losses have been sustained in transit and when the reserve stock will permit.

Change of Address. Six weeks' advance notice must be given when notifying of change of address to ensure proper identification. Please specify name of journal. Send address changes to: THE ANNALS, c/o Sage Publications, Inc., 2455 Teller Road, Newbury Park, CA 91320.

The American Academy of Political and Social Science

3937 Chestnut Street Philadelphia, Pennsylvania 19104

Origin and Purpose. The Academy was organized December 14, 1889, to promote the progress of political and social science, especially through publications and meetings. The Academy does not take sides in controverted questions, but seeks to gather and present reliable information to assist the public in forming an intelligent and accurate judgment.

Meetings. The Academy occasionally holds a meeting in the spring extending over two days.

Publications. THE ANNALS is the bimonthly publication of The Academy. Each issue contains articles on some prominent social or political problem, written at the invitation of the editors. Also, monographs are published from time to time, numbers of which are distributed to pertinent professional organizations. These volumes constitute important reference works on the topics with which they deal, and they are extensively cited by authorities throughout the United States and abroad. The papers presented at the meetings of The Academy are included in THE ANNALS.

Membership. Each member of The Academy receives THE ANNALS and may attend the meetings of The Academy. Membership is open only to individuals. Annual dues: $39.00 for the regular paperbound edition (clothbound, $54.00). California residents must add 7.25% sales tax on all orders ($41.82 paperbound; $57.91 clothbound). Add $9.00 per year for membership outside the U.S.A. Members may also purchase single issues of THE ANNALS for $12.00 each (clothbound, $17.00). California residents: $12.87 paperbound, $18.23 clothbound. Add $1.50 for shipping and handling on all prepaid orders.

Subscriptions. THE ANNALS (ISSN 0002-7162) is published six times annually—in January, March, May, July, September, and November. Institutions may subscribe to THE ANNALS at the annual rate: $120.00 (clothbound, $144.00). California institutions: $128.70 paperbound, $155.44 clothbound. Add $9.00 per year for subscriptions outside the U.S.A. Institutional rates for single issues: $23.00 each (clothbound, $28.00). California institutions: $24.66 paperbound, $30.03 clothbound.

Second class postage paid at Thousand Oaks, California, and at additional mailing offices.

Single issues of THE ANNALS may be obtained by individuals who are not members of The Academy for $15.95 each (clothbound, $25.00). California residents: $17.10 paperbound, $26.81 clothbound. Add $1.50 for shipping and handling on all prepaid orders. Single issues of THE ANNALS have proven to be excellent supplementary texts for classroom use. Direct inquiries regarding adoptions to THE ANNALS c/o Sage Publications (address below).

All correspondence concerning membership in The Academy, dues renewals, inquiries about membership status, and/or purchase of single issues of THE ANNALS should be sent to THE ANNALS c/o Sage Publications, Inc., 2455 Teller Road, Newbury Park, CA 91320. Telephone: (805) 499-0721; FAX/Order line: (805) 499-0871. *Please note that orders under $30 must be prepaid.* Sage affiliates in London and India will assist institutional subscribers abroad with regard to orders, claims, and inquiries for both subscriptions and single issues.

THE ANNALS

of The American Academy *of* Political
and Social Science

RICHARD D. LAMBERT, *Editor*
ALAN W. HESTON, *Associate Editor*

——————————— **FORTHCOMING** ———————————

DRUG ABUSE: LINKING POLICY AND RESEARCH
Special Editor: Eric Wish

Volume 521   May 1992

THE FUTURE: TRENDS INTO
THE TWENTY-FIRST CENTURY
Special Editors: Joseph F. Coates and Jennifer Jarratt

Volume 522   July 1992

AFFIRMATIVE ACTION REVISITED
Special Editors: Harold Orlans and June O'Neill

Volume 523   September 1992

See page 3 for information on Academy membership and
purchase of single volumes of **The Annals.**

CONTENTS

BOOK DEPARTMENT CONTENTS

SOCIOLOGY

ECONOMICS

FOREWORD

The conference "World Literacy in the Year 2000: Research and Policy Dimensions," from which this volume of *The Annals* is derived, brought together more than sixty literacy specialists and policymakers from around the world for four days of debate, conversation, and dialogue. Many topics were explored, as amply demonstrated in the following articles. Plans for future collaborations were made, some of which have already begun to bear fruit. Fortuitously, it was during the conference that the U.S. Department of Education officially announced the establishment of the U.S. National Center on Adult Literacy at the University of Pennsylvania, a research and development effort aimed at many of the very questions raised by the conferees. The conference, held in October 1990 at the University of Pennsylvania, was cosponsored by the U.S. Department of State, the United Nations Educational, Scientific, and Cultural Organization, the United Nations Children's Fund, the International Development Research Centre, the Swedish International Development Agency, the Carnegie Corporation, and the James S. McDonnell Foundation. Support for the editing of this volume was provided in part by the Carnegie Corporation and the U.S. Department of Education (Grant No. R117Q00003).

DANIEL A. WAGNER
LAUREL D. PUCHNER

PREFACE

The set of research papers on literacy in this issue of *The Annals* may come as an eye-opener to many academic social scientists who for years have been pleased to leave the perplexing problems of literacy to elementary school teachers and adult literacy experts.

Because of this lack of acknowledgment of the importance of literacy, for more than thirty years this orphan field was largely devoid of serious research that could be useful for formulating effective policies and programs. Instead, literacy policies were heavily influenced, especially at the international level and throughout the developing world, by an emotion-packed "literacy doctrine" that emerged full blown in the 1950s and swept across the world like a new universal religion. The United Nations Educational, Scientific, and Cultural Organization (UNESCO) led the movement and periodically revived and invoked with enthusiasm the clearly unrealistic goal of "eradicating illiteracy from the world by the end of the decade." But at the end of each decade the absolute number of illiterates, by UNESCO's own calculation, had actually increased—though the estimated percentage of illiterates had declined somewhat.

The past few years, however, have seen an encouraging wave of fresh research on literacy, which, though still limited, has already brought about a broader perception of literacy as viewed by more and more policymakers and program planners. The articles contained in this issue of *The Annals* are representative of this promising new wave of research. They were prepared by well-qualified researchers from all major regions of the world for a unique international conference, "World Literacy in the Year 2000," hosted by the University of Pennsylvania's Literacy Research Center in Philadelphia in October 1990.

The conference served both as a timely celebration of the 1990 U.N. International Literacy Year and as a practical follow-up to the highly successful "World Conference on Education for All: Meeting Basic Learning Needs," convened in Jomtien, Thailand, in March 1990 under the joint sponsorship of UNESCO, the United Nations Children's Fund, the United Nations Development Programme, and the World Bank.

The key papers from the Philadelphia conference focus on six practical themes of importance to literacy policymakers, planners, and program managers, of which a good number were present in Philadelphia to dialogue with the researchers. These themes are research and policy dimensions; targeting literacy efforts; women and literacy; language and literacy; contrasts in literacy between industrialized and developing countries; and health and literacy, all of which are well represented in this *Annals* volume.

The theme papers were discussed in plenary sessions, then echoed in a series of smaller "country roundtables" that examined the practical experiences of a wide variety of countries. These experiences were presented by experts from such countries as Tanzania, Botswana, Chile, China, Jamaica, Indonesia, Canada, and Hungary.

There is not room in this brief preface to discuss the many fascinating substantive points that emerged from the papers and discussions of the conference, but perhaps the following brief appetizers will help entice readers to read the papers themselves.

1. There is a well-documented connection between the literacy levels of women, the size of their families, and the mortality and nutritional status of their children. Unhappily, however, two-thirds of all illiterate adults in the developing world are females, thus minimizing these positive consequences.

2. Recent studies in several of the most highly developed and highly educated nations have revealed a shocking number of functionally illiterate adults, most of whom acquired school literacy but are unable to read a bus or railroad timetable, comprehend their monthly credit card and bank statements, or follow the instructions for filling out their tax return. There are, for example, an estimated 30 million such functionally illiterate adults in North America alone. Moreover, the more sophisticated the information and communications technologies become in these advanced countries, the higher the rate of functional illiteracy will become.

3. Multilingual countries such as India, China, and Nigeria have far greater difficulty spreading literacy through the schools, the mass media, and other means. Nigeria, to cite a relatively extreme case, has more than 400 living languages. The majority of these, however, are not written. Only 19 are sufficiently standardized and utilized to warrant their use for radio and television broadcasts—only three, in fact, dominate the air waves—or in the print media, or as official languages—locally, regionally, or nationally. Yet all 19 are used in local areas as the medium of elementary education. Canada and Belgium, with their bilingual situation, have it easy!

This new venture into literacy research and development is an encouraging beginning, for there can be no doubt that literacy is crucially important in all societies and needs to be guided by something better than emotional enthusiasm. The articles in this volume cover many diverse but crucial facets of the subject of literacy and should act as a vital source of insight and knowledge about literacy and the various issues that surround it.

PHILIP H. COOMBS

Philip Coombs is chairman and director of strategy studies of the International Council for Educational Development, based in Essex, Connecticut. Previously he was founding director of UNESCO's International Institute for Educational Planning in Paris, assistant secretary of state for international educational and cultural affairs under President John F. Kennedy, and program director for education of the Ford Foundation. He has taught at numerous American universities and has more recently been a visiting professor at the University of London and Beijing Normal University in China.

ANNALS, *AAPSS*, 520, March 1992

World Literacy:
Research and Policy in the EFA Decade

By DANIEL A. WAGNER

ABSTRACT: This article reviews research on literacy and makes some educated guesses about literacy research and policy in the current decade and beyond. Issues addressed include defining literacy, literacy acquisition, retention of literacy, and consequences of literacy. The article concludes with some suggestions on future literacy programs in the 1990s, the EFA decade.

Daniel A. Wagner is professor of education and director of the Literacy Research Center at the University of Pennsylvania. He also directs the National Center on Adult Literacy, under the auspices of the U.S. Department of Education. Dr. Wagner has extensive experience in national and international educational issues and has served as an adviser to the U.S. Department of Education, the U.S. Agency for International Development, the United Nations Children's Fund, the United Nations Educational, Scientific, and Cultural Organization, and the World Bank.

NOTE: Support for the writing of this article was provided in part by the U.S. Department of Education (Grant No. R117Q00003). Parts of this article appeared in a special issue of *Literacy Lessons*, a publication of the International Bureau of Education, United Nations Educational, Scientific, and Cultural Organization, Geneva, in conjunction with the International Literacy Year, 1990.

WHEN the word "research" is affixed to a topic of public concern or policy, there is sometimes a reaction of "let's get on with the job" and there is a reluctance to "waste" time and resources on more "studies that lead nowhere." This kind of sentiment is strongly manifested in the field of literacy work. The problems associated with illiteracy and low literacy exist on such a vast scale that we may be tempted to commit all available resources to reaching out to the needy. While such a reaction is understandable, it is unlikely that this way of thinking will be as useful as its advocates might suggest. Indeed, social programs in the twentieth century have been fraught with failure or at least with low rates of success. Reaction to such results often leads, in turn, to a cutoff of funds because a given social program "didn't work well" and to a tendency to move on to a completely new approach to the social problem.

The effort to reduce illiteracy is no exception. While we are beginning to better understand the causes and consequences of literacy and illiteracy, there is much more that needs to be known. Since there exists a great variety of literacy programs for an even larger number of sociocultural contexts, it should come as no surprise that the effectiveness of literacy programs has come under question, not only by policymakers and specialists but also by the larger public. How effective are literacy campaigns? What is the importance of political and ideological commitment? Should writing and reading be taught together or separately? Should literacy programs include numeracy as well?

Is literacy retained following a limited number of years of primary schooling or short-term campaigns? How important is literacy for the workplace? Is it important to teach literacy in the individual's mother tongue? These and similar questions—so central to the core of literacy work around the world—remain without definitive answers, in spite of the occasionally strong rhetoric in support of one position or another. Basic and applied research, along with effective program evaluation, are capable of providing critical information that will not only lead to greater efficiency in particular literacy programs but will also lead to greater public support of literacy programs in these contemporary times of economic constraints.

In the following sections, I would like to review what research on literacy can tell us from the past and the present, and make some educated guesses about literacy and research in the coming decade and beyond. I will conclude with some thoughts and practical suggestions on future adult literacy programs in what I call the EFA decade, the period following the United Nations-sponsored 1990 World Conference on Education for All (EFA) in Jomtien, Thailand.

WHAT LITERACY RESEARCH TELLS US ABOUT PREMODERN TIMES

While a complete review of the history of literacy is well beyond the scope of this short discussion, it is useful to highlight some areas of relevance. Turning points in the production of literate materials—from the

Dead Sea Scrolls to the Gutenberg Bible to the word processor—have served as important markers of social and cultural change. Conversely, historical changes in society have played major roles in the popular use of literate materials, as evidenced, for example, by the need of thirteenth-century British landlords to control the intergenerational transfer of property through legal documents and by the rise of mass public education in nineteenth-century France. What is most impressive in historical accounts of literacy is the importance that reading and writing—often as separate activities—have been given over the centuries. That clergymen of many of the world's great religions were also the possessors of one or both of these skills signifies not only the sometimes restricted nature of literacy but its social and moral power as well.[1] Clearly, what might be termed religious literacy was the predominant form of reading and writing activity before the time of the ancient Greeks and through the Middle Ages. The history of literacy parallels and has been implicated in many of the great changes in social history, such as religion, public schooling, the establishment of democracy, and even social—and socialist—revolutions.

Research indicates that literacy was often transmitted and used outside of what we now call formal schooling. For example, as early as the sixteenth century, reading was widespread in Sweden as a function of family efforts to read the Bible at home. In nineteenth-century Liberia, the Vai people created an indigenous script and have used it ever since for economic and personal written communication. Likewise, the Native American Cree of northern Canada maintain the use of their syllabic script as a source of cultural identity.

Recent efforts to link the rise of mass literacy with economic development during the industrial revolution in Europe and in later decades has become a matter of increasing debate within the research community. It has long been accepted that the rise in literacy and educational levels were basic causes of economic growth. Current research seems to contradict such an assertion by demonstrating that some countries, such as Sweden, had high literacy rates well before the industrial revolution. Conversely, Great Britain had rather low rates of literacy even during periods of rapid economic growth, and increased education and literacy were made possible by the growth of technology, which provided more time for the schooling of children.[2]

Mass literacy programs or campaigns have also been a focus of renewed historical inquiry. For example, the Soviet literacy campaign, which became well-known in the postrevolutionary period, actually began with the so-called peasant initiative in the 1860s. The popularity of literacy classes increased to the extent that, by the 1890s, literacy classes had become more widely available than

1. Cf. Jack Goody, *Literacy in Traditional Societies* (New York: Cambridge University Press, 1968).

2. Michael T. Clanchy, *From Memory to Written Record* (Cambridge, MA: Harvard University Press, 1979).

public schooling, "prompting widespread fear in educated circles about the untoward consequences of unschooled literacy."[3] We see in such reports that prerevolutionary Russia was making important gains in reducing illiteracy well before the famous 1919 Decree of Illiteracy, which required all citizens from age 8 to 50 to become literate. From the Soviet case, we are now beginning to understand that literacy campaigns never take place in cultural and historical isolation. Even prerevolutionary China, where literacy rates were thought to be extremely low, had its popular education movements as well as orthographic reformers long before its contemporary mass campaigns. Recent research suggests that perhaps 30-45 percent of men were literate and up to 10 percent of women, far above the literacy rates that were thought to be extant in traditional China.

Literacy in a historical perspective can tell us a great deal about the causes and consequences of the written word and can help us to avoid some of the pitfalls that continue to hamper literacy work in the present.

WHAT WE KNOW
ABOUT LITERACY IN
CONTEMPORARY TIMES

One of the key differences between historical and present-day research is that the former resides primarily in an old and sometimes unreliable or occasionally biased written record,

while the latter is much easier to reconfirm by conducting new research. Of course, nothing prevents a contemporary piece of research from being inaccurate, unreliable, or biased; however, other researchers have a much better chance of determining credibility in the present than researchers did in the past. In addition, the sheer volume of social science research on literacy has grown tremendously over the past several decades. A great many new books and journals have appeared, sometimes to the distress of the interested observer, who will find that literacy is now dealt with by specialists who might focus their efforts uniquely on spelling, on campaigns, on alphabetic reform, on computer word processing, and so forth. Specialization is a sign that a field of inquiry has come of age, and there is no longer any doubt that literacy has come of age.

Within this increased context of specialization, how might we think about key topics in literacy research? I would like to list four general domains in literacy work with a brief description of the nature of the problem and how research has led to improved understanding. These are issues, I believe, that are likely to be the subject of greater attention in the 1990s, issues that will determine to a large extent whether we are successful at improving global literacy.

Defining and
redefining literacy

With the multitude of experts and published books on the topic, one would suppose that there would be a fair amount of agreement as to how

3. Robert F. Arnove and Harvey J. Graff, eds., *National Literacy Campaigns: Historical and Comparative Aspects* (New York: Plenum Press, 1987), p. 126.

to define the term "literacy." On one hand, most specialists would agree that the term denotes aspects of reading and writing; on the other hand, major debates continue to revolve around such issues as what specific abilities or knowledge count as literacy and what levels can and should be defined for measurement. Thus the United Nations Educational, Scientific, and Cultural Organization (UNESCO) has often used the term "functional literacy," as originally defined by Gray: "A person is functionally literate when he has acquired the knowledge and skills in reading and writing which enable him to engage effectively in all those activities in which literacy is normally assumed in his culture or group."[4]

While functional literacy has a great deal of appeal because of its implied adaptability to a given cultural context, the term can be very awkward for research purposes. For example, it is unclear what level of literacy should be required of all citizens in an industrialized nation like Great Britain. Does a coal miner have different needs from those of a barrister? Similarly, in a Third World country, does an illiterate woman need to learn to read and write in order to take her prescribed medicine correctly, or is it more functional— and cost-effective—to have her school-going son read the instructions to her? The use of the term "functionality," based on norms of a given society, is inadequate precisely because adequate norms are so difficult to establish.

What might, then, be an adequate definition of literacy for today's world? One reasonable approach is the following:

Literacy is a characteristic acquired by individuals in varying degrees from just above none to an indeterminate upper level. Some individuals are more or less literate than others, but it is really not possible to speak of literate and illiterate persons as two distinct categories.[5]

Since there exist dozens of orthographies for hundreds of languages in which innumerable context-specific styles are in use every day, it would seem ill-advised to select a universal operational definition. Attempts to use newspaper-reading skills as a baseline may seriously underestimate literacy if the emphasis is on comprehension of text, especially if the text is in a national language not well understood by the individual. Such tests may overestimate literacy if the individual, as is often the case, is asked simply to read the passage aloud, with little or no attempt at the measurement of comprehension. Surprisingly, there have been relatively few attempts to design a battery of tests that would measure from low literacy ability to high literacy ability and that would be applicable across the complete range of possible languages and literacies in any society, such that a continuum of measurement possibilities might be achieved.

4. William S. Gray, *The Teaching of Reading and Writing* (Paris: United Nations Educational, Scientific, and Cultural Organization, 1956), p. 19.

5. United Nations Educational, Scientific, and Cultural Organization, *World Literacy at Mid-Century* (Paris: United Nations Educational, Scientific, and Cultural Organization, 1957), p. 18.

UNESCO, which provides worldwide statistical comparisons of literacy, relies almost entirely on data provided by its member countries; these, in turn, are based on national census information, where literacy ability is usually measured by self-assessment questionnaires or the number of years of primary schooling. Many specialists would agree that such measures would be unreliable or invalid indicators of real literacy ability.

At least part of the controversy over the definition of literacy lies in how people have attempted to study literacy in the first place. The methodologies chosen, which span the social sciences, usually reflect the disciplinary training of the investigator. Thus we find that anthropologists provide in-depth ethnographic accounts of single communities, while trying to understand how literacy is woven into the fabric of community cultural life. Little or no attempt is made at quantifying levels of particular literacy abilities. By contrast, psychologists and educators have typically chosen to study measurable literacy abilities using tests and questionnaires. While anthropologists primarily use qualitative description to construct a persuasive argument, psychologists tend to use inferential statistics to substantiate claims beyond a numerical level of uncertainty. Both these approaches—as well as those based in history, linguistics, sociology, and computer science—have value in helping us to understand literacy. It often seems, however, that the typical divisions that separate the disciplines from one another make it difficult, in the single domain of literacy, for agree-

ment to be achieved. There is no easy resolution to this problem, but it is clear that a broad-based conception of literacy is required not only for a valid understanding of the term, but also for developing appropriate policy actions.[6]

Because literacy is a cultural phenomenon—adequately defined and understood only within each culture in which it exists—it is not surprising that definitions of literacy may never be permanently fixed. Whether literacy includes computer skills, mental arithmetic, or civic responsibility will depend on how the public and political leaders of each society define this most basic of basic skills. Researchers can help in this effort by trying to be clear about which definition or definitions they choose to employ in their work.

Acquisition of literacy

The study of literacy acquisition appears to be heavily influenced by research undertaken in the industrialized world. Much of this research might be better termed the acquisition of reading and writing skills, with an emphasis on the relationship between cognitive skills, such as perception and memory, and reading skills, such as decoding and comprehension. Most of this work has been carried out with school-age children, rather than with adolescents or adults. Surprisingly little research on literacy acquisition has been undertaken in the Third World, and

6. Richard L. Venezky, Daniel A. Wagner, and Barrie Ciliberti, eds., *Toward Defining Literacy* (Newark, DE: International Reading Association, 1990).

most has typically focused on adult acquisition rather than on children's learning to read. This latter phenomenon appears to be a result of the emphasis by Western and international organizations to promote adult literacy in the developing world, while usually ignoring such problems in Western societies.

Despite these gaps in the research literature, some synthetic statements may be proposed as to how literacy is acquired across different societies. Almost two decades ago, Downing published *Comparative Reading*, which surveyed the acquisition of reading skills across different languages and different orthographies.[7] We know that mastery of the spoken language is a typical prerequisite for fluent reading comprehension in that language, though there exist many exceptions. For example, some Islamic scholars can read and interpret the Koran, even though they cannot speak classical Arabic, the language in which the Koran is written; and, of course, many individuals can read and write languages that they may not speak fluently.

A consensus on the issue of reading abilities is important, since there are also those who would suggest that literacy is more like language in the sense that, while specific abilities do not need to be learned, the individual must be able to interact with a literate environment in order to acquire literacy. This latter approach stems in part from the popular perception of a high correlation between literacy in parents and literacy in their children. It is likely that literate parents provide a variety of opportunities for children to learn to read, including reading practice but also better schools, more textbooks, and the attitudes and values that help children learn in school. In the Third World, however, we know that many parents are illiterate, and yet their children nevertheless may learn how to read and write in school. Nonetheless, recent research on literacy acquisition in children also stresses the impact of early preschool language and literacy skills on subsequent learning. In both the industrialized and developing countries, research has shown that parents who provide such stimulating learning environments for their children—including activities like storybook reading—have produced children with considerably better reading achievement in school.

In a different research approach, some specialists have stressed the importance of class structure and ethnicity/race as explications of differential motivation among young literacy learners. Ogbu, for example, claims that many minority children in America—constituting what is sometimes called the "Fourth World"— are simply unmotivated to learn to read and write in the cultural structure of the school.[8] This approach to understanding social and cultural differences in literacy and school achievement has received increased attention in that it avoids blaming

7. John Downing, *Comparative Reading* (New York: Macmillan, 1973).

8. John U. Ogbu, "Literacy in Subordinate Cultures: The Case of Black Americans" (Paper delivered at the Literacy Conference of the Library of Congress, Washington, DC, 1980).

the child for specific cognitive deficits, while focusing attention more on changes in the social and political structure of schooling. While such a view has been making some progress among Third World social scientists, little psychometric research has been carried out on reading acquisition in the Third World that would substantiate its claims.

Finally, and until fairly recently, it has been assumed that learning to read in one's mother tongue or first language is always the best educational policy for literacy provision, whether for children or adults. Based on some important research studies undertaken in the 1960s, it has generally been assumed that individuals who have had to learn to read in a second language are at a serious disadvantage relative to others who learn in their mother tongue. While this generalization may still be true in many of the world's multilingual societies, more recent research has shown that there may be important exceptions. In one such study, it was found that Berber-speaking children in fifth grade who had to learn to read in standard Arabic in Moroccan schools were able to read just as well as children who were native speakers of Arabic.[9] Adequate research on nonliterate adults who learn to read in a second versus a first language has yet to be undertaken.

In sum, considerable progress has been made in understanding the ac-

9. For more details, see Daniel A. Wagner, Jennifer E. Spratt, and Abdelkader Ezzaki, "Does Learning to Read in a Second Language Always Put the Child at a Disadvantage? Some Counter-Evidence from Morocco," *Applied Psycholinguistics*, 10:31-48 (1989).

quisition of literacy in children and adults, but primarily in industrialized societies. Far less is known about literacy acquisition in a truly global perspective and in multilingual societies. Since the bulk of nonliterate people live in these areas of the world, there is much more that needs to be known if we are to improve literacy provision in the coming decades.

Retention of literacy

The term "educational wastage" is common in the literature on international and comparative education, particularly with respect to the Third World. This term typically refers to the loss, usually by dropping out, of children who do not finish what is thought to be the minimum educational curriculum of a given country, which, often, is 5-8 years of primary school. Most specialists who work within this area gather data on the number of children who enter school each year, the number who progress to the next grade, those who repeat a given year—quite a common occurrence in many Third World countries—and those who quit school altogether. The concept of wastage, then, refers to those children for whom an economic investment in educational resources has already been made but who, literally, waste that investment by not completing the appropriate level of studies.

The issue of literacy retention is crucial here, for it is not actually the number of school leavers or graduates that really matters for a society but, rather, what they learn and retain from their school years, such as literacy skills. When students drop out of an educational program, a society is wasting its resources because those individuals—children, or adults, if the program is in adult education—will not reach some presumed threshold of minimum learning such that what has been acquired will not be lost. Thus retention of learning—or of literacy, in particular—is a key goal of educational planners around the world. There are so far only a small number of research studies published on this question, and their results are highly contradictory. Some show that there is a relapse into illiteracy for those who have not received sufficient instruction, while others demonstrate no serious loss. As yet, there is so much variability in these studies that we can conclude very little about what might be termed the trajectory of literacy ability, once literacy has been acquired to varying degrees. Retention is as complex a topic as acquisition because the same sorts of localized societal and cognitive factors intervene in the retention process. What are the effects of practice on literacy ability? What type of materials, what type of motivation, and how many years are required to retain fluent or partially fluent reading and writing? What types of schools and programs are needed for this retention to take place? Do short-term campaigns have the same retention effects as the longer-term process of formal schooling? Such questions provide a rich and important area of inquiry, and one that will be essential as ever greater numbers of children and adults receive modest levels of literacy as governments move toward universalization of basic education for all citizens.

Individual and social consequences of literacy

The dual rationale for literacy programs is that they result in substantial good for the individual and for the larger society. In the case of the former, it is usually said that employment, self-defense, and cultural enrichment are among the numerous individual consequences of literacy. What does research tell us about this? Interestingly, because the literate world has such a great sense of the importance of literacy in their lives, relatively little formal research has been undertaken in this area. Many assume, for example, that literacy is a key factor in employment in the world's modernizing and increasingly technological economies. While few would dispute the need for literacy in this context, it is far less clear that basic reading and writing skills are sufficient to obtain employment in the modern sectors of many societies. Indeed, recent research emphasizes the need more for advanced skills in problem solving and analytic thinking than for basic reading and writing. And in Third World societies, it is increasingly common for those with a primary or secondary school education to find themselves excluded from white-collar jobs that were once guaranteed for the literate. As basic literacy becomes a commodity more widely available, its purchasing power is diminished. This consequence does not necessarily reduce other benefits of literacy—such as reading for enjoyment—but it has resulted, in countries like the United States, in an increase in the number of high school dropouts.

Let us now look at the argument for the social consequences of literacy. Since World War II, perhaps the most compelling argument for human resource development was that literacy will lead to economic growth. This approach, sometimes referred to as investment in human capital, supported the hypothesis that a minimum adult literacy rate of 40 percent would be required for economic growth. Naturally, this type of claim made use of aggregated data across many countries of the world and was based on a significant correlation between gross national product and literacy rates. Of course, one would probably be just as correct in claiming that literacy rates, like infant mortality rates, are prime indicators of the degree of economic development in most countries. If social and economic progress are being attained, then one usually finds that literacy rates climb and infant mortality rates drop.

Thus it would seem that the intellectual tide is turning against those who have argued that universal literacy would have immediate and important economic outcomes. Increasing numbers of policymakers in the area of educational planning are wondering if nations can bear the burden of ever-expanding educational costs, given fixed or lowered economic resources. Nonetheless, the association of literacy with health, nutrition, and other social goods is such that it is unlikely that governments will cease efforts at universalizing literacy and primary education.

Moreover, high rates of literacy have taken generations to achieve. As may be seen in the realm of economic development, literacy development has not taken place overnight. Literacy certainly brings individual and social benefits, but these benefits are not distributed evenly in all societies. What seems certain is that a minimum level of literacy would be useful for individuals in every society, but that even such minimum levels are not sufficient for certain guaranteed outcomes. Research in this area can be particularly useful for literacy learners and for policymakers, as it will promote a more realistic—as opposed to rhetorical—approach to the provision of basic education.

SOME GUESSES ABOUT LITERACY AFTER THE YEAR 2000

If current trends continue, particularly the universalization of primary schooling, the world of illiteracy will continue to diminish over the next century. Indeed, the number of naive illiterates—those with no knowledge that literacy exists and with no knowledge of the uses of literacy by others—is dwindling as we begin the 1990s. Of course, as many observers have noted, the absolute numbers of individuals with low literacy skills— for example, those with only a few years of primary schooling—continues to increase in many parts of the world. One major implication for the future is that policy attention will focus less on providing such minimal literacy skills than on which kinds and what levels of literacy skill are required for each society. Some obvious examples are now present in industrialized countries where basic arithmetic skills have been substantially replaced by the hand-held calculator. Even spelling—the focus of a great deal of school time in Western primary schools—is beginning to see the effects of spelling-checking computers for children. Why memorize rules when the computer is faster and more accurate? While there is still debate among researchers on this issue, the advent of high technology is compelling social change even before specialists have engaged in the requisite research.

The provision of adult literacy services is another area that appears ripe for major changes. During the twentieth century, many of the most widely known adult literacy programs were undertaken in the form of campaigns, large-scale efforts undertaken over a relatively short period of time, often under revolutionary conditions such as those in the Soviet Union, China, Cuba, and Ethiopia. While some uncertainty remains as to the actual outcomes of such efforts, the advent of universal primary education, the relative scarcity of contemporary social revolution, and the decreased need of a fixed minimum level of literacy among adults would lead one to predict that adult literacy campaigns are unlikely to be a major vehicle for literacy provision in the coming century. Much more likely would be public or private programs designed for the provision of specific types of skills, such as those involved in the use of microcomputers, word processing, data management, and analytic thinking.

Finally, it is not unreasonable to expect that changes in international language use will lead to commensurate changes in world literacy. For example, the advent of English as the predominant force in the publication of books and scientific journals is already having a major effect on social and economic life the world over and has led to corresponding changes in school curricula around the globe. Secondary consequences of the movement toward English use include the increasing importance of the Roman alphabet as a favored orthography. Although China and the Chinese language and script constitute a major demographic component in the world of literacy, recent efforts to promote the use of the Roman alphabet for Chinese literacy is one apparent consequence of the advancement of English literacy. The power of the alphabet is not, of course, limited to the dominance of English but may also be traced to changing technologies. The microcomputer is an important factor here. Software programs and the microcomputer keyboard were designed with the Roman alphabet in mind, and other orthographies— such as Chinese, Japanese, and Arabic—do not adapt well to this technology. A consequence is that orthographies other than the Roman alphabet are unlikely to maintain parity as technology advances in the coming decades.

Of course, reading the future is inherently more difficult than reading the present, that is, doing research in contemporary societies. We now turn to some conclusions and suggestions based on this brief excursion into the realm of literacy research.

SUGGESTIONS FOR
THE EFA DECADE

In the preceding sections, I have attempted to provide a brief sketch of some key areas of literacy research. The importance of research in literacy is that it provides us new paths to greater efficiency in literacy provision. While no social program, including research, is without economic costs, such expenditures must be understood in light of the costs involved in not knowing which path to take. Those who have argued that the literacy crisis is so mammoth that money spent on research is somehow wasteful are, in my view, wrongheaded in this regard. To invest resources in implementation without developing the means to learn from such programs is to call into question any purported gains in the literacy arena.

Investment and interest in literacy received a major boost at the World Conference on Education for All (EFA) in Jomtien, Thailand, in March 1990. In the 1990s EFA decade, it is important to reconsider issues in research and policy. Whether the topic is primary schooling or adult literacy campaigns, most policymakers want to be able to gather and utilize information about the effectiveness of any given intervention. As we learn more about the cultural dimensions of literacy, the evaluation process itself becomes more problematic. In a recent and widely publicized survey of adolescent literacy ability

in the United States, relatively little attention was paid to cultural and linguistic diversity, even though those who are least literate in America are often members of minority ethnic and linguistic groups.[10] This phenomenon repeats itself in much of the developing world as well, where ethnic and linguistic diversity is the rule, not the exception.

Thus, as part of any consideration of the issues associated with a minimum set of basic skills in "education for all," care needs to be taken as to the appropriateness of the learning experience and the material to be learned. It is widely agreed that learning is optimized when individuals are motivated to learn. Yet what is far less known is the nature of the motivation for learning in the population contexts—low income, poor health, female, and agriculturalist—that are likely to be targets of educational intervention in the coming decades. One reason for the purportedly weak results from many national and regional literacy campaigns is that the so-called clients were simply not motivated enough to learn what the government thought was essential to teach. Numerous reasons for disinterest among the target populations have been cited, ranging from ideological rejection of government programs to simple lack of time to attend during seasonal agricultural work cycles. In the case of literacy, one must also add the difficult problem of multilingualism. Government literacy programs are often provided in a

10. Irwin Kirsch and Ann Jungeblut, *Literacy: Profiles of America's Young Adults* (Princeton, NJ: ETS, 1986).

single national language and script, ignoring the often strong social and historical linkages that people have with other languages and other literacies. This issue is among the most nettlesome in the field of literacy and remains to be resolved in many of the countries where adult literacy programs have been and will be initiated.

Based on the foregoing review of research issues, several areas seem particularly ripe for practical application to the field of adult literacy.[11] These are as follows.

Contexts for skill retention

It appears that the retention of skills can be achieved when certain contextual determinants are present, such as a minimum level of initial learning, the availability of texts in the individual's language or languages of literacy, and, most important, the maintenance of the motivation to read and practice one's skills.[12] The level of initial learning required for specific contexts and the probable differences between low-literate children and low-literate adults remain research questions that will need further exploration in the coming years.

11. A more complete presentation of these suggestions is provided in D. A. Wagner, "Literacy: Developing the Future," *UNESCO Yearbook of Education* (Paris: United Nations Educational, Scientific, and Cultural Organization, 1992), vol. 43.

12. Daniel A. Wagner et al., "The Myth of Literacy Relapse: Literacy Retention among Moroccan Primary School Leavers," *International Journal of Educational Development*, 9:307-15 (1989).

Broad-based learning needs

Since the motivation of people to learn new skills will be a function of what they want and need to learn, we should be particularly cautious about top-down approaches that predetermine the meaning of such terms as "minimum skills," "functionally literate," and "educated." A contextually tailored program might take the form of health education, numeracy training in the workplace, and teaching the technical use of scripts and numerical systems for agriculture. Rather than a focus on a single-minded presumed need for a literate citizenry, consideration should be given to a broad range of learning as evidenced by people's expressed needs. In other words, new efforts should build on the dual themes of appropriateness and flexibility.

Build on local and cultural strengths

Although obvious in everyday life, building on strengths is a concept often ignored in educational programming. For example, if a government seeks to promote literacy, then literacy training ought to be built on the languages and scripts that people have the most motivation to learn. Such languages and scripts may not be the same as those of the government elite, and care will have to be taken to support minority language needs. Likewise, if numeracy is a goal, then planners might consider building on, where appropriate, base-five numerical systems, rather than the usual imposition of base-ten systems. The planners' response may be that they know best what constitutes national needs. Clearly, some blending of top-down and bottom-up needs and values must be achieved if successful interventions are to be made.

Long time lines and pilot studies

A well-known problem in development work is the usual brevity in the funding of programs that fall outside the national educational system. Campaigns and nonformal programs may only have one to three years to prove themselves. For this reason, planners sometimes opt for large-scale programs—for example, campaigns—before adequate preparations and planning can be provided. New EFA efforts should attempt to secure a 10-year time line, so that pilot studies can be conducted over the first two or three years in order to optimize the probability of achieving the project goals. Such pilot studies might involve the use of household surveys to determine social and individual motivation for various kinds of possible educational programming, while at the same time affording an opportunity to gain baseline information as to current literacy and other basic skill levels.

Accountability

Program accountability has sometimes taken the form of counting the number of textbooks distributed or the number of persons who completed a given program. Yet the actual goal of educational programs is to provide a set of enabling skills, even though these are rarely assessed after the termination of the actual course of study. Clearly, accountability should not be limited uniquely to the administrative needs of the policymakers but should be focused as well on how much learners learn from the services provided. Such broader measures of accountability can also provide the kind of information critical to obtaining political support for a continuation of funding in future years.

Horizontal and vertical integration

Literacy and other forms of training should be linked horizontally to other types of social interventions and institutions to which individuals have daily access. That is, a literacy program undertaken, say, under the aegis of a ministry of education must not become isolated from other literacy resources in the community, such as a local health clinic. In this case, attention should be paid to potential linkages across ministries and across social service programs. Furthermore, these educational programs should be able to be linked vertically to other programs that provide educational certificates or degrees. For example, a literacy program might be based in the utilization of traditional Islamic schools; ways must be found so that literacy learning in that context is recognized as legitimate by primary and secondary schools. In this way, new opportunities can be developed that promote the growth of human resources.

FINAL THOUGHT

In what I have termed the EFA decade, we have a unique opportunity to support educational efforts on a truly global scale. In spite of the clear needs for cultural sensitivities and specificities, this new effort suggests possible important economies of scale. Methodologies for pilot programs, assessment and evaluation, and computerized textbook preparation, for example, may be transferable with local adaptations to many cultural contexts. The kind of social marketing that will attend EFA efforts can provide a context of international political support, which comes at an ideal time. The needs for literacy and other basic skills have never been greater, and the gap between literate and nonliterate life-styles is becoming ever larger, with parallel growth in income disparities. Yet we must not let ourselves be pushed too rapidly into quick fixes or underdeveloped program proposals. Literacy and learning are a part of the culture of every society. To produce a lasting cultural change in the area of literacy requires both a realistic assessment of the kinds of change that people wish to see in their lives and sustained support to provide appropriate instructional services.

ANNALS, *AAPSS*, **520**, March 1992

Universal Adult Literacy:
Policy Myths and Realities

By STEPHEN P. HEYNEMAN

ABSTRACT: There is not the slightest doubt that literacy is good and its effects significant, but the virtues of literacy have occasionally been promoted in isolation from competing social objectives. This article notes three past mistakes in advocating literacy programs and suggests that future arguments would be more effective if past mistakes were taken into account.

Stephen P. Heyneman is chief of the Population and Human Resources Division in the Technical Department, Europe/USSR and Middle East/North Africa regions of the World Bank, Washington, D.C.

NOTE: The views expressed in this article are those of the author and should in no way be attributed to the World Bank.

REFERRING to the percentage of a population that is literate to denote social progress is traditional, in both economics and sociology. Those who can read constitute a given good, that is, the greater that percentage, the greater the progress. Though this relationship is not assumed to be linear, there is such wide consensus on the virtues of literacy that debate about when and under what circumstances to advocate its promotion is not a primary concern. Errors can be made, however, when advocacy of literacy ignores political realities and programmatic trade-offs. Blind advocacy can manifest itself in three ways:

— a rush to judgment in cases where policymakers are assumed to undervalue the goals of literacy;
— a naïveté about the real forces that motivate policymakers; and
— a misunderstanding about the nature of research and its appropriate role in determining social policy.

Let us look at each in turn.

RUSH TO JUDGMENT

Policymakers may be adjudged to undervalue adult literacy programs because of the low priority afforded to the programs within the budgets of ministries of education. Similarly, development assistance agencies— the regional development banks, the World Bank, and bilateral agencies— that follow suit are believed to be working against the interests of the poor and the downtrodden. The discussion often takes on a derogatory tone, as though these big agencies and ministries were instruments of the status quo, as though they were beholden to vested interests, unresponsive to the true voices of the people.

It is true, of course, that adult literacy programs within ministry budgets are commonly allocated less than 2 percent of total recurrent expenditures. It is false that their low priority is irrational, is a function of conservatism, or denotes a lack of innovation in the education sector. The education sector is large and therefore cumbersome in terms of policy shift. Its public nature implies that it is subject to widespread scrutiny and public pressure. For example, approximately one of four Americans is involved in education as a teacher, a student, or an administrator. In a developing country, the proportion of the population can reach one in three. But neither its cumbersome nature nor its size determines the priority given to adult literacy. The priority is based upon a correct perception of the costs and failures of past programs and the correct estimate of the public interest.

REAL FORCES BEHIND POLICYMAKERS

Whether policymakers are elected or are members of the military, and whether the economy has as its origin the free market or central planning, all policymakers are subject to common pressures. One pressure is their obligation to help people responsible for their welfare during times of difficulty and political uncertainty; such people may include, for example, neighbors from the same province or village, family members, tribal connections, and kinship relations. Lines of authority to party or bureaucracy rule through manifest mechanisms. This is especially true of executive authority in developing countries, where sycophancy is common. Other influences include personal gain, ideology and professional views, and orientations associated with particular graduate schools. Public opinion, program results, and literacy campaigns are three domains that cut across such influences and are crucial to support for adult literacy programs.

Public opinion

Public opinion can be legitimately expressed even within dictatorships. Whereas opinions about a president's competence are usually considered threatening and even traitorous, public claims for local bridge repair, a new school, or a health clinic are considered normal and acceptable. Public claims, therefore, influence and help to establish educational policy and choose between educational priorities.

For example, public opinion often holds that senior policymakers, being disproportionately rich and/or urban, skew the direction of health care toward hospital care and away from primary health care and, in education, toward universities and against elementary education. But there is little evidence to suggest that the low priority given to adult education results from lack of political power among its supporters. It is not that people believe adult literacy programs lack value. Instead, wealthy people favor university or preschool programs for their children, and poor people, especially in rural areas, tend to favor primary education when given a choice. Since votes are rarely taken, this impression may not be substantiated empirically. Nonetheless, it is widely known that if a school is not built, the policymaker feels tangible public pressure. If there is no adult education program, the claim is more likely less frequent and weaker. In essence, the low budgetary priority given to adult literacy programs most probably is a rational reflection of weak demand.

Program results

Lessons learned from past efforts also influence the priority given to adult literacy programs. Most policymakers are aware of the problems; problems are discovered not by complex research effort but by common sense. For instance, the opportunity cost—especially for the poor—of literacy constrains a learner's continuation in a program; when families are hungry, literacy classes have to come second. Literacy as a skill—as opposed to oral rehydration or cattle dipping—is complex and difficult to transfer. Literacy teachers are often volunteers or low-paid service personnel. Quality control is low; personnel turnover is high. The language of literacy programs is politically sensitive. Choices can sometimes alienate ethnic out-groups; linguistic tolerance can increase costs. Program resources are idiosyncratic; they ebb and flow. Private voluntary organizations may play a large role in program delivery, but these organizations can create tension with the state if they have a supplementary message that is inconsistent with governmental goals. Other programs—numeracy, entrepreneurship training, child care, agricultural extension, and marketing—rival literacy programs for resources. While these programs are conceived as companions to good literacy training, they can act as an opportunity cost for an individual's attention. A learner may take a literacy class but may be more interested in shopkeeping skills.

Perhaps most important is the willingness to pay for literacy classes. Unless the classes are attached to the equivalent of an elementary school certificate, the economic demand is generally low.

Literacy campaigns

Literacy campaigns are highly political, highly visible short-term action programs designed to jump-start an end to illiteracy. The shortcomings in these programs are widely known and are, quite understandably, widely ignored when policymakers are contemplating new campaigns. With respect to literacy campaigns, one must recognize that the process is as much an attempt to solidify political legitimacy as an attempt to teach literacy efficiently.

Literacy campaigns often follow on the heels of political revolution; they occur in the midst of high hope and strong levels of consensus. They accompany programs for distributing eye glasses, vaccinations, nutritional supplements, and elementary school equivalency certificates for those previously excluded from the system, for example. They are often nested among many other campaign goals that have equal weight.

Other characteristics of mass campaigns are also widely known but less widely acknowledged. Somalia shut down every postprimary educational institution for one year so that students could be used in the campaign. The students had, of course, no choice in the matter. Cuba's well-known and successful campaign occurred when the country was emerging from its revolution not only with considerable fervor but with a level of literacy—80 percent—considered the highest at the time in Latin America. Such circumstances are not easy to duplicate elsewhere.

COMMUNICATION PROBLEMS BETWEEN RESEARCHER AND POLICYMAKER

Sometimes it is thought that results of research on literacy should determine policy decisions in adult literacy programs. Usually this opinion coincides with those who pose research questions and publish research results. The problem is that research questions, by their nature, can focus only on a small subset of the problem. For instance, while one might conclude from research that one program is more efficient than another, it would be a mistake to generalize as to whether either program was justified. Sometimes researchers conclude that policymakers who ignore findings are irrational and must, therefore, make decisions on the basis of "political" (read "irrational") grounds. This accounts for many types of misunderstandings.

Key to understanding the sources of misunderstanding here is knowing who is the client and who is the producer. Policymakers are clients; researchers are producers. As in marketing a consumer good, the client does not need to improve on his or her adaptability or interest; rather, the producer needs to understand exactly how, whether, and under what circumstances the research might make an impact. The responsibility for making research effective lies with the producer. If the research is not read, if it is ignored, this does not necessarily mean that the policymaker is deficient. All sides must recognize that the policymaker has to decide priorities on the basis of instinct, as well as on scientific underpinning.

SUMMARY

It is entirely reasonable and fitting to value adult literacy, to promote it, and to assess its effects. Adult literacy should not, however, be promoted at the expense of common sense, at the expense of other important services, or at the expense of other demands on people's time. We should remind ourselves, when advocating literacy, what has been learned recently about the effects of schooling. We have learned that some of the most powerful influences of schooling have to do with the attitudes and behavior associated with the schooling process rather than with the skills acquired as a result of the curriculum. We have learned that not all curricular goals are equally effective in influencing behavior, that higher-order understanding is stronger than the mechanics of factual recall.

This implies that the direct behavioral results of the short-term teaching of adults to read may be disappointing compared to the 6- to 10-year process of educating children in primary and secondary schools. No country, so far as I am aware, has achieved universal literacy without also achieving universal schooling. I do not doubt that adult literacy classes are worth selective investment, but the ultimate guarantee of a literate population remains an educated population.

ANNALS, *AAPSS*, 520, March 1992

Literacy in a Larger Context

By MANZOOR AHMED

ABSTRACT: Illiteracy is a social phenomenon reflecting structural problems of society; therefore, the nature of the illiteracy problem can be better understood and the solutions found by looking at the larger social context. The complexity and social ramifications of illiteracy make it inappropriate to talk about eradication of illiteracy by a certain date. Literacy is not merely learning the mechanics of decoding the alphabet. To be meaningful, literacy must help meet people's basic learning needs, and, to that end, it must be reinforced and supplemented by a network of opportunities for diverse and continuing education and post-literacy learning. Effective primary education for children and the use of all channels of communication and education to create a learning society are essential conditions for nurturing a culture of literacy. Participation of all segments of society and additional resources are needed to promote literacy as an integral part of the effort to meet basic education needs. The research agenda in literacy should include, in addition to technical aspects, the exploration of policy issues relating to the role of literacy in a larger social context.

Manzoor Ahmed is special adviser for programs at UNICEF headquarters in New York. He has worked in educational planning, nonformal education, rural development, and social services for children and women in Bangladesh and several other Asian and African countries. Formerly UNICEF representative in China, he has also served as senior education adviser for UNICEF. His main policy and research interests are in finding effective ways of promoting literacy as a component of "basic education for all" and in forming a national human resource development strategy.

THE issue of literacy must be understood in the context of the basic learning needs of children and adults and the specific circumstances for social and economic development involved. Taking the social context of literacy as a starting point, it is useful to remind ourselves that illiteracy is not an isolated social phenomenon either in its causes or in its consequences. Rather, the distribution of illiteracy in society follows certain typical patterns. There is a high concentration of illiteracy, in both developing and industrialized countries, among ethnic and cultural minorities and the poor—those who are outside the mainstream of society. Women, the victims of age-old social discrimination, are also greatly affected; they constitute two-thirds of the world's illiterates.

Looking at the pattern of illiteracy in societies, one cannot but conclude that the degree and persistence of illiteracy reflects structural imbalances in a society, such as the uneven distribution of political and economic power, the uneven way in which political and economic policies and priorities are determined, and the uneven way in which the systems and institutions implementing those policies are organized. The extent of illiteracy in a nation is a measure of that nation's degree of attachment to principles of social justice. Progress in literacy is not tied to a nation's economic status, as illustrated by the estimated 30 million functionally illiterate adults in North America and the fact that some of the poorest countries or regions within countries have made major gains in both adult literacy and primary education in recent times.

The sad irony of illiteracy is that those who most need access to knowledge, information, and skills, by which they might pull themselves out of a disadvantageous situation, are the ones most deprived of this access. The tendency for this legacy to be passed on to one's children, in turn, aggravates the situation. There is a well-established connection between the illiteracy of parents and the failure to enroll children in school as well as early primary school drop-out. There is also a well-documented connection between the literacy levels of women, the size of their families, and the mortality and nutritional status of their children. The cost of large-scale illiteracy to society as a whole is the individual tragedy of unrealized potential in personal growth, self-sufficiency, and economic achievement magnified a million times.

ILLITERACY AND MEETING BASIC LEARNING NEEDS

The complexity and the ramifications of illiteracy as a social phenomenon make it, in my view, inappropriate to talk about eradication of illiteracy by a certain date. It is not an affliction that can be removed by a surgical operation or a disease that can be eliminated by vaccination. If a medical analogy is to be used, promoting and maintaining literacy—and preventing illiteracy—is more like providing life-sustaining nourishment on a continuing basis than like eradicating smallpox.

The programmatic implication is that literacy is not merely a matter of exposing a learner for a certain number of lesson hours to the mechanics of decoding the alphabet, although this is an essential step. It is, therefore, significant and appropriate to set literacy in the larger social context of basic learning needs and opportunities.

Illiteracy is bred by the absence of effective primary education for large numbers of children and is sustained by the absence of opportunities for applying and enhancing literacy skills in an environment conducive to continued learning. Any plan to significantly reduce adult illiteracy must start with a plan to expand the reach of effective primary education. "Effective" is the key word here, as the aim must be to go beyond enrollment to enabling the learner to reach a self-sustaining level of learning. Learning must also be reinforced and supplemented by a network of opportunities for diverse and continuing education and post-literacy learning. All channels of communication and education must be harnessed to create a learning society in which a culture of literacy can be nurtured. The power of communications technology, when fully used to disseminate widely useful knowledge and information, can boost the acquisition and use of literacy and make a difference in people's lives.

In promoting literacy as an integral element of a basic education thrust, a participatory approach has to be developed, both because the job is large and complex and everybody's help is needed and because the beneficiaries themselves must put their hearts into it if they are going to succeed. A broad spectrum of social, cultural, religious, labor, and professional organizations have to contribute to the mass education movement that a literacy effort entails. Voluntary organizations and community groups that address people's urgently felt needs can often be the best vehicles for literacy and continuing education. Rather than attempt to control and run the education programs, the main tasks of governments should be to create a national learning environment in which all sectors of society can participate.

To accomplish the goals and objectives of basic education, additional resources are needed. For one, the priorities in public expenditure in many countries clearly need rethinking. Public education budgets as a proportion of national income and total government budget should be reexamined, as should the share for basic education—primary education, literacy, post-literacy learning, and early-childhood education—in the total national education budget. Ways of mobilizing nongovernmental resources for basic education also have to be considered. Finally, there has to be an increase in external assistance, especially because external assistance for education as a proportion of total international aid has been falling in the past decade.

RESEARCH ISSUES

The agenda for research needs to include exploration, comparison, and analysis of operational aspects of these policy issues. In addition, there are other more technical and methodological aspects that need research attention. For example, there is a need for a more rigorous approach to developing and applying meaningful measures of literacy than the casual methods used today. The present state of literacy statistics is nothing short of scandalous, and if meaningful criteria are applied properly, the magnitude of illiteracy in today's world will prove to be substantially higher than officially stated. Valid and affordable systems for monitoring and assessing individual literacy achievements as well as national progress must be developed and applied systematically.

Other technical issues that call for professional research attention include teaching and learning methods appropriate for adults and children in specific cultural and linguistic settings, the question of the language of instruction in a multilingual situation, the training of adult literacy instructors, appropriate learning content, and the development and production of learning materials. We also need to know how to develop research capacity and how to make research efforts responsive to relevant policy and operational questions. How to put research results to use in a setting of diverse local organizations engaged in literacy efforts is another question that has no categorical answer and that therefore needs to be asked repeatedly.

In this final decade of the twentieth century, illiteracy in both poor and rich countries is a stark reminder of polarities and divisions that persist in the world and in each society. Efforts to solve technical and methodological problems and to attract resources to literacy activities must continue, but these efforts will yield results only when they take fully into account the larger context of societal values and priorities.

ANNALS, *AAPSS,* **520,** March 1992

Literacy Research, Policy, and Practice: The Elusive Triangle

By JOHN RYAN

ABSTRACT: This article explores the interrelationships between literacy research, policy, and practice. The author contends that these three spheres of activity, which in principle should be closely related and mutually supportive, have in fact developed independently of one another and remain separated by mutual misunderstandings. In developing nations, the influence of externally funded research and internationally sanctioned policy objectives has often resulted in research undertakings that fail to illuminate prevailing realities and policy goals out of touch with actual possibilities. The author concludes by noting the growing importance of adult literacy programs and the increasing efforts in both industrialized and developing countries to ensure closer linkages between research, policy formulation, and practice.

John W. Ryan, a UNESCO staff member, served as coordinator for International Literacy Year. From 1973 to 1979, he was director of the International Institute for Adult Literacy Methods in Tehran, Iran. He holds the Ph.D. from Stanford University.

IN principle, the interrelationships between research, policy, and practice are simple, direct, and mutually supportive: research advances knowledge and understanding, thereby illuminating policy choices and guiding practice; policymaking, in turn, draws upon the insights deriving from research and the experience gained through practice in order to formulate more effective strategies and approaches; improved practice is the consequence of research and policy as well as being their testing ground.

In reality, these relationships are, of course, more complex and problematic. First of all, researchers do not march to the drums of either policymakers or practitioners but follow their own rhythms, determined, inter alia, by the direction of research in particular academic disciplines, personal interests, and available opportunities. There is no evil in this. Academic research may, indeed, prove more valuable in orienting policy and practice in useful directions than would a research agenda directly linked to operational issues and problems. During the past quarter century, basic research in psychology, linguistics, and other disciplines has, for example, fundamentally transformed our conception of the reading process and has had a profound, if gradual, impact upon the manner in which reading is taught. Once viewed largely as an exercise in decoding, reading is now recognized as an active search for meaning to which both study of text and knowledge of context contribute. In the future, it is probable, to cite but one example,

that research in the cognitive sciences, including brain research, will further advance our understanding of reading and especially of reading problems and how to cope with them. Thus the choice is not between applied and basic research. It is evident that we need both and many types of research in between, in which theory and practice interact.

Yet, a discontent with literacy research persists. Policymakers complain that most research fails to illuminate the policy choices with which they are confronted or to guide them in policy formulation. Why is this so? In part, it may be that policymakers, faced with difficult choices and, more especially, with hard-to-please constituencies, are seeking scientific solutions to choices that are essentially ethical and political. They are searching for answers from without when what is required is strength within. This discontent may also be the consequence of the fundamentally different outlooks and objectives of researchers as compared to those of policymakers. The researcher's focus is usually upon the individual or, in certain cases, the family or a particular community. The purpose of the research, explicitly or implicitly, is to distinguish between individuals, families, communities, and situations. Thus the researcher insists—and rightly so—that there is not one autonomous literacy; there is rather an infinite variety of situationally specific forms and degrees of literacy and illiteracy. This, while accurate, is not necessarily helpful to the policymaker who, consciously or otherwise, is engaged in a search for common denominators. Policy, as the etymology of the term suggests, is concerned with the polity or collectivity. Literacy practice may be individually tailored, but literacy policy has to have a broader perspective. It must be applicable to an entire community or a clearly defined portion thereof. To the researcher, this search for common denominators often seems a simplification or distortion of reality. To the policymaker, on the other hand, it is an essential averaging-out of different situations and circumstances in order to be able to formulate broadly applicable public policies. The researcher's endless categories of literacy and illiteracy, in turn, seem to the policymaker a pointless obfuscation—an inability to see the forest for the trees—which needlessly complicates and potentially enfeebles the formulation of policies and the actions that ensue from them.

The practitioner's outlook, in this instance at least, is likely to be closer to that of the researcher than the policymaker. Experience teaches the practitioner that each learner is unique, a fact of which policy—especially that applicable in the so-called formal education system—fails to take adequate account and for which it makes insufficient provision.

FAMILIAR RESPONSES
TO UNFAMILIAR REALITIES

In the developing nations, where many studies are financed by external agencies, the complaint is heard that research better reflects foreign interests, styles, trends, and methods than it does domestic needs and realities. American or European paradigms and protocols are applied or adapted to African or Asian realities and the results published in American or European journals. The evident need is not to halt research by foreigners but to complement and correct it with a growing volume of research by nationals.

Indeed, the most fundamental problem in many developing countries, and especially in Africa, is not the quality or relevance of research but its paucity. Research on learning in schools is limited and, with the exception of a few countries, research on adult literacy is practically nonexistent. The single factor of salaries often accounts for over 90 percent of public educational expenditures. Evidently, little remains for books, materials, and equipment and rarely anything at all for research and development. As a consequence, countries struggle to apply policies, often concocted by external agencies, to realities sometimes very different from those assumed. Policy tends to be normative: concerned with what should be rather than with what is or what might be possible or feasible. Policy documents call for doing all of several programs—for example, universal primary education, expanded adult literacy programs, and vocational training for out-of-school youths—whereas the resources available can finance only half of only one program. In such cases, policy is little more than an elaborate platitude. Effective policy has to take account of the economic and demographic facts of life, facts that better data and more study would help to clarify. The ultimate goal may remain to do all that the policy statement mandates, but the immediate need is to know how and where to begin with best effect and with the best hope of overall success. The tendency has been—and this applies as well to adult literacy in the industrialized countries—for policy to trail far behind rhetoric, and financing and enabling measures far behind policy. A lot is being said, but relatively little is being done.

MUTUAL MISUNDERSTANDINGS

Practitioners, too, have their misgivings about research. Research, they complain, often fails to address their problems and, even when it does so, rarely divulges its findings in terms that are easy to understand and apply. This is not only a question of language but also, more profoundly, of culture: of differences between these two professions in background, education and training, clients, work conditions, goals, rewards, values, and so forth. One sign of this difficulty is that while more and more conferences and meetings seek to bring researchers and practitioners together, the two groups usually remain separate under the same roof. Practitioners attend sessions run by other practitioners; researchers, sessions run by other researchers. Policymakers—unless directly engaged in funding the activities under discussion, in which case they must be humored, if not honored—are usually shunned by both groups: researchers question their understanding and theoretical knowledge,

and practitioners doubt their intentions and situational knowledge.

In conditions of extreme austerity —alas, more and more common in the developing nations—much research, whether internally or, as is more often the case, externally funded, must seem a conspicuous luxury to the practitioner. Does it make sense to study and evaluate achievement levels in schools or adult literacy programs that lack everything: trained teachers; sound, safe, and sanitary buildings; equipment; textbooks and materials; even pencils and paper? Would not funds be better used to provide, however modestly, a few of the things that existing research reveals can make a difference and that conscience and common sense alike indicate to be priorities? The argument here is not against research per se but rather against the extreme poverty that enfeebles education in much of the developing world. Research linked to a serious effort to improve conditions would be welcome, indeed essential, but neither research nor improved policy can contribute much to education when even the barest minimum of resources for effective practice are lacking.

A diversity of perspectives among researchers, policymakers, and practitioners is inevitable and can often prove a source of strength rather than weakness. Yet, in a world where resources are in short supply and where more than one adult in four is illiterate and over 100 million children between the ages of 6 and 11 years do not attend school, efficiency is imperative. Achieving it need not—and should not—require any rigid or even formalized linkages, but it does call for a more symbiotic relationship, a greater interplay between the points of the triangle: research, policy, and practice.

The origin of the present disharmony is that these spheres of activity have grown up separately, not together. What has passed for research and development in adult literacy has normally been the artisanal fabrication of methods and approaches by committed practitioners, many of whom lacked specialized training in relevant disciplines. This occurred not by choice but from necessity. Until quite recently—roughly 25 years ago—adult literacy practitioners could turn neither to policymakers nor to researchers for guidance and support. With the exception of the Soviet Union, where a concern with literacy was born with the revolution, there were no policies addressing problems of adult literacy. Literacy work, whether at home or abroad, was considered an activity for the voluntary sectors, especially for churches and missionaries. The developing nations, afflicted with a situation of mass illiteracy that could hardly be overlooked, were among the first to seek to formulate policies for promoting literacy. Nor was there a body of research findings on adult literacy. School-based research on the teaching and acquisition of reading skills may have provided some insights, but practitioners were quick to recognize that adult literacy presented many special problems as well as the evident advantage of being able to draw upon adult knowledge and experience.

EXPANDED POSSIBILITIES AND NEW REQUIREMENTS

Today, the situation is dramatically different. First, adult literacy is no longer a marginal activity to be left to volunteers and missionaries, although the nongovernmental sector continues to play an important and innovative role. The knowledge explosion has profoundly transformed working and living environments, systematically eliminating low-skill jobs and accelerating the tempo of change within and between occupations. As a consequence, even in highly industrialized countries, some 10 to 20 percent or more of the population may be classified as "functionally illiterate," an elastic term that stretches or contracts to fit the needs of the user. Hence illiteracy has clearly become a mainstream concern.

The same knowledge explosion has also affected literacy work as a professional pursuit. There is now a sizable body of literature deriving from research in many disciplines and practice in countless settings capable of illuminating and guiding the preparation and implementation of programs. Thus the increased need for knowledge, implicit in expanded and more sophisticated programming, is matched by a growing body of research findings, project documents, evaluation, and inquiries. The challenge is to put such knowledge to work: for researchers, by keeping their thinking abreast of current development in their own and especially allied disciplines; for policymakers, by being alert to relevant developments in other states and countries and by elucidating the calculus of cause and effect between a policy decision and its consequences; and for practitioners, by having a body of information deriving from research findings and experimental programs and, more important, instructional methods and materials incorporating such up-to-date and tested knowledge.

While the problems and needs can be readily delineated, solutions are less easy and evident. In the simplest terms, the need is for closer interactions between practice, policy, and research and for institutional settings that permit and encourage such exchanges. In countries as diverse as India and the United States, adult literacy resource centers have been established to forge the needed links. The Indian experience is now nearly a decade old and has shown promising results as well as some expected problems. The greatest of these is the need for decentralization, that is, the need to reach practitioners who usually operate on distant frontiers socially, culturally, and geographically. In recent years, satellite resource centers have been established at state and district levels. But the gap remains great, and there is a clear need to complement trickle-down with bubble-up approaches. Local-level program administrators and practitioners have to be induced to diagnose their problems and actively seek out support in solving them. In the United States, the efforts of the federal government to make systematic provision for the support of adult literacy programs are recent. These new initiatives aim at establishing an interplay between policy, practice, and research, consolidating what, to date, has been an elusive relationship between the actors who must pull together to create a more literate world.

Literacy and Human Resources Development: An Integrated Approach

By JOHN E. S. LAWRENCE

ABSTRACT: The persistently high number of illiterate persons, and exacerbated conditions of stress on education, training, and employment systems worldwide necessitate major alterations in approaches to human resources development. Accordingly, this article overviews the widening scope of human resources problems facing countries at all points on the development spectrum and outlines some broad initiatives being taken by the United Nations Development Program to assist countries in addressing these issues. In particular, it is argued that strategies for improving literacy and basic learning programs must be more participatory and must explicitly acknowledge the mutualities between several social sectors. Broader, more intersectoral research, policies, and procedures are indicated that look as much at the linkages between sectors as they do at intrasectoral mechanisms. The United Nations Development Program's Human Development Index is defined, and an operational framework for more integrated human resources development is discussed.

John Lawrence is currently principal technical adviser for human resources development at the United Nations Development Program. Formerly he was senior research psychologist for the Research Triangle Institute and adjunct associate professor of psychology at North Carolina State University.

NOTE: A more detailed version of this article was delivered at the Comparative International Education Society Annual Meeting at the University of Pittsburgh, 15 March 1991. Opinions expressed in the present article are those of the author and are not necessarily those of the United Nations Development Program, its Governing Council, or other member governments.

ALL countries, and particularly those in earlier stages of development, are facing extraordinary and growing human resources problems. It is a distressing reality that, despite enormous expenditures and some advances, these problems have in many ways been growing worse worldwide for several years. Few countries anywhere on the development scale have escaped, for example, marked degradation in their education systems, including persistent illiteracy; growing health care inequities, particularly for the young and the aging; shortage of adequate urban shelter in large cities; serious environmental deterioration; and acute un- and underemployment.

Certainly the wealthier nations are not immune, suggesting that wealth is not itself the answer. As Rahman has noted, "in some of the most 'developed' societies we are witnessing social disease formations which are going beyond human control."[1] It is nevertheless in the less developed and poorer countries that human resources problems are most severe. Accordingly, the United Nations Development Program (UNDP) is examining new measures that quantify the human aspects of development and supplement conventional economic indices. Within this conceptual structure, human resources development (HRD) is also being reassessed as a broader, more intersectoral approach that acknowledges mutualities between, for example, literacy and enhanced individual choice, education and work, learning and environment, and between community, family, teacher, and student. The awesome scope and complexity of the problems in each of the five sectors listed at the beginning of this article, however, obstruct progress and so far defy solution.

EDUCATION

At the 1990 Jomtien Conference on Education for All, more than 150 countries testified to the rising numbers of illiterates worldwide and, importantly, in rich and poor countries alike. The conference was timely and tapped into a latent but strong international consensus that business as usual in education is no longer tolerable. Hallak[2] and others have documented the 1980s' decline in real public spending on education even in the more developed countries, which spent 6.0 percent of gross national product on education in 1980 and 5.8 percent in 1986. Moreover, the percentages of total population, by major world region, with no education were estimated by Horn and Arriagada as follows: East Asia and Pacific, 17 percent; Latin America and the Caribbean, 22 percent; East Africa, 38 percent; South Asia, 58 percent; Middle East and North Africa, 66 percent; and West Africa, 70 percent.[3]

1. M. A. Rahman, "Towards an Alternative Development Paradigm" (Inaugural address at the Biennial Conference of the Bangladesh Economic Association, Dhaka, 23 Nov. 1990), p. 7.

2. Jacques Hallak, *Investing in the Future: Setting Educational Priorities in the Developing World* (Paris: United Nations Development Program and United Nations Educational, Scientific, and Cultural Organization [hereinafter cited as UNESCO] Institute for Educational Planning, 1990).

3. Robin Horn and Ana-Maria Arriagada, "The Educational Attainment of the World's Population: Three Decades of Progress" (World

For no one is this picture bleaker than for women. According to the United Nations Educational, Scientific, and Cultural Organization, more than 60 million school-age girls—aged 6 to 11 years—worldwide do not enter the schoolhouse door. Female net enrollment ratios at the primary level in 1984-86 exceeded 50 percent in only 9 of the 21 low-income countries reporting these figures. Gross female enrollment ratios for primary school were less than or equal to 50 percent in 17 of the 41 reporting low-income economies and were equal to or below 20 percent in 6 countries.[4] The first UNDP *Human Development Report* identifies five low-income countries where the 1986-88 primary female-male ratio was less than 50 percent. Female primary school enrollment was at or above 90 percent of male enrollment in only 8 of the 39 low-income economies. At the secondary level, disparities were even more marked, despite the overwhelming evidence for positive social gains in women's education, such as improved longevity and economic productivity, lower fertility, and reduction in infant and maternal mortality.[5] Strong human rights arguments for equity in educational opportunity are thus buttressed by the measurable socioeconomic costs of ignoring such policies. Yet, despite notable gains, the persistent de facto discrimination of many educational systems against women remains a blight on development today.

We can discern, furthermore, a loss of faith in education as a guarantor of improved skill acquisition in increasingly competitive labor markets. Rural education in India, for example, is described as a "sick industry"[6] and utterly discouraging to the rural poor. The number of illiterate persons, already estimated at over 1 billion worldwide, thus continues to advance.

HEALTH

More than 100 million children will die from disease and malnutrition this decade from known and, in many cases, treatable conditions.[7] The most common are diarrhea and respiratory disease, which can be cured quite simply with, respectively, oral rehydration therapy and orally administered antibiotics usually costing less than $1. In addition, acquired immune deficiency syndrome threatens most of the countries where the problem is recognized least, and it cruelly afflicts those in the young and productive years. Education of communities and parents can assist in reversing such decimation of a nation's future human resources.

Knowledge about relationships between health status—particularly malnutrition—and cognitive func-

Bank Education and Training Department Discussion Paper EDT #37, 1986).

4. UNESCO, Office of Statistics, *UNESCO Statistical Year Book 1989* (Paris: UNESCO, 1989).

5. United Nations Development Program, *Human Development Report* (New York: Oxford University Press, 1990).

6. A. K. Jalaluddin et al., *Basic Education and National Development: The Indian Scene* (New Delhi: United Nations Children's Fund, 1990).

7. United Nations Children's Fund, *State of the World's Children* (New York: United Nations Children's Fund, 1990).

tion is embryonic at present. The U.N. Administrative Committee on Coordination, however, stated that nutritional deficiencies and health conditions negatively affect school enrollment, aptitudes, time spent in school—attendance and dropout rates—and achievement.[8]

The number of out-of-school children correlates positively with the number of underweight children— under the age of five, below minus two standard deviations from the median weight-for-age of the reference population—for countries reporting these data in the 1990 *Human Development Report*. Yet school-age children in developing countries generally have been neglected epidemiologically, despite the fact that the pattern of relevant health problems in this age group appears to be unique.[9] School feeding programs are one of a relatively few measures that can benefit a broad range of constituencies, from the farmer to the developing-country planner, not to mention the schoolchildren and the local communities themselves. They are, furthermore, politically popular and constitute an important tangible sign of a national government's commitment to helping the poor.[10] Yet they are not cheap and require administrative commitment.

8. United Nations Administrative Committee on Coordination, Subcommittee on Nutrition, *Summary Report of the Sixteenth Session* (Paris: UNESCO, 1990), p. 2.

9. Dean T. Jamison and Joanne Leslie, "Health and Nutrition Considerations in Educational Planning" (Paper prepared for UNESCO and the U.N. Administrative Committee on Coordination, Subcommittee on Nutrition, Feb. 1990).

10. B. Levinger, *School Feeding Programs in Developing Countries: An Analysis of Actual*

URBAN SHELTER

Large cities are usually associated with cultural diversity, commercial creativity, and productivity. Chronic rural-urban migration, however, overloads city financial resources, infrastructures, and services and attenuates sociocultural controls. In 1960, only 3 of the world's 10 largest cities were in developing countries. In 2000, that will change to 8 of the 10. Urban populations will grow by 70 percent in developing countries but by only 13 percent in industrial countries.[11]

The healthier and more educated members of the rural populations are those who migrate to the cities, and they take with them correspondingly elevated initial expectations. This pool of human resources offers high potential for development. All too often, however, they remain marginalized in insecure informal-sector employment, with correspondingly reduced access to shelter and services. Formal-sector housing seldom accounts for more than one-fifth of new housing in large cities in the developing world. As a consequence, rural immigrants are forced into squatting and other undesirable and usually illegal dwelling arrangements, with all of the concomitant sanitation, health, logistical, and domestic problems.

Given the inevitability of this massive shift of human resources, and the inherent push-pull incentives of

and Potential Impact, AID Evaluation Special Study no 30. (Washington, DC: U.S. Agency for International Development, 1986).

11. United Nations Development Program, *Human Development Report*, 1990, chap. 5.

rural necessity and urban opportunity, the HRD needs of these populations present a stark challenge to those education, health, and employment systems that have traditionally been the province of the elites.

ENVIRONMENT

Industrialized countries are waking up to the disastrous consequences of ignoring the exacerbated pollution of our planet. "The greatest potential threat to [our] future comes not from the prospects of a clash of arms or from the ravages of economic depression. It arises instead from the slow and insidious deterioration of the environment, undramatic in any one year but devastating over time."[12]

Problems in the less industrialized countries include the continuing destruction of primary forest, desertification, and dumping of untreated and unregulated organic, chemical, and other wastes into the water and the air. While environmental protection is closely related to the degree to which there are incentives and technologies for measuring and/or reducing pollution, the costs of prevention are often less than the costs of the cure. Thus the issues—besides the central issue of financial resources—become fostering the awareness, positive attitudes, and will to change and then improving capacities to obtain and apply the necessary technologies.

Education can contribute to both of these goals. In fact, environmental literacy, as a component in the education-for-all effort, is considered an essential ingredient for a nation's sustainable development.[13]

EMPLOYMENT

In industrialized countries, annual average economic growth—as a percentage of gross domestic product—has been declining overall since the 1960s.[14] High unemployment rates, balance-of-trade deficits, and the specter of regional protectionism have all accompanied this reversal. In less industrialized countries, the "1980s have . . . particularly in Africa and Latin America, been a lost decade,"[15] characterized, for example, by the debt crisis and resulting net capital outflow, deteriorating terms of trade, and decelerating employment creation as well as reduction in the quality—wages, working conditions—of jobs created. Yet the International Labour Office has estimated that almost 40 million people per year will be actively seeking work in the decade 1991-2000, with more than 90 percent of them in developing countries. While the Asian region, primarily India and China, will account for the largest numbers in this increase—47 percent, at over 100 million people—the rate of growth will be more rapid in Africa and Latin

12. Aspen Institute, *The Americas in a New World: The 1990 Report of the Inter-American Dialogue* (Washington, DC: Aspen Institute, 1990), p. 31.

13. UNESCO and the United Nations Environment Program, International Environmental Education Programme, "Environmental Education" (Special study for the World Conference on Education for All, Jomtien, Thailand, 5-9 Mar. 1990).

14. International Labour Office, *Recovery and Employment: Report of the Director General* (Geneva: International Labour Office, 1989).

15. Ibid., p. 5.

America—68 percent and 63 percent, respectively.

The assumed positive association between the number of years of schooling and the probability of finding a rewarding, remunerative job is proving repeatedly fallible. Individuals reliably cite their expectations of better jobs as the major reason for education for themselves or their children.[16] Yet graduate under- and unemployment remain widespread, reflecting tighter labor markets; so-called qualifications creep, as employers hire the more educated for work that once required less education; high and often unrealistic expectations of graduates themselves; and lack of correspondence between schooling and work. The majority of economically active persons in the developing world will receive only primary education at best. Average social rates of return to primary schooling are routinely stated as substantially higher to primary than either to secondary or tertiary education. Yet recent studies in Kenya, for example, suggest that "today's primary school completer is fortunate to get even a menial blue-collar job in the wage sector, and [the] chance of obtaining a white-collar job is virtually nil."[17] In South Nyanza, Kenya, "there is generally no significant link between (primary) school subjects and . . . work, and schooling is iso-lated from the immediate social and physical environment of the school."[18]

The informal sector, an amorphous residual category of self-employment, micro-enterprise, and alternative business style, reflects at its roots the premise that "livelihoods are more important than wage employment."[19] By no means confined to the Third World, as anyone knows who is familiar with the residential apartment bazaars and street services of Manhattan, this emerging sector is adding new dimensions to HRD in many countries. Difficult to penetrate from several perspectives, such as research and policy, it draws obscure and often hostile reactions from governments. It exhibits very different characteristics in Africa from those in either Latin America or Asia.[20] It also presents a stubborn hurdle to would-be young entrants, since apprenticeship roles or on-the-job training, while not unknown particularly in Africa,[21] are unlikely to be well defined or even welcomed in situations where job skills exemplify survival. Moreover, the average age of

16. Harvard University, *Planning Education for Development*, vol. 1 (Cambridge, MA: Harvard University, Center for Studies in Education and Development, 1980).

17. World Bank, *Education in Sub-Saharan Africa: Policies for Adjustment, Revitalization and Expansion* (Washington, DC: World Bank, 1988).

18. J. O. Shiundu, *Primary Education and Self-Employment in the Rural Informal Sector in Kenya: A Study of Primary School Leavers in Suna, South Nyanza* (Nairobi: Kenyatta University, Bureau of Education Research; Montreal: McGill University, School of Education, 1987).

19. Paul Streeten, *Mobilizing Human Potential: The Challenge of Unemployment*, UNDP Policy Discussion Paper (New York: United Nations Development Program, Bureau for Programme Policy and Evaluation, Policy Division, 1989), p. 9.

20. F. Fluitman, ed., *Training for Work in the Informal Sector* (Geneva: International Labour Office, 1989).

21. F. Fluitman and A. K. Sangare, "Some Recent Evidence of Informal Sector Appren-

informal-sector workers is quite high: for example, 36 years in African case studies[22] and 27 years in Bangkok.[23]

Technology is reshaping the structure of industry and occupational wage employment as well as the skill requirements of the jobs themselves.[24] Amin and others demonstrate that Asian informal sectors may be much less technologically stagnant than commonly thought, with extensive experimentation with self-made machinery and adaptations of secondhand machines in small enterprises, for example.[25] In Africa, structural and technical changes in informal-sector equipment are occurring faster than the skills and knowledge of the users.[26]

Displacement of workers as a function of capital-intensive technology and higher productivity in manufacturing is well documented. Economic growth and employment growth thus do not necessarily go hand in hand. In the formal sector, compensatory

sectoral shifts in employment from manufacturing to services has been associated with larger numbers of low-wage jobs. Thus employment creation and poverty in some cases can be positively correlated. We must therefore understand better the complex relationship between literacy, skills, employment, and productivity and economic growth and reflect these mutualities in HRD policy.

To summarize, major and interrelated problems of unprecedented difficulty are facing HRD decision makers over the next decade and beyond. In education, stringent competition for funds, inequitable access, reduced quality, and charges of obsolescence, even irrelevance, are shaking educational establishments worldwide, while the basic learning needs[27] of hundreds of millions remain unmet. In the health sector, malnutrition and infectious diseases continue to thwart human progress and sap the human resources of the poorer regions. Urbanization of large segments of the stronger rural poor overloads infrastructure and services and threatens to overwhelm both the education and health systems. Consequent degradation of urban environments results through rampant industrial, commercial, and other kinds of pollution, as well as overexploitation of remaining natural resources in rural areas. Spiraling labor force growth, sluggish private sector development, radical readjustments to

ticeship in Abidjan, Cote d'Ivoire," in Fluitman, ed., *Training for Work in the Informal Sector*, pp. 107-16.

22. Jobs and Skills Programme for Africa, *Africa Employment Report 1988* (Addis Ababa: International Labour Organization, 1988).

23. A.T.M.N. Amin, "Technology Adaptation in Bangkok's Informal Sector" (Working paper, World Employment Programme Research, International Labour Office, Geneva, 1989).

24. John E. S. Lawrence, "HRD Impacts of Technological Change: Implications for Basic Learning Needs" (Paper delivered at the World Conference on Education for All, Round Table on the Implications of Technological Change for Basic Learning Needs for Children and Adults. Jomtien, Thailand, 5-9 Mar. 1990).

25. Amin, "Technology Adaptation in Bangkok's Informal Sector."

26. Jobs and Skills Programme for Africa, *Africa Employment Report 1988*, p. 124.

27. Defined in background documentation for the World Conference on Education for All, 5-9 Mar. 1990, as "knowledge, skills, attitudes and values necessary for people to survive, to improve the quality of their lives, and to continue learning."

public sector occupational structures, and widespread unemployment and underemployment even of educated youths further discourage potentially productive work force entrants. A flourishing informal sector provides some hope for both labor force absorption and economic growth, but it is in many ways relatively impervious to current policy and particularly to the young, new labor force entrants.

SOLUTIONS

More integrated HRD strategies offer potential solutions to this extraordinary array of problems. The need for such strategies has been recognized for many years, but there has been a resurgence in several recent U.N. statements. UNDP, in its new annual *Human Development Report* series,[28] redefines human development operationally in terms of enlarging people's choices and offers quantification through comparison of selected social indicators across time and between countries. A Human Development Index is constructed from data on longevity, knowledge, and decent living standards. Adult literacy rates are used in the knowledge component of the Human Development Index.

Of course, the process of the development of human beings reflects multidimensional interactions between neurobiological maturation and individual exposure to learning experiences and contains elements

currently inaccessible to public policy. In addition, there is no single established path to successful development. All individuals will, as must each nation, unfold their own cultural, spiritual, economic, and political order relative to their freedom to act, and their own interpretations of the best information available. But it is the extension of alternatives, and the explicit measurement of progress toward human development goals, that are the central propositions in the UNDP approach.

Within the overall human development domain as outlined previously, HRD is a critical subcomponent, addressing specifically those policies or activities that foster opportunities for people to develop or apply their knowledge and skills in socially or economically useful ways. In view of residual confusion from the common yet imprecise substitution of the terms "human development" and "human resources development" for each other, I thus propose a clear distinction of HRD that focuses on the contributory capacity of human beings as explained in the following.

HRD has been defined in several ways over the years. For example, it has been defined as roughly synonymous with manpower development planning in relation to theories of human capital formation; as remedial programs for those perceived to be at some disadvantage in competition for or performance of jobs; as personnel administration and advancement and/or training policies and programs of agencies or organizations; or as simply education or training to improve skills and knowledge. Each of these definitions is use-

28. United Nations Development Program, *Human Development Report* (New York: Oxford University Press, 1991).

ful for the restrictive purposes for which it is designed, but they also have distinct shortcomings, as detailed elsewhere.[29]

Manpower planning is associated with an overly mechanistic and demand-oriented approach to occupational affiliation that has been all too often methodologically unsound, gender insensitive, and, at best, highly time dependent. It also presumes a degree of correspondence between education/training and job entry and performance that has been difficult to demonstrate empirically. A remedial program, however well intentioned, by targeting the disadvantaged is likely to find itself quickly marginalized and at best finds insufficient resources to do more than scrape the surface of the problems it is intended to solve. Personnel administration approaches to HRD within large organizations are inherently complicated by contrasts between individual and organizational goals; although, at best, these approaches will maximize both, they often err in the direction of the second at the expense of the first. The view of HRD as dealing simply with the supply side, or the institutional preparation of people for work, ignores the fundamentally developmental aspects of all life outside of institutions, and of work itself.

29. John E. S. Lawrence, "Intersectoral Approaches to HRD for the 1990s and Beyond" (Paper delivered at the Comparative and International Education Society Meeting, University of Pittsburgh, 14-17 Mar. 1991); idem, *Occupational Information and International Development*, Occasional Paper no. 1 (Washington, DC: National Occupational Information Coordinating Committee, 1990).

A more comprehensive and integrated definition of HRD therefore should incorporate the best of the foregoing approaches and extend both development and utilization of human capabilities toward economically productive and/or otherwise socially useful ends. This idea of building the self-helping and other-helping capacities of all humans permits HRD to start at the grass-roots level of the individual and the immediate social grouping and becomes the keystone for poverty alleviation.

In recognition of the awesome problems referenced earlier, HRD must be participatory and action oriented, and it must be applicable to both short-term and long-term needs. We therefore define the HRD concept from this public policy perspective as follows: sustaining equitable opportunities for continued acquisition and application of skills, knowledge, and competencies that promote individual self-sufficiency and are mutually beneficial to individuals, the community, and the larger environment of which they are a part.

Four basic, interactive elements are implied in this definition. The first is access to assets such as credit and shelter, without which human capabilities are stunted at the source. Among populations marginalized by economic status and/or by location— for example, inner-city or peri-urban slums, refugee camps—the needs are for composite services including infrastructure, building materials, and financial assistance for shelter and entrepreneurial activities.

The second element is initial and continuing acquisition of knowledge or skills necessary for the performance of chosen roles that contribute economically and/or socially to self or to the immediate social grouping. The type and nature of these roles are discussed further with the third element, application. The acquisition process may be preservice and formative prior to taking up a particular role or roles, or in-service as part of self-improvement with an ongoing or future role in mind. Acquisition will persist over the lifetime span of the individual, with literacy as the fundamental necessary condition. It may be pre-institutional, such as kindergarten or early childhood development; institutional, such as education or training; or noninstitutional —nonformal education or training, work experience, public communication media, contacts with peers or others in a household, and so forth— but it will be a source of or mechanism for learning.

Third is the productive application of individual skills and knowledge in a chosen role or roles in mutually rewarding ways for both individuals and the larger group, establishment, or community of which they are a part. Such roles may not necessarily be for direct economic compensation—that is, work—and may, for example, include inspired community leadership or responsible parenthood but should be directed toward a clearly value-added contribution to the larger group—family, community, enterprise, or society—of which the individual is a functioning member; the value added will, of course, depend on each national, cultural, or social setting. Since most individuals work for the majority of their lives in

either formal or informal work settings, application of skills and knowledge to occupational roles—for wage, salary, or other compensation—will be central, although HRD strategies should be sensitive also to the acquisition and application of nonoccupational skills and knowledge.

The fourth and final element is conservation and sustenance of human resources in support of both acquisition and application of skills and knowledge. This means strategies and policies—with legislative and statutory foundations as appropriate— that promote equitable opportunities for access to schooling, training, and employment, underpinning such opportunities with social infrastructures for maintaining adequate health and nutrition levels for both learning and performance, as well as occupationally supportive, environmentally sensitive, safe, and healthy physical and psychosocial dimensions in the workplace. This implies that HRD policies articulate educational, training, employment, economic, health, and environmental aspects in a more integrated fashion that facilitates rather than inhibits human learning and performance.

HRD, from this public policy perspective, therefore seeks intersectorally to focus relevant actors and agencies—governmental, nongovernmental, private—on improving the autonomous and contributory functioning of individuals in their own chosen roles and status hierarchies, whether the individuals be unemployed or working at one or more occupations, whether for self or for an employer, part-time or full-time, partially disabled or not, or young or old.

The ultimate goal of HRD is to tap into and nurture in explicit and measurable ways the underlying human resourcefulness in all individuals so as to promote their socioeconomic autonomy and facilitate their participation in their own and others' development. To effectively implement such an HRD approach, a more dynamic, less time-dependent and traditional view is needed of the process by which we acquire knowledge and skills, and more attention must be given to possible reentry points into the education and training cycle. Above all, education and training systems will have to be winched closer to actual settings in which competencies are applied. This does not mean simply "vocationalizing" all of education or necessarily linking education exclusively to occupations or even to the workplace. It means providing people with the opportunities to learn useful knowledge and skills that can then be applied to shape their own and others' futures.

At the root of all HRD policies must be sound and flexible guidance in adapting the process and content of programs constructed to meet basic learning needs. Increasingly, adults are demonstrating by their behavior that learning must be lifelong. Today's context for knowledge and skills seems to change even faster than yesterday's. Literacy and numeracy alone are probably not enough to survive adequately in tomorrow's world. Thus even the most basic education will need to be flexible enough to meet different cultural demands as they evolve. Students will be required to become more active in the educational pro-

cess, and teachers must acknowledge that they are learning, too.

What are needed therefore are augmented concepts of literacy and numeracy that will be sensitive to each national and cultural setting and that go beyond simple reading, writing, and counting. The new concepts will build on the old, not replace them. As Caxton's printing press revolutionized the transmission of knowledge, the computer is altering cognition itself. The abstraction of reading and writing, as manipulating, comprehending, and reflecting on symbolic representations, can be successfully incorporated into the teaching of literacy, as the ball-stick-bird method has so dramatically demonstrated.[30] Ideally, innovative concepts of literacy will result in enhanced teacher training that encourages teachers to go beyond simple "black-boxing" of students, where one expects a given set of inputs to produce a given set of outputs with little attention paid to the students' information processing.

Above all, we should remember that people have basic learning needs that endure throughout the life span. In a sense, therefore, we all have a continuing stake in basic education for social and occupational survival. Formal education systems in the past, faced with relatively stable intragenerational environments over time and enjoying a respected tradition and status within societies, have focused mainly on the early initiation of children and young people into responsible and productive roles

30. Rene Fuller, *In Search of the IQ Correlation* (Stony Brook, NY: Ball-Stick-Bird Publications, 1977).

through staged access to existing bodies of knowledge.

No longer is the environment for education as stable as in the past, however, and adults increasingly need periodic booster shots to supplement initial—purported—educational vaccinations against ignorance. The bodies of knowledge are becoming larger, the pace of change faster, and the needs of youths more demanding. Consequently, traditional approaches to meeting basic learning needs are at a real risk of losing credibility altogether. The solution is for new coalitions to extend into more cohesive and integrated strategies for HRD, including but not limited to the educational sector alone.[31] Such strategies must address both the acquisition and the application of knowledge and skills simultaneously.

The new coalitions should involve communities, families, and public and private sectors at the grass-roots level. Such local-level efforts, however, must be supported by improved national-level research and by the necessary national data systems and diagnostic and analytical capabilities to provide timely information on types and rates of changes in social and economic contexts for basic learning and to monitor such issues as equity and accountability. Only if this kind of flexibility, coordination, and adaptability is built into modern educational systems will they be able to compensate for the inertia of the past and meet even the most basic learning needs of the societies they serve.

31. Jacques Hallak, *Investing in the Future: Setting Educational Priorities in the Developing World* (Paris: United Nations Development Program and UNESCO Institute for Educational Planning, 1990), pp. 287-88.

Women and Literacy: Promises and Constraints

By NELLY P. STROMQUIST

ABSTRACT: In almost every country, illiteracy rates are higher among women than among men. This gender disparity can be explained in terms of (1) the sexual division of labor that assigns women many domestic tasks, especially, among poor and rural families, time-consuming chores, and (2) men's control of women's sexuality, which creates both physical and psychological constraints in women's lives. Research has identified various benefits of literacy for women, such as better maternal behaviors regarding child health and child rearing, and effective family planning. Although women could use literacy to increase their access to new knowledge, most literacy programs do not encourage this because their curricula are still designed along sexually stereotyped lines that emphasize women's roles as mothers and household managers. This article argues that these messages do not convey emancipatory knowledge and may solidify values and attitudes that cause women to accept current gender relations rather than to question them.

Nelly P. Stromquist (Ph.D. in international education, Stanford University, 1975) is an associate professor at the University of Southern California. Her research interests focus on the dynamics between education and gender relations and social change, particularly in Latin America and West Africa. Her most recent works include Daring to Be Different: The Choice of Nonconventional Fields of Study by International Women Students *(1991) and* Women and Education in Latin America: Knowledge, Power, and Change *(1992). She has published in journals such as the* Comparative Education Review, *the* Review of Educational Research, *and* Convergence.

ILLITERACY is generally considered to be a major impediment to the understanding of one's world and to the securing of a good place in it. The role of literacy as a prerequisite for the acquisition of other skills and the development of more rational attitudes is universally accepted. In today's rapidly advancing technological society, the written word has become the dominant mode of complex communication; those without the ability to read and write will be condemned to the lowest roles in society.

And yet illiteracy is far from being eliminated throughout the world. It is estimated that in less than 10 years from now, the world will have 1 billion illiterates, 98 percent of whom will be in developing regions.

Illiteracy is far from being a mere technical problem, that is, the inability to decode and encode the written word. It is linked to contextual factors in which social-class distinctions, linguistic affiliations, general levels of socioeconomic development, and marginalization of certain groups play important and mutually supportive roles.

While there is diversity in the causes operating in any given country, a persistent phenomenon observed in most societies is that women constitute the majority of illiterates.[1] Moreover, the numbers of illiterate women have been increasing not only in absolute but also in

1. There are some exceptions in the pattern of women's composing the majority of illiterates. These are usually small countries characterized by heavy male out-migration, such as Lesotho, or a preponderance of female heads of households, such as Jamaica and a few other Caribbean islands.

relative terms: according to data from the United Nations Educational, Scientific, and Cultural Organization (UNESCO), they represented 63 percent of the illiterates in 1983, up from 58 percent in 1960. Two of every three adult women in Africa and one of every two in Asia are illiterate. In the African and Asian areas there is a literacy gap of 21 percentage points in favor of men (Table 1), a gap that clearly spells out economic and social inequality for many women.

UNDERSTANDING THE SUBORDINATION OF WOMEN

Observers of literacy programs note that neither adult literacy studies nor "women in development" studies have focused on women's literacy. From a theoretical perspective, the conditions of women's illiteracy can be easily explained in the context of women's overall inferior status in society. For a variety of historical and technological reasons, industrialization brought with it a division of social life into public and private spheres. Soon, a patriarchal ideology that defined women as inferiors and subordinate to men developed in most countries. This ideology was promptly codified in the laws of the emerging nation-states through regulations affecting institutions such as the family, work, landownership, and voting rights. Although these institutions have undergone modification over time, the two essential mechanisms for the persistence of patriarchal ideologies—the sexual division of labor and the control of women's sexuality by men—continue

TABLE 1

UNESCO ESTIMATES OF ILLITERACY RATES, BY GENDER, 1985

Region	Gender		Gender Gap
	Female	Male	
Developed countries	2.6	1.7	0.9
Developing countries	48.9	27.9	21.0
Africa	64.5	43.3	21.2
Asia	47.4	25.6	21.8
Latin America and the Caribbean	19.2	15.3	3.9

SOURCE: United Nations Educational, Scientific, and Cultural Organization, *Compendium of Statistics on Illiteracy*, no. 30 (Paris: United Nations Educational, Scientific, and Cultural Organization, 1988).

in effect. Although these forces are substantially modified by class position, the country's level of technological development, and cultural beliefs, the influence of gender is strong and remarkably stable across societies.

The sexual division of labor

According to statistics of the International Labor Organization, women account for two-thirds of the working hours in the world. Poor women in rural areas perform heavy and arduous tasks daily to ensure family subsistence. In Africa, women provide 60 to 80 percent of the labor in food production and a considerable contribution to cash agricultural production. In Asia and Latin America, men contribute a greater share than in Africa to agricultural work, but the domestic burden of women remains considerable. Given the demands of rural domestic life in many developing countries—which includes walking long distances to obtain water and wood for fuel, growing subsistence crops and processing foods that require a considerable investment of physical energy and time, and facing pregnancy and related illnesses with a minimum of medical technologies —women and girls in rural areas face a daily existence that is indisputably more demanding in terms of time and effort than that experienced by men. Social beliefs that women should take care of children and home lead poor social groups to consider education—even literacy—an element less crucial than others to the everyday survival of the family.

Control of women's sexuality

In addition to the sexual division of labor that places poor women in inescapable domestic servitude, men's control of women's sexuality places additional constraints on women's lives. This sexuality control, which operates mainly in Asian and Latin American countries, is manifested by strict supervision of women's movement outside the home and of the friendships they develop with members of the opposite sex. In many societies, it is also manifested by the withdrawal of daughters from school as soon as they reach puberty for fear that the young girls may lose their virginity.

A more serious manifestation of the control of women's sexuality is wife beating, which creates among women an attitude of conflict avoidance, which in turn produces a reluctance to engage in any action that might trigger the husband's attack.[2] That this may have a bearing on decisions such as attendance in literacy classes has been documented through life-history methods.[3] The existence of intensive domestic work coupled with conflictual family dynamics renders literacy an unattainable dream for a large number of women and merely a dream for some of their children—particularly their daughters, who early in life tend to be assigned the same domestic and subsistence roles that their mothers perform.

Control of women's sexuality affects their participation in literacy programs because often the places available for classes are considered unsuitable in terms of safety and accessibility for women. Reports from India indicate that obstacles imposed by family members, particularly husbands and in-laws, prevent women from participating in literacy programs. The experience of a recent national literacy campaign in Ecuador detected similar effects.

These two fundamental causes, the sexual division of labor and the control by men of women's sexuality, are socially constructed realities. They exist by virtue of social understandings rather than because they are the only ways in which societies can exist. In traditional societies and, to a surprising degree, even in modern nations, women are defined primarily as mothers and wives rather than as autonomous citizens or workers. Women attain legitimacy when they marry and form families. Subsequent legitimacy is gained when they produce children, especially sons.

Patriarchal ideologies are generally supported by religiocultural norms, even though within a given religion variations may be found as a result of historical differences that have led to different interpretations of sacred texts. Islam and Hinduism tend to be more gender restrictive than either Christianity or Buddhism regarding social norms. In India, for instance, the traditional laws of Manu make women noneligible for all scholastic activities. The three countries in West Asia with the lowest rates of female literacy and the highest gender gap in literacy are Muslim: Yemen, Syria, and Afghanistan. Confucianism, a cohesive set of moral precepts, is also highly oppressive of women, and its legacy is still evident in rural areas of today's socialist China.

2. Wife beating is a widespread social practice. Formal studies of its incidence in the United States have declared it the single greatest source of injury to women. Wife beating in certain developing countries, such as Papua New Guinea, affects as much as two-thirds of the adult women.

3. See, for instance, Kathleen Rockhill, "Literacy as Threat/Desire: Theorizing Women's Oppression" (Paper delivered at the Comparative and International Education Society, Toronto, Ontario, Canada, Mar. 1986).

WOMEN AND LITERACY

Not only is illiteracy higher among women than men, but it is higher in less industrialized and in agrarian societies than in urban societies. One explanation for the low levels of literacy among women in nonindustrial societies is that in these societies the maternal roles do not require high levels of education. Literacy indeed may not be necessary if the main reproductive and productive tasks that women carry out—having babies, raising children, managing a low-budget household, growing subsistence crops—can be learned through informal, oral-tradition methods. In all countries, illiteracy rates are higher in rural than in urban areas. UNESCO data for 15 Latin American countries show that rural areas have greater levels of illiteracy than urban areas regardless of sex, although women have a slightly greater disadvantage compared to men—a 27.5 percent illiteracy gap exists between urban and rural women compared to a 25.4 percent gap between urban and rural men. It is striking, however, to observe that the gender gap in rural areas is almost double that in urban areas—12.0 versus 6.3 percentage points. The disadvantage of rural women is most likely due to the sexual division of labor that places upon them major burdens for domestic work, subsistence production, and various family responsibilities.

With the expansion of schooling, poor families today are more inclined than former generations to allow their daughters to be educated. Girls' enrollment rates in primary school are gradually reaching parity with those of boys in many developing countries. Yet the early withdrawal of girls from school, as happens in many African and Asian countries, does not allow the retention of literacy skills. Three or four years of schooling characterized by numerous absences do not amount to much education for the girls; thus a significant loss of literacy skills follows. As adults, their limited physical mobility, their contacts mostly with women of their own community—who tend to be illiterates like them—and their own socialization into accepting the norm that women do not need as much education as do men create a strong mindset among women that further prevents them from seeking basic literacy skills.

BENEFITS OF LITERACY FOR WOMEN

Do women benefit from access to literacy? There have been relatively few studies measuring the impact of literacy per se—as opposed to levels of schooling—and even fewer studies focusing on literacy while controlling for other, confounding variables.

We have substantial evidence about the positive effect of education on a number of individual and maternal outcomes, but such studies are based mainly on examinations of the impacts of years of schooling. Nonetheless, it could be inferred that literacy—a critical component of formal education—also offers the same benefits. Several findings support this inference. First, mother's schooling has been found to have a monotonically negative relationship with infant and child mortality rates and fertility rates. This suggests that every amount of additional schooling—of which literacy represents the first step—makes a difference. Second, because education makes a difference even in places where the quality of education is low, the effects of schooling are probably less due to the curriculum or the instructional program than to "something very general about schooling."[4] This general factor could be literacy since most schooling experiences at least provide literacy skills. Third, if we conceptualize adult literacy as the precursor to the establishment of literate practices—that is, regular access to the printed word—then the effects of literacy should be akin to those of the number of years of schooling.

In numerous countries, education is so strongly associated with reduced fertility and decreased infant and child mortality that it is accepted now as a causal factor.[5] Some of the critical mechanisms that account for the literacy-fertility relationship have been found to be knowledge of and access to birth control and increased husband-wife communication. Not surprisingly, the level of education of women has an effect on fertility that is three times stronger than that of men. Regardless of social class, the more educated a woman is, the fewer children she will have; this effect seems to be stronger in urban than in rural areas. Education seems to have more positive effects when the society in which people live is also literate; Cochrane's review of data for 23 countries found that the inverse relation between education and fertility was strongest in societies where the aggregate literacy was at least 40 percent.[6] Moreover, the more educated a woman is, the better will be the health of her children and the greater will be their life expectancy at birth. Various studies have found more powerful benefits associated with the education of mothers than of fathers on outcomes such as improved nutrition of children. The latter effect is part of an indirect causal chain: mothers with more education tend to enter the labor force in greater numbers; as they earn wages, they spend their income on improving the family diet. Educated women have been found to marry at a later age and to provide their children with much more verbal and physical stimulation than do women with little or no education; this stimulation is in turn associated with greater cognitive development on the part of the child.

Studies relating literacy to cognitive and various social outcomes are few in number. A Nigerian study comparing literate with illiterate women found that educated mothers have different maternal behaviors in that they practice less force-feeding, talk

4. Robert LeVine, "Women's Schooling, Patterns of Fertility, and Child Survival," *Educational Researcher*, Dec. 1987, p. 23.

5. See ibid., pp. 21-27, for an extensive reference to the research literature supporting this claim.

6. Susan Cochrane, "Education and Fertility: An Expanded Examination of the Evidence," in *Women's Education in the Third World: Comparative Perspectives*, ed. Gail Kelly and Carolyn Elliott (Albany: State University of New York Press, 1982), pp. 311-30.

more to their babies, and use less physical punishment.[7] A study of rural women in Sri Lanka found that illiterate women visited maternal and child health clinics less often, were less inclined to seek immunization against tetanus, had unattended home deliveries, and had a higher incidence of prenatal and neonatal mortality among their infants.[8] A study of short-term literacy outcomes conducted in Kenya, where approximately 70 percent of the participants in literacy programs were women, found that literacy skills facilitated the acquisition of functional knowledge regarding agriculture, health, and family planning; further, they produced more positive individual attitudes toward innovation.[9]

Those studies that focus on the number of years of schooling as their measurement of education assert that important processes—still not well documented—materialize through the school and through classroom experiences. They also assert that education allows substantial cognitive growth and that this ability allows women to detect relationships between means and ends. If literacy allows cognitive growth, then its effect may be similar to that of the number of years of schooling. Nonetheless, the point at which literacy makes an impact remains unclear. The ability to read and write as segmented skills probably is less valuable than literacy skills nurtured by content that conveys to women important messages and perspectives about their social reality. If so, the importance of literacy is really in post-literacy, in the kinds of activities and learning that take place after reading and writing skills are mastered.

While the findings are not always unambiguous and positive, the overall results indicate that literate women make better maternal and family decisions and engage in more desirable practices than do women who do not have access to the written word. The evidence reviewed previously makes it clear that benefits do accrue to women from access to education, including literacy. These benefits have been measured primarily in terms of women's contribution to families and society as presently constituted; in other words, they have been measured in terms of serving the social status quo. Nonetheless, the acquisition of skills to process new and more distant forms of knowledge has a potential that can be channeled to meet women's needs.

7. Robert LeVine, "Influences of Women's Schooling on Maternal Behavior in the Third World," in *Women's Education in the Third World*, ed. Kelly and Elliot, pp. 283-310. This study, conducted by Barbara Lloyd and associates, focused on Yoruba women; it also found that educated mothers tended to discourage aggression less, to practice less the postpartum taboo of their society, and to engage in shorter periods of breast-feeding than the illiterate, traditional mothers. These findings suggest that not all behaviors associated with literacy are positive.

8. Swarna Jayaweera, "Women and Literacy: The Sri Lanka Experience" (Paper delivered at the "Symposium on Women and Literacy: Yesterday, Today, and Tomorrow," Hasselby Slott, Sweden, 8-10 June 1989).

9. Francoise Caillods, "Women's Literacy for Development: A Brief Overview of the Situation Today" (Paper delivered at the "Symposium on Women and Literacy").

THE CONSTRAINTS OF LITERACY PROGRAMS

Literacy is increasingly being recognized as a basic human right. Yet very few governments have conducted serious literacy programs, much less taken specific measures to expand the education of adult women, even though women are recognized—especially after the 1975-85 U.N. Decade for Women—as intended beneficiaries. Most literacy programs conducted by governments have tended to assume that programs can be designed to serve both men and women simultaneously. Close examination of these programs, however, reveals that they offer little in the line of supportive services for women—for example, child-care services, flexible class schedules, alternative class settings—that would facilitate their attendance. There is little also in terms of instructional methodologies to appeal to adult, generally fatigued and harassed women. While more women than men tend to enroll in literacy classes, this is probably a consequence of the larger numbers of women who are illiterate. At the same time, the participation of women is sporadic and many never complete their programs.

Literacy programs for women have offered limited attention both to the deep causes of women's subordination and to the immediate constraints they face in participating in literacy programs. As a result, these programs tend to solidify the existing social order. The explicit justification for many literacy programs for women is that women need to be "incorporated into development efforts." This argument implies that women are not part of the economy and society. It would be more correct to state that women are not incorporated under equal conditions. The problem of uneducated women is not their failure to contribute but rather that their contribution takes place under exploitative and oppressive conditions. The discourse about helping women "to contribute more fully to economic and social development"[10] is misguided in that it does not recognize the current contribution being made by women and does not examine the conditions under which further contributions might be exacted.

When governments do offer literacy programs for women, the similarity of their objectives is remarkable. Common features are their content emphasis on family health, child care, nutrition, and family planning. To a lesser extent, information on income generation is being introduced, but even here the activities are designed so that they are totally compatible with women's traditional domestic and family roles. Most damaging of all is the fact that the curricular content of many literacy programs conveys traditional notions of male superiority. These messages are commonly disguised under the notion of "complementary" roles, whereby men assume economic and political responsibilities in public life and women concentrate their energy and devotion to husband and children.

10. World Bank, *Sub-Saharan Africa: From Crisis to Sustainable Growth* (Washington, DC: World Bank, 1989), p. 60.

In the governmental discourse that puts a premium on the provision of literacy education to women, it is clear that literacy for women is advocated as an instrument for rendering them better mothers and house managers. Less often does one hear that literacy can also help women become independent and involved citizens. Many of the literacy programs for women today center on giving women literacy skills so that they can read information on child care, nutrition, hygiene, family planning, pre- and postnatal care, and water-pump management. While these programs are described as "functional literacy," it is clear that it is a functionality conceived along traditional, narrow roles for women.

This emphasis on social and biological reproduction has been observed in numerous programs, from Indonesia to Argentina. Evidence from the curricula of various governmental literacy programs for women confirms the reproductive objectives of these programs. The case of India is particularly relevant. India is a country with long-standing literacy programs, including some centering on women. The National Adult Education Program (NAEP), initiated in 1978, specifically identified women as intended beneficiaries and sought to provide them with knowledge of their rights and responsibilities in society, with an understanding of the manifest and concealed causes of women's oppression, with skills for economic viability, and with knowledge related to health, child care, nutrition, family planning, and so on. Several studies of the implementation of the NAEP, however, coincide

in describing this program as one that has emphasized the traditional, reproductive role of women by concentrating on drilling them in nutrition, health, and family planning.[11] The primers used in some of the NAEP literacy classes for women reveal a content that would perpetuate women's dependence on men and that leaves gender relations at home and in society untouched. Content analysis of the reader used in the state of Gujarat found a focus on marriage, housework, child care, and family planning that portrayed women in the roles of wives and mothers in a happy nuclear patriarchal family. The income-generating activities proposed for women built on "feminine" home-based activities such as sewing, embroidery, and preparing and processing food, "thereby ensuring that the domestic sphere is not disturbed."[12] A curriculum for literacy programs that heavily emphasizes a home economics content has also been identified in the National Literacy Program of Botswana.[13]

Literacy primers reproduce gender relations also by omitting discussion of important knowledge. In Tanzania, a socialist country well known

11. Anita Dighe, "Programmes with Focus on Women's Involvement: The Case of India," in *Issues in Planning and Implementing National Literacy Programs*, ed. G. Carron and A. Bordia (Paris: International Institute for Educational Planning, 1985), pp. 141-58.

12. Ila Patel, "Policy and Practice of Adult Education for Women in India, 1970-1984" (Paper delivered at the Sixth World Congress of Comparative Education, Rio de Janeiro, Brazil, 6-10 July 1987).

13. Samora Gaborone, "Gender and Literacy: The Case of Botswana" (Paper delivered at the "Symposium on Women and Literacy").

for its inspiring educational philosophies, primers do not mention the domestic labor of women, their work load in the family, or issues of sexuality and sexual harassment.[14]

Information about basic needs and skills in nutrition, child care, and hygiene is important. It will help rural and poor women reduce their hours of toil and suffering. On the other hand, if the messages conveyed to women gravitate essentially around reproductive roles, the women's social definition as mothers and wives will be consolidated, not transformed.

I referred earlier to the programs' ability to respond to women's needs. The notion of needs requires discussion. Government officials usually describe women's needs as those that derive from their traditionally feminine roles. From a feminist perspective, women's needs are those that link women to processes of social questioning and transformation. At the program level, there emerges a tension between providing women with knowledge for ordinary life— knowledge that addresses basic survival needs tied to social and biological reproduction—and knowledge and skills needed to change social relations—a critical understanding of reality, political mobilization, and organization. There is much to be said about improving also the knowledge that women receive regarding necessary skills for subsistence, particularly those skills needed for increasing agricultural productivity. A recent study found that women culti-

vators in Kenya, even though they had literacy skills and were able to read instructions for applying agricultural chemicals to their crops, still did not have the ability to utilize such inputs safely and effectively. The researchers concluded that if literacy were to make a difference, instruction in science and agriculture would have to improve to enable women farmers to understand basic scientific principles.[15]

As an implementation strategy, it would make sense to start literacy programs that appeal to women's conventional roles and thus their immediate responsibilities. But these programs should progressively expand to include knowledge that is more emancipatory in nature, moving from basic needs to political information. The question that now emerges is, How willing will the state be to endorse such programs? The state has responded to programs with emancipatory content in either of two ways: (1) by failing to implement such programs altogether, or (2) by conducting one or two of them as progressive pilot programs but delaying their large-scale implementation.

Women need literacy programs that will make them aware of their subordinate status in society and in the family. They need programs that inspire in them the questioning of the prevailing sexual division of labor and the norms that control their sexuality and thus their physical and mental freedom. Literacy for women has to provide access not only to the

14. Aikael Kweka, "Women in Literacy Programs and Underdevelopment: The Case of Tanzania" (Paper delivered at the "Symposium on Women and Literacy").

15. Thomas Eisemon and Andrew Nyamete, "School Literacy and Agricultural Modernization in Kenya," *Comparative Education Review*, 34(2):161-76 (1990).

written word but also to the information they need to transform their world. The programs, therefore, will have to be designed so that not only the content but also the process of knowledge acquisition is emancipatory. A process that promotes an active role for women will have to include them in the design and implementation of literacy programs. This is a notion to which many government bureaucrats react with ridicule and that few of them are willing to undertake. Yet, a woman who is not empowered will do little with her new literacy.

Illiteracy is a social condition that reflects structural inequalities and the discrimination built into social institutions. A major constraint on women's acquisition of literacy lies in the material benefits that women's illiteracy produces for others. Women's work at home and in the informal sector reduces the price of labor in general and facilitates capital accumulation in free-market systems. Therefore, women's role in the informal sector and in household labor, far from being a "holdout from capitalist modernization," is an important element in the modernization process,[16] making changes in their socioeconomic position difficult as the changes will call for a complex realignment of forces.

Who can provide the literacy programs that women need? Certainly not the state, which relies on the traditional family to keep society stable. Because of the constraints imposed

16. Elaine Draper, "Women's Work and Development in Latin America, *Studies in Comparative International Development*, 20(1):3-30 (Spring 1985).

on gender issues by some religions, it is doubtful that Muslim religious schools such as the *maktab* and the *madrasah* could provide women and their daughters with literacy knowledge that is emancipatory in nature. The possibility for change will, I believe, come from the women themselves, through local programs willing to undertake small-scale but radical steps to transform society at both micro—household—and macro—community—levels. The role of nongovernmental organizations, and particularly women-run nongovernmental organizations, will be important here. Their possibilities for state support are very small; hence this is an area where external funding sources may have to play a crucial role.

That most governments have done little to address the problem of illiteracy can be widely observed. In recent years, initiatives outside the state have taken place to encourage greater attention to the problem of illiteracy and to put pressure on governments to act. Several international and national nongovernmental organizations in developed countries conducted efforts beginning in 1981 to have the United Nations proclaim a year devoted to literacy. This finally happened in 1989, when the U.N. General Assembly declared 1990 the International Literacy Year and asked UNESCO, as the leading international agency on education, to coordinate the activities for the year.

The objectives of the International Literacy Year specifically identified "women and girls" among the intended beneficiaries of literacy. The objectives also sought to "increase action by the governments of member states afflicted by illiteracy or functional illiteracy to eliminate these problems" and to "increase popular participation particularly through activities of governmental and nongovernmental organizations, voluntary associations and community groups."[17] While these are noble aims, those seeking the advancement of women will have to ensure that governments allocate substantial funds for literacy and post-literacy programs, that these programs do not continue their patriarchal message to women, and that they do not construe "popular participation of nongovernmental organizations" to mean unpaid, voluntary efforts.

It would be a mistake to see illiteracy as mainly an individual's failure to develop literacy skills. The emergence of conditions fostering illiteracy is deeply embedded in social definitions of the role of women in society. These definitions, part and parcel of patriarchal ideologies, are reenacted on a day-to-day basis. The quotidian nature of their reenactment makes patriarchal ideologies most difficult to question and change. The problem of illiteracy among women therefore is best understood as a manifestation of gender inequality in society, which necessitates a solution that goes far beyond educational strategies.

Efforts to enable poor and marginal women to become literate will need the pressure of people committed to social change on numerous fronts, which must include employment, marriage and household relations, legal rights, and increased primary education. If literacy for women does not bring with it an emancipatory content and participatory methods of instruction, there is a greater danger that the state may be using literacy not to release women from subordinate positions but to indoctrinate them more effectively with asymmetrical gender relations.

17. United Nations Educational, Scientific, and Cultural Organization, *1990: International Literacy Year, Information Document, June 1989* (Paris: United Nations Educational, Scientific, and Cultural Organization, 1989).

Functional Literacy:
North-South Perspectives

By ADAMA OUANE

ABSTRACT: Can we postulate that a line of distinction could be drawn between developing and developed countries with regard to the functionality of prevailing literacies? The multilayered perception of literacy and the interpretive ambiguity surrounding functionality, in addition to the lack of focused treatment of the issue in the literature, complicate such an attempt considerably. Functionality can be referred to as a moving range to be located and periodically relocated on the illiteracy-literacy continuum. Two notions are found to be of interest in this analysis: restricted literacy in the sense used by Goody; and functional penetration, referred to by Levine as the range of activities and transactions in which literacy is institutionalized for a human group.

Dr. Adama Ouane holds a Ph.D. in linguistics from the Institute of Linguistics of the Academy of Sciences of the USSR (1976). Research specialist at the UNESCO Institute for Education (UIE) since 1983, he is responsible for the research and research-based programs on basic nonformal education for out-of-school children, youths, and adults in both developing and industrialized countries. He is editor, author, and / or coauthor of eight volumes in the UIE series published on this theme and has had articles on literacy, post-literacy, evaluation, and the use of national languages published in a number of journals.

DEFINITIONS of literacy are numerous and varied. One sees, for example, the influence of development ideology, of educational objectives, and of a desire for educational reform; links to cultural, social, and ecological contexts have been frequently pointed out as well. Questions are raised concerning the distribution of literacy skills across social groups, resulting power and status shifts, the use of literacy, and its resulting value. In their analysis of a corpus of literacy definitions, Giere et al. demonstrate that such definitions range from short-term pragmatic and utilitarian approaches to idealistic, broad, humanitarian ones, depending on the ways in which authors interpret, combine, and highlight the core elements involved, as well as the contextual constraints, the predominant forces that determine the operational objectives, and the standards set.[1]

Functional literacy is an old concept that has recently become popular. By seeking to establish a relationship between the learner and his or her surroundings, functionality cuts across all the aforementioned elements and hence holds a wide interpretive potential that is appreciated by some as a sign of richness and by others as a reflection of confusion. This conflict is evident in statements such as the following: "There is no non-functional, non-related literacy"[2]

and "All literacy is functional"[3] as compared to "Literacy per se is not functional for the act of learning is an individual one."[4] It would appear that the more broadly literacy is defined, the wider is its functionality. It has also been found that the degree of functionality and the need for it are closely related to participant age, meaning that if a functional approach is appropriate in literacy programs for youths and adults, it will not necessarily be appropriate for children.[5] A related factor is that different approaches are called for by different constituencies. For example, governments, state bodies, and businesses tend to advocate and adopt short-term approaches based on utilitarian considerations, while humanistic scholars and voluntary organizations, on the other hand, call for long-term, broad objectives.

Although the terms are not easily definable, it is clear that a dichotomy does exist between functional and nonfunctional literacy. An interesting and related question is whether a distinction can also be made between "developing" and industrialized countries with respect to functionality, a topic to which I now turn.

1. Ursula Giere, Adama Ouane, and Mahinda Ranaweera, "Literacy in Developing Countries: An Analytical Bibliography," *Bulletin of the International Bureau of Education*, 254-57:35-36 (Jan.-Dec. 1990).

2. Malcolm S. Adiseshiah, "Functionalities of Literacy," in *A Turning Point for Literacy*, ed. Leon Bataille (Oxford: Pergamon, 1976), p. 65.

3. International Bureau of Education, International Conference on Education, 42d Session, *The Struggle against Illiteracy: Policies, Strategies and Emerging Operational Action for the 1990s*, ED/B1E/CONFINTED 42/3 (Geneva: IBE, July 1990), p. 27.

4. International Bureau of Education, International Conference on Education, 42d Session, *Report of Working Group II*, ED/B1E/CONFINTED 42/Ref 2 (Geneva: IBE, 1990), p. 3.

5. Ibid.

DEFINING FUNCTIONALITY IN LITERACY

The notions of functional literacy and illiteracy stem from analyses of the meaning of literacy use and its effects on individuals in their interactions in the physical and social milieu. The role of context is key in functional literacy, but a look at the historical evolution of literacy concepts and definitions confirms that a consensus is far from being reached regarding what literacy is, what it is used for, and what it means to be literate or illiterate for the individual in various social contexts.[6] Goals cited as desirable outcomes of literacy attainment for the individual or society include empowerment, self-reliance, control, transformation, and autonomy. Studies linked to functional literacy highlight the use of literacy as a communication tool, its contextual relation to institutions and the social structures embedded

in them, and the societal distribution of literacy skills and its influence on social groups, the individual, and state agencies.

To disentangle this conceptual complexity, some authors refer to "literacies" instead of "literacy."[7] As Lankshear and Lawler put it:

There are also very important contemporary dimensions to the claim that we should identify and examine different literacies rather than assert or assume a single unitary literacy. We find present day writers distinguishing between "basic" and "critical," "domesticating" and "liberating" literacy, "improper" and "proper" literacy, "functional" and "full" literacy, and even between different "functional" literacies. In addition, some identify and elaborate different literacies by social class, culture/sub-culture, ethnic group, etc.[8]

The most widely accepted definition of functional literacy, however, comes from Gray's now classical survey of reading and writing carried out for the United Nations Educational, Scientific, and Cultural Organization (UNESCO). He claims that "a person is functionally literate when he [sic] has acquired the knowledge and skills in reading and writing which enable him to engage in all those activities in which literacy is normally assumed in his culture or group."[9]

6. The various points of view and a historical treatment of the issue are to be found in the following publications: Jack Goody, ed., *Literacy in Traditional Societies* (New York: Cambridge University Press, 1968); Harvey J. Graff, *The Labyrinths of Literacy: Reflections on Literacy, Past and Present* (New York: Falmer, 1987); Carman St. J. Hunter, "Literacy the Moving Target," in *Adult Education: International Perspectives from China*, ed. Chris Duke (London: Croom Helm, 1987); Jonathan Kozol, *Illiterate America* (Garden City, NY: Anchor, Doubleday, 1985); Kenneth Levine, *The Social Context of Literacy* (New York: Routledge & Kegan Paul, 1986); Brian Street, *Literacy in Theory and Practice* (New York: Cambridge University Press, 1984); Richard Venezky et al., eds., *Toward Defining Literacy* (Newark, DE: International Reading Association, 1990); Daniel A. Wagner, ed., *The Future of Literacy in a Changing World* (Oxford: Pergamon, 1987).

7. Peter Easton, "Structuring Learning Environments: Lessons from the Organisation of Post-Literacy Programs," *International Review of Education*, 35(4):389-408 (1989); Levine, *Social Context of Literacy*, p. 43.

8. Colin Lankshear and Moira Lawler, *Literacy, Schooling and Revolution* (New York: Falmer, 1987), p. 48.

9. William S. Gray, *The Teaching of Reading and Writing: An International Survey*

FUNCTIONAL LITERACY
IN DEVELOPING COUNTRIES

Gray's definition of functionality in literacy found a resonance in developing countries and was instrumental in bringing about a shift from narrow, work-oriented, economic considerations of literacy to broader sociopolitical and cultural ones. Literacy moved from so-called traditional literacy, where it was seen as an end in itself, to a modern notion, where it is linked with economic development and social transformation. Many feel that literacy is an essential ingredient of individual and social development. For example, Thompson reported how:

literacy would act as the bridge between fatalistic passivity and uncomprehending acceptance, which has been thought of as characterizing many rural peoples, and a real participation both in promoting and in determining the nature of the social transformation thought to be necessary. It would act in this way by facilitating a flow of vital ideals and information to the masses, increasing their awareness of the situation in which they live, and of the possibilities and choices before them.[10]

A conflicting view is summarized by Duke, who stated that there is

no proof: that literacy was historically a prerequisite of economic and social development; that literacy efforts have of themselves diminished exploitation and poverty; that literacy is a prerequisite for the intelligent understanding and handling of life; or that it necessarily and directly relates to attaining participative

structures, achieving liberation and abolishing oppression.[11]

Researchers have treated the major approaches to literacy development in the recent history of developing countries by emphasizing the following foci: fundamental education, basic education, functional literacy, and literacy for liberation. These trends are sometimes chronologically defined and their prominence is evident in events such as the international adult education conferences as well as in landmark events such as the Teheran Conference of Ministers of Education on Literacy, marking the proclamation of the well-known Experimental World Literacy Program, and the Persepolis Declaration, which was influenced by the ideas of Paulo Freire and which marked the consecration of literacy for liberation. Finally, the influence of these trends is also evident in the four major approaches to literacy education identified by Lind and Johnston in their review of objectives and strategies of adult literacy in the Third World. These are, the authors assert, "the 'fundamental education' approach (in today's terminology, 'basic education' or 'general literacy'); the 'selective-intensive' functional approach practiced as 'functional literacy'; the 'conscientization' approach; and the 'mass campaign' approach. None of these are complete or exclusive strategies."[12]

(Paris: United Nations Educational, Scientific, and Cultural Organization, 1956), p. 24.

10. A. R. Thompson, *Education and Development in Africa* (London: Macmillan, 1981), p. 224.

11. Chris Duke, *Combatting Poverty through Adult Education: National Development Strategies* (London: Croom Helm, 1985), p. 7.

12. Agneta Lind and A. Johnston, *Adult Literacy in the Third World: A Review of Objectives and Strategies* (Stockholm: Swedish International Development Authority, 1986), p. 49.

In operational terms, programs vary in the importance they accord to fundamental, basic, functional, or liberating aspects of literacy. One approach that stresses functionality is the attempt to link the actual application of skills acquired through literacy and post-literacy provision to the field of economic development. Whether and how much literacy is actually used for this purpose, however, depends on many variables such as local perceptions and social organization. There are numerous examples of this approach in francophone Africa, such as the Literacy for Income Generation Program for Women in Togo; other programs include the Employment-Oriented Learning Program in Indonesia, the Skill Training Program in Jamaica, and the Small Farmers Development Project in Nepal. The main objective of the Employment-Oriented Learning Program in Indonesia, for instance, is to enable learners organized into groups to market the skills they already possess. The organization and management of small business and income-generating skills are thereby improved. Learning takes place in an actual work situation, and the learners are expected to expand their businesses with the help of special learning funds, ranging from Rp50 thousand to Rp150 thousand—approximately US$4000 to 12,000—depending on the type of business enterprise. Other national development plans assign a major functional role to literacy without necessarily focusing on economic development, targeting instead the social development of communities, for example.

In this context, some programs have adopted an individualistic orientation while others are more society or community oriented. The former pursue mainly personal growth and development, which in turn is expected to produce some impact on the family and social environment of the individual. Some of these offer an academic or general education, while others are vocationally oriented.[13] In community-action and group-oriented programs, on the other hand, although the role of individual learning is recognized, education is primarily conceived of as an instrument for economic and social change for the community as a whole, and goals are explicitly stated at a collective level.

Although literacy definitions vary from country to country, and even from situation to situation, most seem to use a broad, functional definition focusing on the application of literacy skills and on literacy's relation to technical progress and economic development. An example of a campaign approach with functional literacy goals can be found in Burkina Faso. Here the strategy is to train local self-help leaders so that they may implement literacy programs in local communities. These leaders, or literacy commandos, trained in situ within 48 days, cover a variety of regions, operating in 10 different languages. They work with different economic operators, such as leaders of cooperatives, primary

13. Ravindra Dave, Adama Ouane, and Peter Sutton, "Issues in Post-Literacy," *International Review of Education*, 35(4):397 (1989).

health care workers, women and youths, and leaders of traditional associations, with the objective of mounting a network of pedagogical and organizational support services. After the launching of the program, the hope is that the programs will be able to sustain the campaign at the local level.

Since functional literacy as an approach is closely linked to the field activities of many development agencies, another common approach is to integrate literacy into development projects. In Mali, for example, the literacy campaigns are part of development action carried out by the Opération de Développement Rural, which includes the Opération de Développement Intégré pour la Production Arachidiere et Céréaliere, the Opération Riz Ségou, and the Opération Mil Mopti, to name a few. In Senegal, they are labeled "sociétés d'intervention," and they may cover one whole region, as in the case of the Société des Fibres et Textiles; in other cases they intervene in more than one region, an example being the Office National de Commercialisation Agricole. In Burkina Faso, examples are the Organismes Régionaux de Développement, which include the Autorité des Aménagements des Vallées des Voltas, the Fonds de Développement Rural, and the Service d'Éducation et de Participation des Femmes au Développement. Similar agencies can be found in other countries throughout this region.

In order to correct the urban bias of development undertakings, literacy-provision efforts are mainly directed to rural areas. Until recently most of the programs in Burkina Faso and Mali, for example, had a content directed solely toward the rural population, with literacy centers spread only in rural areas. Niger and Senegal, on the other hand, have a mix of rural and urban centers, with a predominance of the former. Logically, program content varies depending on its urban or rural orientation, with the core content of programs aimed at rural populations emphasizing basic literacy, functional literacy, vocational training, work productivity, income generation, and cooperative management, while the focus of urban programs is on industry, manual work, and low-grade clerical work.[14]

Many of these programs have also widened their vision of functionality to include animation and participation leading to critical sociopolitical questioning of the existing reality. Two Latin American movements that demonstrate this wider scope are the Popular Education movement and the Literacy for Conscientization and Liberation movement. In these cases, literacy work is seen as a political act leading to conscientization of the masses and thus to a qualitative transformation of sociopolitical and cultural conditions.[15]

14. Adama Ouane and Yvette Amon-Tanoh, "Literacy in French-Speaking Africa: A Situational Analysis," *African Study Review*, Dec. 1990 no. 3.

15. See the following publications for reference: Bataille, ed., *Turning Point for Literacy*; Paulo Freire, "The Adult Literacy Process as Cultural Action for Freedom," *Harvard Educational Review*, 40(2):205-25 (1970); idem, "Cultural Action and Conscientization," ibid., 40(3):452-77; Paulo Freire and Donald Macedo, *Literacy: Reading the Word and the*

FUNCTIONAL LITERACY IN INDUSTRIALIZED COUNTRIES

The study of functional literacy is receiving increasing interest in industrialized countries as well. After an investigation of trends of formation and development in literacy research in industrialized countries, Barton and Hamilton described how literacy research has moved from the simple technical aspects of learning to read and write to looking at how reading and writing are used in particular social situations. Instead of meaning an ability to read and write, the authors assert, literacy becomes "being able to operate effectively in the literate world of books, signs and forms."[16]

Reviews of the history of education in industrialized countries often quote the following definitions from the United States Department of Education and the U.S. National Reading Center. The Department of Education defines a literate person as

one who has acquired the essential knowledge and skills in reading, writing and computation required for effective functioning in society, and whose attainment in such skills makes it possible for him [sic] to develop new aptitudes and to participate actively in the life of his times.[17]

The National Reading Center's definition, as reported in the manifesto of the British movement A Right to Read, states that a " 'person is functionally literate when he [sic] has command of reading skills that permit him to go about his daily activities successfully on the job, or to move about society normally with comprehension of the usual printed expressions and messages he encounters.' "[18]

Variations in definitions are based on the skills demanded or required and on the adequacy of the supply of and demand for what is deemed essential for survival as perceived by governments, businesses, groups, and individuals. An interesting variation is that put forth by Hunter, who considers literacy as the possession of reading and writing skills that permit individuals to participate in their chosen life roles, whether they be family, community, citizenship, consumer, or occupational.[19] Thus literacy does not even necessarily need to be restricted to the skills of reading and writing. As Tanguiane states,

Minimum functional literacy is that level of knowledge and skills, especially in reading and writing, rising as society advances and individual's needs grow, required to play a full and effective part in the economic, political, civic, social and cultural life of society and the country, to contribute to their progress and to ensure the individual's own personal development.[20]

World (New York: Routledge & Kegan Paul, 1987); Lê Thành Khôi, "Literacy Training and Revolution: The Vietnamese Experience," in *Turning Point for Literacy*, ed. Bataille; Lankshear and Lawler, *Literacy, Schooling and Revolution*.

16. David Barton and Marie Hamilton, *Researching Literacy in Industrialized Countries: Trends and Prospects*, UIE Reports 2 (Hamburg: UNESCO Institute for Education, 1990), p. 12.

17. Quoted in Levine, *Social Context of Literacy*, p. 34; Lankshear and Lawler, *Literacy, Schooling and Revolution*, p. 62.

18. Levine, *Social Context of Literacy*, p. 62; Lankshear and Lawler, *Literacy, Schooling and Revolution*, p. 35.

19. Carman St. J. Hunter, "Literacy: What Do the Definitions Tell Us?" *Convergence*, 20 (3-4):25 (1987).

20. Sema Tanguiane, *World Literacy: Issues and Trends* (Geneva: IBE, International Yearbook of Education, 1990), p. 125.

Paulo Freire's critical pedagogy is found to be of relevance in industrialized countries, as exemplified by programs in the Netherlands, Germany, and the United Kingdom. The pertinence of this movement is formulated by Lankshear and Lawler as follows:

The fact that a given conception and practice of functional literacy is open to challenge, and is challenged, in no way guarantees that a single shared alternative will emerge in its place. Competing views as to what comprises an optimal or ideal functional literacy seem inevitable.... Freire does not himself speak of functional literacy in respect of his theory and practice. Yet, I believe, a notion of functionality is entirely appropriate here.[21]

COMPARISONS AND PERSPECTIVES

A quick appraisal of the definitions of literacy in industrialized countries reveals several features common with those in developing countries. This section of this article will compare the two situations, looking in particular at the minimum survival skills deemed essential, mass versus residual illiteracy, and post-literacy.

The literacy level minimally required for survival is viewed differently in industrialized and developing situations. A number of factors lead to such differentiated perceptions and prospects. As Tanguiane put it:

Quite clearly the threshold and limit of functional literacy and illiteracy can depend on the level of development of the country concerned, on the complexity of

its economic, social and civil environment, of its technical infrastructure, and on its administrative machinery and on daily living conditions. For this reason someone who may be considered functionally literate under the conditions prevailing in one country may prove to be functionally illiterate in those of another country.[22]

In other aspects, however, the differences are not so great. A study carried out by the UNESCO Institute for Education in Hamburg, in more than twenty developing countries, arrived at a typology of national literacy situations in which the two opposing extremes were termed as mass illiteracy and residual illiteracy, or, more positively, restricted literacy—in the sense of the spread, not the use[23]—and mass literacy.[24] Three elements were found to play a determining influence in shaping these situations: the medium of instruction and its distance from the learner's mother tongue, the role of written communication in the culture concerned, and the educational tradition. The situation in developing countries that have achieved mass literacy—defined by an arbitrary threshold of 90 percent—is similar in many respects to what is largely observed in industrialized countries. For instance, the sociopsychological

21. Lankshear and Lawler, Literacy, Schooling and Revolution, p. 63.

22. Tanguiane, World Literacy, pp. 122-23.

23. Jack Goody, ed., Literacy in Traditional Society, pp. 11-20, cited in Levine, Social Context of Literacy, p. 16.

24. Ravindra Dave, Adama Ouane, and D. A. Perera, Learning Strategies for Post-Literacy and Continuing Education: A Cross-National Perspective, revised version, UIE Studies on Post-Literacy and Continuing Education, no. 1 (Hamburg: UNESCO Institute for Education, 1988), pp. 17-26.

problems of guilt and shame become more prominent in the situation of residual illiteracy, and even the use of standard terms such as "literacy" or "post-literacy" becomes unacceptable to potential learners. Semantic perceptions, among other factors, therefore have to be taken into account when institutions, programs, and learning strategies are devised.[25]

In addition to the psychological aspects, both industrialized and developing countries have also been concerned with the practical implications resulting from the spread of what has been called hidden illiteracy. The latter refers to the situation of a large number of people passing through basic literacy—at schools or in literacy centers—yet not having access to postprimary learning and whose virtual illiteracy is disclosed when confronted with tasks requiring higher-order communication skills.

"Functional penetration" refers to the range of activities and transactions in which literacy is institutionalized—or routinely expected—preferred, or required for a given group.[26] Its degree in any given society is important, and it must be nurtured in order for literacy efforts to succeed. If the provision of opportunities to use literacy skills does not follow the spread of functional literacy, a large number of people might relapse into illiteracy. To prevent this sort of relapse, literacy workers try to provide a variety of activities to ensure literacy use and practice.

These activities are called post-literacy activities in developing countries, and the creation of a reading or learned society in industrialized countries. A close examination of the aims of these broad prevention measures, however, shows that they are very similar. In both cases, the aims are to prevent a relapse into illiteracy, to provide multiple opportunities to continue learning, and to increase motivation through application of acquired literacy skills in everyday life in order to enhance the quality of life.

Finally, and importantly, it should be said that functional illiteracy is stressed in situations where people are living in literacy-based conditions in which communication is dependent on reading and writing. As a growing number of developing countries' cultures are becoming more literate, the gap between industrialized and developing countries is decreasing. In this sense, whatever distinction could traditionally be drawn between developing countries and industrialized ones along these lines is decreasing as well. At the same time, it is becoming increasingly clear in both developing and industrialized settings that functional definitions of literacy are most appropriate in the majority of circumstances and that the contrast between literacy and illiteracy is becoming outmoded as a definitional contrast.

CONCLUSION

An observation frequently made nowadays is that illiteracy and literacy are always relative, hence functional, as far as knowledge and the

25. Dave, Ouane, and Sutton, "Issues in Post-Literacy," p. 405.

26. Levine, *Social Context of Literacy*, p. 16.

general areas of skills are concerned. It is the obsolescence of the skills mastered, along with the inadequacy of the already acquired knowledge to cope with emerging demands, that is at stake. In both developing and industrialized nations, literacy and illiteracy are gaining new meaning, shifting from skill acquisition and performance improvement to the search and determination of an evolutive and sometimes changing basic education. Literacy education is defined, then, not as a training or formation process but rather as a continual search for other means of communication and means of changing the perception one has of illiteracy. Literacy in all nations—industrialized or developing—needs to be seen as the capacity to express oneself in writing, to establish oneself in society, to get recognition from others, to master and transmit one's cultural features, and to participate with full autonomy in today's societies.

ANNALS, *AAPSS,* **520**, March 1992

Reading Instructions for Using Commercial Medicines

By THOMAS OWEN EISEMON, JEANNE RATZLAFF,
and VIMLA L. PATEL

ABSTRACT: Reading product labels is a common and important use of literacy and numeracy skills in daily life. Instructions for commercial oral-rehydration-therapy salt solutions were examined. The products are widely available in rural Kenya, where they are purchased for alleviating the symptoms of life-threatening diarrheal dehydration. Many features of these texts do not facilitate comprehension. Information about preparation, dosage, administration, storage, and precautions is difficult to locate, few discourse conventions are used to enable readers to efficiently process information, and much tacit knowledge is presumed—including knowledge of English even when a Kiswahili translation is provided. Numeracy tasks associated with compliance with the treatment regime cannot be easily performed with school-learned mathematical algorithms. Measuring and teaching functional literacy and numeracy skills necessitates a better understanding of the kinds of texts that readers will encounter and analyzing the comprehension and problem-solving skills they require.

Thomas Owen Eisemon is a professor in the Department of Educational Psychology and Counselling at McGill University and codirector of the Centre for Cognitive and Ethnographic Studies.

Jeanne Ratzlaff is a student in the Department of Applied Linguistics at Concordia University. She has worked as a literacy instructor and secondary-school teacher in Kenya and Canada.

Vimla L. Patel is a professor in the Department of Medicine at McGill University and associate director of the Centre for Medical Education.

NOTE: Funding for the fieldwork in Kenya was supported by a grant from the International Development Research Centre to McGill University and Kenyatta University. Dr. Sarone Ole Sena of Kenyatta University participated in designing the initial study and in the collection of data from mothers in Kajiado district. Miss Barbara Graves, a doctoral candidate in the Department of Educational Psychology and Counselling at McGill, assisted in the analysis of some of the data presented in this article.

C ONCERN for functional literacy and numeracy is a prominent theme in literacy research in both developed and developing countries. Quantification of adult illiteracy creates a political rationale for greater investments in adult education and in the expansion and qualitative improvement of basic education. For instance, a recent Canadian literacy survey produced the startling finding that about a fourth of the country's adult population was functionally "illiterate."[1] A significant proportion of adults, including many university graduates, were found to be unable to perform seemingly simple literacy and numeracy tasks like computing taxes from information provided in a schedule of tax rates, reading a bus schedule, or understanding the printed instructions for using a cough syrup. A major literacy initiative funded by the federal government was announced shortly afterward.

Typically, functional literacy and numeracy are measured by proxy, that is, by assuming that performance in comprehending school-like texts and tasks measures underlying information-processing and problem-solving skills applicable in any domain in which literacy is involved. The weakness of this assumption, of course, is that the literacy of school leavers is assessed in relation to texts and tasks that are familiar and meaningful only to schoolchildren. An example is an education module from a recent living-standard survey used by the World Bank in Ghana.[2] Short narrative texts similar to the type used to teach literacy in primary schools were prepared with multiple-choice questions. Assessment tasks were constructed to measure the recall skills except for some questions requiring readers to select the best title for the stories. Numeracy skills were assessed separately in a series of computational tasks requiring basic arithmetic operations. That the literacy and numeracy skills measured are central to functional literacy can only be conjectured.

We focus in this article on the skills involved in processing printed information for using commercial medicines and present data from an ongoing study in Kenya to show the complexity of measuring and teaching functional literacy and numeracy. We have selected the genre of printed instructions for commercial medicines because of its practical importance. Not only are pharmaceutical instructions one of the most common uses of literacy in daily life in Kenya, and many developed countries as well, but misuse of these products is pervasive and a common illustration of functional illiteracy.[3]

Commercial oral rehydration therapy (ORT) salt solutions are widely available in Kenya through the public and private health care delivery sectors, reflecting concern for the high rate of infant and child mortal-

1. Southam News, *Broken Words: Why Five Million Canadians are Illiterate* (Toronto: Southam News, 1987).

2. World Bank, *Ghana Living Standards Survey: Education Module*, mimeographed (Washington, DC: World Bank, 1988).

3. Thomas O. Eisemon, *Benefiting from Basic Education, School Quality and Functional Literacy in Kenya* (Elmsford, NY: Pergamon Press, 1988).

ity that results from diarrheal dehydration. The printed instructions for using such products are the subject of this study. The article is divided into four sections, the first of which summarizes the findings of our previous studies of how mothers use commercial ORT salt solutions. The second examines characteristics of the printed instructions that affect comprehension. The information-processing and problem-solving skills associated with compliance with the procedures for preparing and administering a commercial ORT solution are then described. The concluding section considers how the skills involved in processing these and similar texts might be taught.

MAASAI MOTHERS' USE OF COMMERCIAL ORT SOLUTIONS

This research follows studies initiated in 1986 of Maasai mothers' use of ORT salt solutions carried out in Kajiado district, which is located south of the capital city of Nairobi and borders Tanzania.[4] These studies were, in turn, based on surveys, interviews, and observations carried out

4. Thomas O. Eisemon, Vimla L. Patel, and Sarone Ole Sena, "Use of Formal and Informal Knowledge in the Comprehension of Instruction for Oral Rehydration Therapy in Kenya," *Social Science and Medicine*, 25:1225-34 (1987); Thomas O. Eisemon and Vimla L. Patel, "Strengthening the Effects of Schooling on Health Practices in Kenya," *International Journal of Health Education*, 10:21-29 (1990); Vimla L. Patel, Thomas O. Eisemon, and Jose F. Arocha, "Causal Reasoning and the Treatment of Diarrhoeal Disease by Mothers in Kenya," *Social Science and Medicine*, 27:1277-86 (1988); idem, "Comprehending Instructions for Using Pharmaceutical Products in Rural Kenya," *Instructional Science*, 19:1-14 (1989).

in several districts in Kenya that dealt with the ways school leavers use literacy and numeracy in daily life.[5] Reading printed instructions for using pharmaceutical products and agricultural chemicals was found to be one of the most common uses of school-acquired literacy and numeracy.

In Kajiado district, commercial ORT salt solutions are available from the well-baby clinic at the district hospital, from village dispensaries, and from a large number of small shops or *dukas* that sell medicines for controlling the symptoms of dysentery, malaria, intestinal worms, and other diseases in addition to various household goods. Oral rehydration therapy has been widely promoted by local and national health authorities. While products are manufactured for this purpose, ORT solutions can be prepared with ordinary household supplies—salt, sugar, and water.

There is much controversy concerning the promotion of commercial ORT salt solutions when homemade solutions are equally effective. Nevertheless, the commercial ORT solutions are perceived as modern medicines with connotations very different from those associated with home remedies. Promotion of these products by community health care workers is seen as effective in encouraging adoption of oral rehydration therapy particularly by mothers with little or no schooling. It is ironic that a primary health care strategy intended for largely illiterate poor mothers should involve commercial distribution of products whose use requires literacy and numeracy.

5. Eisemon, "Benefiting from Basic Education."

Mothers obtain information on preparing and administering commercial ORT salt solutions from many sources: from other mothers who have used the products, from the individuals who distribute or sell medicines, as well as from the printed instructions for using them. At the time the initial fieldwork was carried out, five products were being test marketed. The instructions for using each of these products are different, though their chemical composition is nearly identical. They differ primarily in the quantity of the solution that can be made and, consequently, in the regime of administration. Because commercial ORT salt solutions are more widely available from local shops, exchanges between sellers and consumers in Meto and other market centers in Kajiado district were observed. Mothers obtained little information about using the products from the individuals who sold them apart from often incorrect instruction on the number of times the medicine should be administered.[6] Few sellers were found to understand the products well enough to communicate the instructions to consumers, and many were unable to read the instructions at all. Except for one product, the printed instructions were given only in English, without translation into Kiswahili or any other vernacular language.

Observations of mothers revealed several strategies for performing the tasks associated with preparing and administering the commercial ORT salt solutions. Mothers with previous

experience of the product relied on prior knowledge for the information needed to perform these tasks and did not examine the printed instructions. Mothers with previous experience with similar products employed this knowledge for using the product purchased, simply inferring that the procedures were identical without ascertaining whether this was the case from the printed instructions. Some mothers elicited the necessary information orally from the sellers or more knowledgeable consumers, usually a friend or neighbor. If the procedural information was presented in graphics, mothers relied on that information and on any prior knowledge and experience they possessed. Only very rarely did even the most well-educated mothers make use of the textual information provided in the printed instructions. In other words, reading the instructions was the strategy of last resort. But much important information necessary for safe and effective administration of the products is presented in the texts such as information on correct dosages, the regime of administration, procedures for storage, as well as precautions for using them.

One product was selected for examination, and experiments were designed to measure mothers' comprehension of the instructions for its use. Mothers with some primary, complete primary, and lower secondary schooling who were familiar with the product were sampled. All were literate in English and Kiswahili in the sense that they could encode or decode oral and printed information in these languages as well as in Maa, their first language. Data were also

6. Eisemon, Patel, and Ole Sena, "Use of Formal and Informal Knowledge."

collected from mothers who had not been to school or participated in adult education programs and were not literate in any language. Subjects were presented with various stimulus texts, the unrevised English printed instructions, and different manipulations of this text involving translation, simplification, and elaboration of the procedures to be followed in preparing an ORT solution. In the case of unschooled mothers, the stimulus texts were presented orally. The comprehension tasks involved recalling information, making inferences from text propositions and procedures represented in the graphics, integrating graphic and textual information, and problem solving using both sources of information.

Literate mothers used the graphics in performing most comprehension tasks with the original instructions even when the texts were translated into Kiswahili and Maa. Simplification and elaboration of the original instructions significantly increased performance, especially manipulations involving temporal ordering of text procedures to correspond to the graphics, use of common measures, and explanation of procedures and precautions eliciting prior knowledge obtained from schooling or social experience. The highest levels of performance were achieved for the translated manipulations of the original instructions, with the manipulations having more impact than did translation on comprehension. Still, many well-educated mothers who read the revised texts had difficulty in comprehending them.

While the findings indicate that better design of printed instructions for commercial medicines may improve safe and effective use, they also draw attention to the complexity of these texts and of the comprehension skills they require.[7] Moreover, they suggest that school-acquired literacy may be necessary, but it is certainly not sufficient to perform many functional literacy and numeracy tasks.[8]

CHARACTERISTICS OF PRINTED INSTRUCTIONS

The printed instructions for commercial ORT solutions (see Figure 1) and for other modern medicines have many features that do not facilitate comprehension. Typically, they are brief texts with a high density of information. Crucial information is seldom marked with text cues apart from those setting off different kinds of information. Procedural information is sequentially ordered and often expressed in conditional statements to enable competent task performance. Nevertheless, the number of procedures to be learned may exceed what can be stored in short-term memory. That necessitates rereading of the texts in order to accurately represent the information. Although their purpose is instructional, these texts often assume familiarity with the subject and some related expertise. Much tacit knowledge is involved in comprehension. Finally, the

7. Eisemon and Patel, "Strengthening the Effects."

8. Eisemon, Patel, and Ole Sena, "Use of Formal and Informal Knowledge"; Patel, Eisemon, and Arocha, "Causal Reasoning."

FIGURE 1
SAMPLE TEXTS

ELECTROLYTE POWDER

1 2 3 4

1. Open Sachet.

2. Pour contents into glass or container.

3. Add 250 ml of water. (The water should be freshly boiled and cooled.). Do not boil solution after adding contents of Sachet. Stir the contents until dissolved.

4. Drink while fresh, any unused solution should be discarded. A fresh solution should be made each time.

   Always use in the recommended dilution.

Dosage:
Mild to moderate dehydration:
Replacement of losses 50-120 ml/Kg in 6 hours.
Maintenance 100-200 ml/Kg in 24 hours.
Adults may need up to 1000 per hour.

For maintenance therapy with Oral fluids in cases of severe dehydration Initially corrected with I.V. fluids: 15 ml/Kg hourly until diarrhea stops.

Keep out of the reach of Children.

Store in a cool dry place.

Compound Sodium Chloride and Dextrose Oral Powder B.P.

Dissolve contents in sufficient freshly boiled and cooled water to make up to 200 ml (7 fl. oz). Any solution unused after one hour should be discarded. Solutions may be used for up to 24 hours if stored in a refrigerator immediately after reconstitution but the reconstituted solution must not be boiled.

Keep out of reach of children.

structure of this genre of printed information is highly varied. There are relatively few conventions to which discourse must conform that might enable readers to efficiently process information. Instructions for four of the five commercial ORT salt solutions being test marketed in rural Kenya in 1986 were analyzed for this article. The fifth was manufactured by a pharmaceutical company distributing another ORT product under a different name but with the same contents and identical instructions for its use.

Variability of text format, content, and organization

The format and the length of the instructions varied greatly. Three of the product instructions had graphics illustrating procedures for preparing the ORT salt solutions. The other did not. Graphics account for 14 percent, 11 percent, and 8 percent of instructional space, respectively. The number of words in the English instructions ranged from 80 to 228, the longest texts being those that contained illustrations. Graphics do not seem to reduce the length of printed instructions because, in these and in other examples of procedural texts, they usually provide redundant information to facilitate comprehension.[9]

There is evidence in our previous research[10] and in related studies[11]

that readers of procedural texts rely on graphics for much information needed to perform tasks associated with the texts. The graphics used for the products studied require a high level of visual literacy, which schooling might be expected to develop. Two of the three sets of graphics employ two-dimensional multicolor representations. The third uses three-dimensional illustrations. All are expressed in the narrative episode format, similar to illustrations in children's books, depicting four or five events. The representations of objects and human beings are highly stylized, using conventions of textbook art such as cutaway drawings simultaneously revealing the inside and outside of containers. There is some effort to emphasize the familiar. The graphic for one of the products shows the typical East African pot, the *suferia*, used for boiling water. Another shows a pot with a handle and lid that is found only in well-to-do homes in urban areas, which are unlikely to have much need for the product.

The graphics are related in different ways to the portions of the texts elaborating procedures for preparing the product for administration. In one case, the four numbered events depicted match the procedures enumerated in the instructions below them. Boiling water prior to adding the product is not shown. Another set has the graphics alongside each procedure, including some illustrations that cannot be interpreted without the aid of the text, such as measuring

9. Harold R. Booher, "Relative Comprehensibility of Pictorial Information and Printed Words in Proceduralized Instructions," *Human Factors*, 17:266-77 (1975).

10. Patel, Eisemon, and Arocha, "Comprehending Instructions."

11. David E. Stone and Marvin D. Glock, "How Do Young Adults Read Directions with

and without Pictures?" *Journal of Educational Psychology*, 73:419-26 (1981).

and cooling the water prior to boiling. The graphics for the third product appear on the front of the packet below the trade name while the instructions are on the opposite side.

Despite the fact that the four products are nearly identical, there is little similarity in the scope of information provided, in the amount of attention given to different kinds of information, or, more surprising, in the procedures mentioned for preparation, dosage, administration, and storage or in the precautions given for using the products. The instructions for one product state simply that the contents of the packet should be dissolved "in freshly boiled and cooled water to make up to 200 ml (7 fl oz.)." The others provide detailed instructions for boiling and cooling a specific quantity of water and mixing the solution for administration. As many as six procedures are involved, beginning with measuring a quantity of water for boiling. The proportion of instructional space used to describe procedures for preparing an ORT salt solution varied from 6 percent to 30 percent, with the lowest and highest being those for two products that illustrated these procedures with graphics.

Two texts provide little or no information about administration, one no information about dosages, and another no information about storage of the product or the solution. For three of the four products, information about dosages constitutes about a third of the texts, about the same proportion of the text that is used to describe precautions. The precautions are not the same across the products, however. Some products

advise consumers to discard any unused solution, presumably because of the possibility of bacterial contamination. One presents this precaution as a plausible but difficult inference: "solutions may be used for up to 24 hours if stored in a refrigerator immediately after reconstitution." Two emphasize that consumers should "keep [the product] out of reach of children," which is probably intended to reinforce this practice as a good one for all household medicines.

Text markers and
coherence devices

Text markers are important devices for alerting readers to different kinds of information and facilitating location of essential information. These structural signals may be more important for pharmaceutical instructions than for other instructional genres. Only information given about precautions reveals any conventions used by the pharmaceutical industry in writing instructions. In all texts, precautions are mentioned at the end of the text and are set off by different kinds of text markers; the information is boxed in two cases, given in bold letters in a third, and set off by spaces in the fourth. Two texts separate information about preparation of the product from that given for dosage and administration, while one combines this information into one passage and the fourth incorporates information about storing the product into information about its preparation and administration. In brief, there seem to be few conventions requiring separation of information pertaining to different purposes.

Procedures that are described in one text are presented sequentially in another. Information for preparing the products may be given partly in what Chambliss and Calfee[12] characterize as a sequential linear string—"1. Open Sachet. 2. Pour contents into glass or container."—sometimes with reversals of temporal order: "3. Add 250 ml of water. The water should be freshly boiled and cooled." The devices used for connecting descriptive information are often very complex, as the following passage, about storing one of the products, illustrates: "Any solution unused after one hour should be discarded. Solutions may be used for up to 24 hours if stored in a refrigerator immediately after reconstitution but the reconstituted solution must not be boiled." Disparate information is organized into some kind of topical net, storage being the topic to which this information is related in different ways: causally if the condition of refrigeration of the unused solution is satisfied, temporally if it is not. The instruction about not boiling unused solution stored in a refrigerator is neither connected causally nor temporally to the topic of storage but to the condition of refrigeration.

Tacit knowledge

Comprehension of these texts presumes different kinds of tacit or prior knowledge on the part of readers, literacy in English being a prerequisite for all of the texts. This is also

12. Marilyn J. Chambliss and Robert C. Calfee, "Designing Science Textbooks to Enhance Student Understanding," *Educational Psychologist*, 24:307-22 (1989).

true for the only text with a Kiswahili translation of the procedures for preparing the product for administration—this text provides no information in Kiswahili about dosage or administration of the product. A comparison of the English and Kiswahili versions of the procedures for preparation indicates that the Kiswahili text, which is probably a translation from the English original, is in some respects clearer. For example, while the English text begins with the instruction to "pour enough *fresh* water to fill a large beer bottle (500 ml) into a clean pan," the Kiswahili version makes it explicit that the water must be clean (*"Mwanga maji safi . . ."*). The instruction to "cool it" is translated into Kiswahili as "leave it to cool," which is a better description of the procedure. Similarly, the final instruction in Kiswahili suggests that the solution should be given with a spoon while the English only states that it "is ready to drink."

Determining how much of the product to purchase and prepare and how much and how often to administer the solution requires both numeracy and modern health knowledge. The instructions employ three different units of liquid measure for preparing the products for administration: metric measures, English measures, and common measures such as a beer bottle, glass, or tumbler. Metric weights are provided for estimating how much of the solution should be prepared and given to infants and children, while measures of time use the division of the day in European languages for purposes of describing the regime of administration. Three of the four products provide common equivalencies for metric liquid measures. The other provides only the English equivalent of the metric liquid measure used. The packets make between 250 milliliters to 1 liter of solution. Estimating body weights in kilos is necessary for two of the products in order to determine how much of the solution should be mixed and given in equal periods of up to six hours; however, the day in Kiswahili and some other East African languages is divided into four unequal periods. Two products do not require estimation of body weight. One makes the amount to be prepared and given contingent on a patient's age and condition, and the other states an amount to be administered without any qualifications.

Although it is necessary for users to relate dehydration to diarrhea and diagnose the seriousness of its symptoms for effective treatment, only two of the products require this for determining the correct dosage. And only one provides definitions of the stages of diarrheal dehydration. In that case, the definitions are technical and the symptoms are ambiguously associated with the purpose of administration rather than with the stage of the illness; for example, "For Mild Rehydration: thirsty, reduced skin elasticity." Significantly, only one product mentions the importance of continuing nutrition, which is essential to successful treatment. All products presume the consumer's knowledge of oral rehydration therapy. That many consumers do not have such knowledge is strongly suggested by the findings of the pilot studies that revealed several instances of well-educated, literate mothers using commercial ORT salt solutions in combination with the administration of traditional purgatives likely to worsen a child's condition.[13]

PROCESSING INFORMATION FOR USING COMMERCIAL ORT SALT SOLUTIONS

Attention has been drawn to characteristics of the four ORT texts that increase the difficulty of locating essential information. To summarize, information about preparation, dosage, administration, storage, and precautions is located in different places, designated with different text markers, and often combined in different ways. Moreover, important information may be absent altogether and must be inferred from prior knowledge.

Maasai mothers were asked to locate information regarding what the product is used for and about preparation, dosage, administration, and precautions. Typically, even when these tasks were preceded by reading the text aloud, the mothers tried to locate such information in the graphics, although only procedures for preparation are illustrated.[14] Sometimes incorrect inferences can be made from the graphics. For instance, illustrations for one of the products, showing preparation of a solution for administration to a baby, suggested to a mother who was a medical secretary at a district hospital that it was intended only for children. Under probing, precautionary

13. Eisemon and Patel, "Strengthening the Effects."

14. Patel, Eisemon, and Arocha, "Comprehending Instructions."

information was found to be easiest to locate if indicated by a text marker. Additional precautions included in other parts of the texts were usually not noted. Information on dosages and administration was located if clearly marked. Information about what the product is used for was the most difficult to find as it is usually sandwiched between the trade and common names for the product, on one hand, and information given about manufacturing and its chemical components, on the other—information that most experienced readers recognize as irrelevant.

Users of commercial ORT salt solutions must make sense of many procedures and precautions that are not self-evidently necessary. For example, for most of the products the instructions require boiling some water prior to preparing a solution. This instruction is not explained, and the boiling of water is not a normal household practice in many rural areas with contaminated water supplies. Rainwater is usually used for drinking. Boiling water makes sense mainly to mothers who have been to school and have learned that boiling is necessary to kill the germs that cause diarrhea.[15] Another example concerns the combining of the medicine and water. The instructions for all of the products that require boiling and cooling warn that the medicine should not be mixed with the water prior to boiling. Again, no explanation is given for a procedure and related precaution that are not intuitive. Yet mothers usually had no

15. Eisemon, Patel, and Ole Sena, "Use of Formal and Informal Knowledge."

difficulty in explaining and complying with this procedure; heating was thought to dilute the strength of the medicine. Subjects also invoked a rule from experience with popular commercial medicines such as antacids; powder is always added to cold water. In the absence of explanations for unfamiliar procedures, users apply rules and theories based on their prior knowledge and experience, selectively complying with those instructions that make sense to them.

The complexity of many practical numeracy tasks requires novel problem-solving strategies such as those associated with complying with instructions for using medicines. They are normally too complex for computational solutions of the kind learned in school. The information needed from the instructions to ascertain how much of the ORT medicine to purchase for the three products providing this information is given in Table 1. The instructions have been extracted from different parts of these texts and reordered for purposes of comparison.

Only the information needed for administration of the product to infants and children is given. Consumers must determine with this information how much of the product to purchase. That, in turn, requires deciding the length of treatment and the regime of administration. The instructions for Product C describe a two-day regime of administration and suggest that the treatment should be discontinued after that time if the patient has not improved. Products A and B say nothing about the length of treatment. This will be in-

TABLE 1

INFORMATION NEEDED FOR PROBLEM SOLVING WITH ORT TEXTS

Product A	Product B	Product C
Pour contents into glass or container. Add 250 ml of water. Any unused solution should be discarded. A fresh solution should be made each time.	Pour enough water to fill a large beer bottle (500 ml) into a clean pan. Any portion of the solution remaining after 24 hrs. should be discarded.	Fill tumbler with water up to mark (300 ml). Add ALL powder from sachet.
Mild to moderate dehydration 50-120 ml/kg in 6 hrs.	*For mild rehydration* 50-120 ml/kg every 4-6 hrs.	*(Mild or moderate dehydration)* Give 2 or 3 tumblers during the first 4 to 6 hrs.
	For severe continuing diarrhoea 15 ml/kg every hr.	
Maintenance 100-200 ml/kg in 24 hrs.	*(Maintenance)* 100-200 ml/kg every 24 hrs. until diarrhoea stops.	*(Maintenance)* Give 2 or 3 more tumblers over next 18 to 24 hrs.
		Give 2 more tumblers in the following 24 hrs.
		Do not give more than 6 tumblers in 24 hrs.

fluenced by the patient's condition, that is, whether the symptoms of diarrheal dehydration are moderate or severe. To determine the length of treatment, the user must make a judgment about the patient's condition and then decide how long to administer the medicine. To facilitate judgment, Product B describes the symptoms for "mild rehydration" and for mild as well as severe continuing diarrhea.

Judgments about the patient's condition and estimation of the length of treatment involve prior knowledge and experience. Most mothers employ general rules in such situations and vary them according to circumstances. A common rule, according to the medical secretary who advises patients on using drugs distributed at the district hospital, is that commercial ORT solutions are to be administered for two to three days. The child should be taken to the hospital or clinic if there is no improvement. The period of treatment may be shortened or lengthened depending on the severity of the child's condition. Estimating this period is usually the first step in determining how much of the product to buy.

The next is to ascertain the number of administrations and the amount of the product to be used for each. The instructions for the three products were obviously not written to facilitate these computations and, not surprisingly, most mothers we studied could not perform them. Consider, for instance, the instructions for Product B in relation to a hypothetical example: a child weighing about twenty kilos who has continuing diarrhea requiring mild rehydration. A judgment must be made about the amount of the solution to be given for each administration—between 50 to 120 milliliters per kilogram in 6 hours—as well as a prediction concerning the number of initial treatments for replacement of fluid lost prior to beginning maintenance therapy, which specifies a different dosage—100-200 milliliters per kilogram. It is then necessary to compute the quantity of the solution required for each administration with the information that the contents of the packet make 250 milliliters of solution. The problem could now be solved with a multistep computation were it not for the instruction that "any unused solution should be discarded." Thus each administration requires one packet of the product. Alternatively, the reader can derive the number of packets to be purchased by estimating the number of administrations, disregarding the information given about dosage rates. The application of school mathematical algorithms would not produce a correct solution. Unlike a good story problem, this one contains information that interferes with an accurate representation of the problem for solution.

In practice, mothers disregarded information leading to complex calculations. They took short cuts based on experience. One packet of any medicine is normally needed for one administration. Children will drink as much of the solution as they require. The amount of medicine given and the frequency of administrations may be increased if no improvement is observed. If the child does not improve in two or three days, he or she will be taken to a hospital or clinic. More of the product should be purchased than may be needed because of difficulties in obtaining it. These rules enable estimation and practical problem solving. Information provided in the printed instructions seems to be used to reinforce or modify these rules. The strategies for comprehending texts for problem solving employed by the users of these products whom we have studied have little to do with those that are taught and tested in school.

CONCLUSION

The instructions for using the commercial medicines described in this article, like those for using agricultural chemicals and many other products of modern technology, require consumers to perform complex cognitive tasks. Reading product labels for medicines is a common and important use of literacy. Intuitively, skills in comprehending printed instructions have much to do with the mechanisms through which literacy lowers infant mortality, increases life expectancy, and improves health status.

There are several implications of our studies for teaching and assessing functional literacy and numeracy.

The most obvious have to do with the texts used for instruction. While comprehension skills such as decoding and encoding are involved in performing any literacy task, higher-level information-processing skills are closely related to familiarity with a particular genre of texts. Procedural texts should figure prominently in literacy instruction particularly in developing countries, for both adult education and primary schooling, as primary schooling is the terminal stage of schooling for many students.[16] These texts are readily accessible, unlike textbooks for primary schools and adult education programs.

Literacy in more than one language is required for processing many procedural texts in societies where a metropolitan language is used for school instruction. In Kenya and a large number of African countries, students are taught in their mother tongue for the first few years of primary schooling and then in English or French. Their literacy skills in the metropolitan language are weak even if the students complete primary school.[17] Until vernacular languages are used as both the languages of instruction in science, health, and agriculture in primary school and as the languages of ordinary scientific discourse, metropolitan language instruction will have to be improved, perhaps by introducing these languages earlier in the school curricula—and by teaching literacy in metropolitan languages to adults.[18]

The numeracy skills embedded in functional literacy tasks involve estimating and approximating solutions to practical problems. The use of story problems to teach high-level numeracy skills and of testing practices that penalize guessing may actually inhibit development of functional numeracy. Naturalistic problems requiring numeracy skills are not presented as stories with all of the information needed for problem solving. Procedural texts provide incomplete and sometimes contradictory information that does not lend itself to the application of school-learned algorithms. Mathematics instruction designed to support functional literacy and numeracy should emphasize skills in comprehending texts and tasks that are transferable to daily life.

Finally, we have shown that functional illiteracy is difficult to define without identifying the kinds of text that literates will encounter and analyzing the comprehension and problem-solving skills they require. The studies previously summarized were carried out to inform product labeling. The findings have implications for improving product labeling—for translation of texts, topical, hierarchial organization of information, use of common text markers, providing

16. Thomas O. Eisemon and John Schwille, "Should Schools Prepare Students for Secondary Education or for Self-Employment? Addressing a Dilemma of Primary Schooling in Burundi and Kenya," *Elementary School Journal* (in press).

17. Eisemon, "Benefiting from Basic Education."

18. Thomas O. Eisemon, Robert Prouty, and John Schwille, "What Language Should Be Used for Teaching? Language Policy and School Reform in Burundi," *Journal of Multilingual and Multicultural Development*, 10: 473-98 (1990).

explanations for unfamiliar procedures, and so on—some of which have already been incorporated into Kenya's labeling legislation. The producers of these texts also have a responsibility to facilitate performance of literacy and numeracy tasks through better text design.

Increasing functional literacy and numeracy is central to proposals for educational reform and development strategies in Kenya and other countries. It is the object of many governmental and nongovernmental initiatives. But little progress is likely to be achieved in the absence of a much better understanding of everyday experiences involving literacy and numeracy, the cognitive tasks associated with these experiences, and the information-processing and problem-solving skills they require.

Mother-Tongue Literacy in Nigeria

By J. T. OKEDARA and C. A. OKEDARA

ABSTRACT: The importance of mother-tongue literacy cannot be overemphasized. Regrettably, contemporary language literacy in Nigeria is fraught with constraints, such as the lack of orthography for a large proportion of Nigerian languages. The prospects for mass literacy are not encouraging, unless the federal government of Nigeria directs its efforts to developing orthography and literature in many unwritten indigenous languages. Moreover, there is a need to clarify, in terms of policy, what it means to be literate locally, regionally, and nationally. The newly established Commission for Adult and Non-Formal Education is charged with working out language policy for an adult literacy program in the country. The hope is that the commission will soon provide a realistic solution to the problem. Nigeria could thereby present a model program for other countries in similar circumstances to emulate, as necessary and appropriate.

Joseph Okedara is currently professor and head, Department of Adult Education, University of Ibadan, Nigeria.

Caroline Okedara is a reader in language education, Department of Teacher Education, University of Ibadan, Nigeria.

NOTE: The authors would like to express their appreciation for the use of facilities provided by the Literacy Research Center at the University of Pennsylvania and for support from the Carnegie Corporation of New York for the present work.

LITERACY education within the context of this article refers to the acquisition of sufficient reading, writing, speaking, and numeracy skills to enable the individual to communicate to others, to understand communications from others, and to be able to function properly in community situations in which literacy is required. Language, or the body of words, forms, and patterns of sounds and structure making up the speech of a people, nation, or group of people, plays a key role as the medium of literacy education.

A local language or mother tongue facilitates the acquisition of literacy. The term "mother tongue" refers to the initial, or first, language of contact, naturally or normally acquired. A second language, then, is any language acquired after having mastered the initial language. In Africa, the second language more often than not offers communication with a wider group of speakers.

In our view, the initial, or mother-tongue, language appears to be the best medium for literacy, for psychological, educational, and sociological reasons. Psychologically, it is the system of meaningful signs that works most automatically in one's mind for the expression and understanding of facts. Educationally, one learns more quickly through it than through an unfamiliar linguistic medium.[1] Sociologically, it is a means of identification among members of the community to which one belongs; the language of a community is also the most potent symbolic representation of its culture. Every human being already possesses the basic structure and vocabulary of his or her initial language and can add words from the common written stock contained in dictionaries to his or her personal vocabulary very easily, if he or she makes the necessary effort.

Gudschinsky sees the teaching of literacy in the mother tongue as a bridge to the acquisition of a second language.[2] She declares it a pedagogical truism that learning must begin with the known and proceed to the unknown, and she uses monolingual Indians in Latin America to illustrate this. In her illustration, the known for the monolingual Indian is the oral control of his or her own language; the unknown includes both the basic skills and concepts of reading and writing in his or her own language and the oral skills of the second language—in this case, the national language. She claims that an individual can be taught oral and written control of the second language by either of two teaching sequences: (1) by instruction in literacy skills in his or her own language, followed by instruction in speaking and reading the regional or national language; or (2) by oral instruction in speaking the national language, followed by instruction in literacy skills in that language. Gudschinsky feels that the ac-

1. United Nations Educational, Scientific, and Cultural Organization, *The Use of Vernacular Languages in Education*, Monographs of Fundamental Education no. 8 (Paris: United Nations Educational, Scientific, and Cultural Organization, 1953).

2. Sarah C. Gudschinsky, "Techniques for Functional Literacy in Indigenous Language and the National Language," in *Language and Literacy: Current Issues and Research*, by T. P. Gorman (Tehran: International Methods, 1977), p. 65.

quisition of first-language literacy facilitates the acquisition of second-language literacy, and this point is supported by other theories proposed in the literature. Among these are the results of Baker's work on the development of cognitive skills and the development of children in their native language,[3] and Cummins's developmental interdependence hypothesis, which holds that the level of second-language competence that a child acquires is partly dependent on the level of competence achieved in the first language, as a result of a "common underlying proficiency."[4]

Other research findings from developed and developing countries agree with the preceding findings. In Sweden, Skutnabb-Kangas and Toukoma found that older Finnish immigrants, whose academic ability in the first language is better established than that of the younger immigrants, became more proficient in their first-language literacy skills as well as in their second-language literacy skills.[5] In Nigeria, in a six-year primary school experiment using Yoruba as the medium of instruction for English taught as a foreign language, Fafunwa found that pupils in the experimental classes seemed to express themselves more fluently in Yoruba and in English as compared with those in control classes.[6] Furthermore, between 1969 and 1971, the Institute of African Adult Education at the University of Ibadan, Nigeria, carried out an experiment on the "role of the mother tongue in learning a second language." The experimental group, made up of literate tobacco farmers, acquired literacy in their mother tongue, Yoruba, during a work-oriented functional-literacy program. The control group was made up of illiterates. Both groups were taught English as a second language. The experimental group learned English faster than the control group, suggesting that acquiring literacy in the mother tongue could be an advantage in becoming literate in a second language.[7] A study by Wagner et al. on linguistic communities—Moroccan, Arabic, and Berber—in Morocco showed that the transfer of literacy skills takes place in spite of the lack of similarity of the scripts in the two languages—Arabic and French. The transfer is due principally to decoding skills based on the first-language literacy experience.[8]

3. Colin Baker, *Key Issues in Bilingualism and Bilingual Education*, Multilingual Matters 5 (Philadelphia: Multilingual Matters, 1988), p. 182.

4. James Cummins, "The Entry and Exit Fallacy in Bilingual Education," *NABE Journal*, 4(3):25-29 (1980).

5. Tove Skutnabb-Kangas and Pertti Toukoma, *Teaching Migrant Children's Mother Tongue and Learning the Language of the Host Country in the Context of the Socio-Cultural Situation of the Migrant Family* (Helsinki: Finnish National Commission for UNESCO, 1976).

6. Babs Fafunwa, "Education in the Mother Tongue, a Nigerian Experience: The Six-Year (Yoruba Medium) Primary Education Project at the University of Ife, Nigeria," *West African Journal of Education*, 19(2):213-28 (June 1975).

7. Sunday H. O. Tomori and Joseph Taiwo Okedara, "A Comparative Study of the Learning of English as a Second Language by Literate and Illiterate Tobacco Farmers of Oyo North District, Western State of Nigeria," *Journal of Nigeria English Studies Association*, Dec. 1975, nos. 1 and 2, pp. 89-101.

8. Daniel A. Wagner, Jennifer E. Spratt, and Abdelkader Ezzaki, "Does Learning to Read in a Second Language Always Put the Child at a Disadvantage? Some Counter Evidence from

An important aspect of mother-tongue literacy is its cultural and motivational value. Reporting on the six-year Yoruba Medium Primary Education Project at the University of Ife—now Obafemi Awolowo University, Ife-Ife, Nigeria—Fafunwa found that "generally, the children in the experimental classes [showed] more evidence of self-reliance, resourcefulness, and [were] relatively happier as a group as compared with the control group."[9] Apparently the acquisition of literacy in Yoruba, the language of their cultural heritage, gave the children enough confidence, enthusiasm, and motivation to learn English and its associated cultural values.

The account thus far provides us with concepts and processes demonstrating the importance of acquiring adult literacy through first-language literacy. How far these variables have been taken into account in the language policies in Nigeria is the subject of the next section of this article.

LANGUAGE POLICIES IN SUPPORT OF LITERACY EFFORTS IN NIGERIA

The early missionaries in Nigeria realized that they needed to have an intimate knowledge of the indigenous African languages in order to understand African ways and successfully accomplish their goals. In 1831, in an attempt to carry out a policy of teaching indigenous-language literacy skills, the first lesson in Yoruba-language literacy was given at Charlotte's Girls School in Freetown.[10] This initial effort was followed by an intensive study of selected African languages by missionaries. Among the early missionaries to undertake such studies was S. W. Koelle, who worked with the Kanuri and Vai and compiled the *Polyglotta Africana* in 1854, consisting of 283 words in 156 languages.[11]

Missionary linguistic studies contributed greatly to the development of mother-tongue literacy in Nigeria by making orthography and resource materials available for the teaching of African languages. The missionaries used these materials as part of an intensive effort to convert people to their religions through mother-tongue literacy. The practice continues today, with the United Bible Society of the Nigeria Bible Translation Center actively engaged in language study in support of the production of Christian literature, especially the Bible, in indigenous languages.

The missionaries did not retain a free hand in the control of literacy development for long, as the British colonial government soon intervened with its own policy; subsequently, the Nigerian government followed suit. The British Colonial Education Ordinance for West Africa in 1882 regulated the educational practices in Lagos, Nigeria, and the Gold Coast (now Ghana). As a result of missionary protests, however, the colonial government emphasized that the ordinance did not forbid the teaching of mother-tongue literacy but rather

Morocco," *Journal of Applied Psycholinguistics*, 10:31-48 (1989).

9. Fafunwa, "Education in the Mother Tongue," p. 226.

10. Paul E. H. Hair, *The Early Study of Nigerian Languages* (New York: Cambridge University Press, 1967), p. 8.

11. Ibid., pp. 4-81.

that such teaching was expected to pay for itself. Missionaries who were having financial troubles at the time would receive financial aid from the colonial government for English-literacy training only.

A European Language Examination Scheme was initiated in 1895, requiring colonial Europeans in Nigeria to be conversant in one or more local indigenous languages. The object of the policy was to solve the problem of communication between the colonial officials and the non-English-speaking Africans, and it apparently contributed to raising the interest of the British colonial power in the development of indigenous-language literacy among Africans. Coupled with this development was the financing by the Phelps-Stokes Fund of two commissions to assess the quantity and quality of education that was provided to Africans. The Phelps-Stokes report of 1922 criticized the lukewarm attitudes toward the teaching of mother-tongue literacy on the grounds that the latter was a "means of giving expression to their [the Africans'] personality however primitive they may be." The British government subsequently became interested in the report and considered it a sufficiently accurate appraisal of the educational policy of the colonial government upon which to base their language policy. Among other things, the report recommended the use of "the tribal language" in the lower primary classes and "the language of the European nation in control" in the upper classes. Similar reports by the Advisory Committee, which was appointed by the secretary of state for the colonies in 1925, 1927, 1935, and 1943, emphasized the importance of teaching and acquiring mother-tongue literacy in primary education but promoted the teaching and acquisition of English-language literacy as well at both primary and postprimary institutions. This practice was extended to the teaching of adults at basic and post-literacy levels. Such reports became the guidelines for the British colonial government's language literacy policy throughout the period of the British Empire in Nigeria.

One consequence of this rising interest in mother-tongue literacy was the establishment of the International Institute of African Languages and Cultures in 1926. The objectives of the institute, which was set up by the British colonial government, were to study languages and cultures of native Africans and to assist in the production of an educational literature in the mother tongue. The institute established its own journal in 1928 and in 1930 produced a pamphlet on practical orthography for African languages. The School of Oriental Studies—later the School of Oriental and African Studies—was formally opened in 1917 in London. Since then, the school has been associated with the training of West Africans in the analysis of their mother tongues. Local enthusiasm for mother-tongue usage grew among Western-educated Nigerians, and many of them started mother-tongue monolingual or bilingual newspapers. There were seven mother-tongue newspapers published in Yoruba between 1900 and 1940 as well as others in Hausa and Igbo languages, mostly in the Northern and Eastern parts of the country.[12]

Some indigenous languages, such as Hausa, Igbo, and Yoruba, received recognition in public examinations. For instance, from 1931 to 1951, provision was made by the University of Cambridge Local Examination Syndicate to offer papers in Yoruba at the London Matriculation Examinations. The West African Examinations Council was established in 1951 and was responsible for moderating the West African School Certificate Examinations in Anglophone West Africa as well as the London General Certificate Examinations. The institutions of higher learning, starting with the University College in Ibadan (now the University of Ibadan) and others that followed, took an interest in the study and teaching of indigenous Nigerian languages in addition to the English language. Common features in these institutions at that time included the establishment of departments of English, linguistics, local languages, and, later, other languages such as French, Latin, and Russian. There were institutes of African studies that carried out research in indigenous languages and institutes of education and departments of education that taught mother-tongue and English methodology courses and produced future classroom teachers for both mother-tongue and European —especially English and French— languages.

As early as 1953, the United Nations Educational, Scientific, and Cultural Organization supported a survey of the orthographies of some Nigerian languages and recommended their use in the Nigerian educational system. These included orthographies of Idoma, Nupe, Kanuri, and Fulani.[13] Other support for the use of indigenous languages in Nigeria came from the West African Language Survey, which was established in 1960 with funds from the Ford Foundation; the Ford Foundation also funded scholars to carry out specific research into several West African languages.

In the 1970s, several other events took place to support the development of indigenous literacy. For example, the federal Ministry of Education set up the National Language Center for the development of indigenous Nigerian languages and English. The center, now part of the Nigerian Educational Research and Development Council and based in Abuja, is also currently concerned with improving the quality of instruction in multilingualism and multilingual education. Second, in 1975 the federal government sponsored the preparation of books and materials for teaching and learning certain indigenous languages, including Edo, Efik, Hausa, Igbo, Yoruba, Fulfude, and Kanuri.[14] Finally, the National Television Authority made it a regu-

12. Timothy A. Awoniyi, "The Role and Status of the Yoruba Language in the Formal School System of Western Nigeria, 1846-1971" (Ph.D. diss., University of Ibadan, Nigeria 1973), pp. 172-279.

13. Hans Wolff, *Nigerian Orthography* (Zaria: Nigeria Gaskya, 1954), pp. 1-62.

14. C. O. Taiwo, "Nigeria: Language Problems and Solutions," *Prospects*, 6(3):388-92 (1976).

lar practice to broadcast the summary of its national news in these indigenous languages as well as in Tiv and Ijaw, with full details given normally in English. The practice continues today.

The National Policy on Education, revised in 1981, attempts to clarify the use of both indigenous and English languages in literacy development, especially at the various levels of education in the country. The relevant clauses are as follows:

1. At the preprimary level, the government will ensure that the medium of instruction will be principally the mother tongue or the language of the immediate community.

2. At the primary level, the government will see to it that the medium of instruction in the primary school is initially the mother tongue or the language of the immediate community and, at a later stage, English.

3. For adult education, the National Commission for the Development of Adult Education will work out the overall strategy for the inclusion of Nigerian arts, culture, and languages in adult education programs.[15]

It is evident that at least partial promotion of mother-tongue literacy as a policy goes far back to the beginnings of the Nigerian nation. The next section takes up the question of how the national language policies promoted the development of mother-tongue literacy in Nigeria.

15. Federal Republic of Nigeria, *National Policy on Education* (Lagos: Federal Ministry of Information, Printing Division, 1977), p. 8.

CONTEMPORARY LANGUAGE AND LITERACY USE IN NIGERIA

A former British colony, Nigeria has, as of 1984, an estimated population of 97 million. Of these, Christians constitute an estimated 49 percent, Muslims an estimated 36 percent, and citizens embracing traditional religions about 15 percent. The latest information shows that there are 420 languages in Nigeria; 413 of these are still in use, and 7 have fallen into extinction.

Languages that have no orthography at the moment constitute about half—198 out of 420—of the known languages in the country. These 198 languages cannot, therefore, be useful for literacy activities among their speakers. Of course, these speakers can acquire literacy skills in other languages, indigenous or foreign, that have an orthography and where communication takes place at the local, regional, or national level. Some languages are not indigenous to only one state but rather are spoken in several states. A case in point is Fulfude, which is spoken in Bauchi, Plateau Kano, and Katsina states.

The languages with orthographies include 215 of the known languages in Nigeria, but these orthographies vary considerably in their applicability to literacy. Those with only a word list—25.0 percent of the known languages—have established orthographies but are not used actively. They have not been used in teaching literacy because written primers or booklets in these languages are not available. Languages with word lists and portions—11.2 percent—are so labeled because portions, chapters, or a part of a book, such as the Bible, are available in these languages, and they thus have some utility in literacy teaching.

The third category of languages with established orthographies comprises those languages that have been used in book production, especially in religious literature, such as a component of the Bible—for example, the New Testament—or full Bibles. This category is more advanced in literacy use than the previous two categories. Almost half of these languages are found in Cross River, Gongola, Plateau, and Borno states.

The fourth category constitutes 4.5 percent of known Nigerian languages, a tiny minority. These languages are used for literacy learning and teaching locally, regionally, or nationally and also as an official language on radio and television and in the print media. Many of them are rich in spiritual and scholarly literature, and almost all of them are used in primary education as well as in adult literacy programs. The English language tops the list as an official language of literacy in both public and private business in all the 21 states, including the Federal Capital Territory of Abuja; however, less than 10 percent of the entire population of Nigeria speaks English. Hausa is also an official language of literacy. In addition, it is the mother tongue of literacy in Sokoto, Kaduna, Kano, Bauchi, and Niger states and is a second language of literacy in other Northern states. Like English, Hausa is used on radio and television, in print media, in primary, secondary, and tertiary education, and in adult

literacy programs. It has both Roman and Ajumi scripts.

Yoruba, Igbo, and Pidgin English constitute another set of regional languages. Yoruba is used as an official language of literacy in six states. Other languages used as official languages in the areas where they are spoken include Kanuri in Borno State; Idoma in Benue State; Edo in Bendel State; Efik in Cross River State; Esan in Bendel State; Igala in Benue and Anambra states; Ijaw in Rivers, Bendel, and Ondo states; Ikwere in Rivers State; Isekiri and Isoko in Bendel State; Nwagharul in Plateau State; Nupe in Niger and Kwara states; Tiv in Benue, Plateau, and Gongola states; and Urhobo in Bendel State. These are also used on radio and television and in print media, and literature for primary and adult literacy education has been produced in these languages. Nonetheless, literacy work does not take place in any of the languages except English, Hausa, Yoruba, and Igbo. The first serves as a national language, while the second, third, and fourth, respectively, are regional languages for the Northern, Western, and Eastern regions of the country. This has implications for adult literacy efforts in the country, which is the topic of the next section of this article.

ADULT LITERACY EFFORTS

Have language policies advanced or hindered adult literacy in Nigeria? The following account of past and present literacy efforts in Nigeria reviews this issue.

Free slaves who left Sierra Leone brought written English literacy to

Nigeria in 1841. From 1842 to 1968, however, many Christian missions—Methodist, Baptist, Church of Scotland—taught their converts in Nigeria how to read and write in mother tongues as well as in English. As stated in the previous section, these missionaries helped produce orthographies for the indigenous languages. For instance, J. F. Schon succeeded in transcribing the Hausa language into writing, and J. C. Raban, A. C. Gollwer, and Samuel Ajayi Crowther worked successfully on the Yoruba language.[16] In the 1970s the Summer Institute of Linguistics engaged in the application of linguistics to literacy and translation work and printed 15,000 primers and other booklets in four Nigerian languages and 43,000 leaflets in five languages. The Summer Institute of Linguistics completed translations of the New Testament and of summaries and selections from the Old Testament in at least ten Nigerian languages.

The British government became interested in literacy around 1941, after the outbreak of World War II, because of the need for literate colonial military personnel.[17] At that time, an adult education department was set up in each of the three regional ministries of education. Adults were taught in their mother tongues, such as Hausa, Kanuri, Yoruba, Tiv, Idoma, Igala, and Igbira, and prim-

ers were prepared with approved orthographies for these languages. The North Literature Agency was established, which helped in the production, translation, and distribution of literature on adult literacy education throughout the Northern Region. Some adults who were versed in Koranic education were indifferent or averse to Western-style adult literacy education. But many of those who received Arabic instruction in special Koranic schools, such as the Sanhuchi School in Kano, were encouraged to extend their studies to include literacy in Roman characters and to impart their knowledge to pupils at the ordinary Koranic schools.[18]

Immediately after World War II, adult literacy education was established nationwide. The objective was to help illiterate adults to read and write in their mother tongues and thus to play a more intelligent role in their social, economic, and political development. The responsibility of actually running the adult literacy centers was placed on village adult education committees, under control of a local government. In the Eastern Region the adult literacy program was patterned along those of the other two regions, with the exception that literacy classes were taught mostly in English because Pidgin English was used widely as a medium of expression. The adult literacy programs in both the North and South were supported by the print news media. For instance, the *Gaskiya ta fi kwabo*, a Hausa newspaper in the

16. Hair, *Early Study of Nigerian Languages*, pp. 11-41.

17. Great Britain, Advisory Committee on Education in the Colonies, *Mass Education in African Society*, Colonial no. 186, HMSO, 1943, p. 11.

18. Clement N. Anyanwu, *Adult Education in Nigeria* (Ibadan: Nigeria Moba Printers, 1981), p. 28.

North, and *Irohin*, a Yoruba newspaper in the West, were published for neoliterates. This practice contributed to the development of a vernacular literature and of civic enlightenment among new literates. Similarly, news from different parts of the Eastern Region was printed in the Igbo and Efik languages, in newspapers such as the *Dawn*, published at Aba, and the *Eastern Nigeria Guardian*, published at Onitsha. By the 1960s, mass literacy campaigns were organized in all three regions of Nigeria, and more and more reading materials were provided as village libraries sprang up.[19]

The adult literacy programs of the 1960s clearly contributed greatly to the positive changes in the customs and habits of many people in the three regions of Nigeria. The practice of functional literacy education has not, however, materialized on a wide scale in Nigeria.[20] Obstacles include inadequate funding by state and federal governments, a lack of written materials, and insufficient data on literacy education in the country. Thus the illiteracy problem in Nigeria has continued to mount. To find solutions to these problems, the federal government of Nigeria recently earmarked a sum of 10 million naira —N10 million—for literacy educa-

tion in the Fourth National Development Plan (1981-85). In addition, the government launched the 10-year National Mass Literacy Campaign in 1982, in accordance with the new National Policy on Education. The policy document states:

In character and content all mass literacy programs will be adapted in each case to local cultural and sociological conditions and each will also contain basic civic instruction aimed at generating qualities of good citizenship and active involvement by all in the national development process.[21]

Evaluations of the 1982-83 National Mass Literacy Campaign in Nigeria have not been positive. They found that the average enrollment rate was 2.8 percent of the illiterate population and that the number of literacy classes decreased compared to previous years. The illiteracy rate was high in the country, conservatively estimated at 70 percent of the population, and the number of people who had completed an adult literacy program by 1982-83 increased over those for 1981-82 in only two states. Many illiterates were enrolled in basic literacy classes that ran for nine months, but only a few continued in post-literacy classes that ran for an additional one or two years. Consequently, many neoliterates reverted to illiteracy before reaching a permanent literacy level. At the same time, the newly created illiterates, that is, dropouts from the primary-school-age population, continue to increase the number of adult illiterates.[22]

19. Joseph Taiwo Okedara, "Adult Literacy Education in Nigeria," in *The Right to Read: Literacy around the World*, ed. Eve Malmquist (Evanston, IL: Rotary International, 1985); Taiwo, "Nigeria: Language Problems and Solutions."

20. United Nations Educational, Scientific, and Cultural Organization, Third International Conference on Adult Education, *Final Report* (Paris: United Nations Educational, Scientific, and Cultural Organization, 1972).

21. Federal Republic of Nigeria, *National Policy on Education*, p. 21.

The problems have been attributed, to a lesser extent, to occupational factors, migration, and turnover of learners and, to a greater extent, to a lack of funds and a lack of motivation on the part of learners and instructors. Low priority accorded adult literacy programs by federal and state governments is another important factor. Policymakers at the federal, state, and local levels have yet to accord adult literacy education—be it functional literacy programs or mass literacy campaigns—a high priority. Policies are formulated but never executed. The paucity of adult literacy funding certainly hampers development of audiovisual and other material for mass literacy campaigns. Of particular note is the scarcity of basic and post-literacy primers, in mother tongues and in English, appropriate to the different levels and needs of adult literacy participants. Using primary school or other unsuitable literature or none at all by adult literacy instructors certainly adversely affects the morale of participants and goes against the objective stated in the new National Policy on Education. Moreover, the efforts of the adult literacy instructors are adversely affected by irregular payment of their honoraria. In addition, the radio, television, and print media have yet to play a positive role in the national mass literacy campaign in this decade compared to the 1950s and 1960s.

CONCLUSION

The new National Policy on Education in Nigeria states, "The mass literacy campaign will be planned within a limited duration of ten years during which all available resources will be mobilized towards the achievement of total eradication of illiteracy."[23] The importance and relevance of this policy statement cannot be overemphasized, as Nigeria, like other developing nations, is geared toward literacy for all in the year 2000.

The launching of the International Literacy Year and the establishment of the National Commission for Mass Literacy, Adult and Non-Formal Education in June 1990 are two policy steps in the right direction. They make us aware of the intention of the federal government, and they are necessary—though not sufficient—for achieving literacy for all in the year 2000. To succeed, they must be backed up with policy actions that call for making adult literacy education a priority in fund allocation; this includes getting the national commission off the ground and functioning without further delay and making sure that orthographies are established for languages without orthographies through well-funded research programs at the university level. It is also very important that governments at the federal and state levels immediately commission the production of relevant instructional materials, especially syllabi, primers, and follow-up booklets for basic and post-literacy programs through-

22. Joseph Taiwo Okedara, "An Assessment of the 1982/83 National Mass Literacy Campaign in Nigeria," *Literacy Voices*, 1(1) (Apr. 1988).

23. Federal Republic of Nigeria, *National Policy on Education*, p. 21.

out the country. Mass literacy campaigns by the media—radio, television, and print—and other organs of information dissemination are as vital today as they were in the past campaigns.

Finally, language policy with regard to national mass literacy campaigns has to be strengthened and practiced. Nigeria is a multilingual country with three categories of languages: English, the official language; Hausa, Igbo, and Yoruba, the regional languages in the Northern, Eastern, and Western parts of the country, respectively; and local minority languages. An individual illiterate may thus end up being bilingual or even multilingual before he or she can be truly regarded as functionally literate since he or she has to be able to communicate not only with neighbors but also with the wider community covered by his or her occupational, social, religious, or political functions. For the major ethnic groups that speak Hausa, Igbo, or Yoruba, literacy can be attained in two languages: the mother tongue and English. For others, literacy can be attained in at least three languages: the mother tongue, the regional language, and English. Until a policy concerning this language issue is clarified, the questions surrounding what it means to be literate and how literacy instruction should be carried out will not be resolved.

ANNALS, *AAPSS*, 520, March 1992

Functional Literacy,
Health, and Quality of Life

By A. EL BINDARI HAMMAD
in collaboration with C. MULHOLLAND

ABSTRACT: Many policymakers and development planners now realize that people are fundamental to all development processes and that investment in human development provides the highest rate of economic return. This return is enormously increased when one is dealing with an educated population. The human development approach brings together the production and distribution of material resources as well as the expansion and use of human resources through focusing on increasing people's self-reliance and choice. In this approach, functional literacy has a major role to play. This article addresses two aspects of functional literacy: first, the role of education as an essential factor in preparing people to lead healthy, socially rewarding, and economically productive lives; and, second, the relevance of functional literacy to the improvement of health status, especially that of women. An interlinking approach to improving health status and quality of life through interventions that combine functional literacy, local health services, and viable economic activities is presented. This approach can be incorporated into development planning and processes so that improvement in health status and quality of life is attained along with economic objectives.

Aleya El Bindari Hammad is adviser to the director-general of the World Health Organization on health and development policies. She has a wide range of experience in public health and education. Dr. Hammad has organized international and national conferences and seminars on intersectoral action for health and the impacts of development policies on health. She is the author of numerous publications on the subject.

Catherine Mulholland, a technical officer with the World Health Organization, has participated in seminars and workshops and has contributed to publications pertaining to intersectoral action for health. She has been closely involved with projects in Africa to improve women's health through functional literacy and intersectoral action.

THE director-general of the World Health Organization recently described the 1980s as a lost decade.[1] For those of us working in the health sector, much could have been achieved to improve health status with the knowledge and technology we had at our disposal, if we had had the political will and perseverance to do so. In contrast to the 1980s, the decade of the 1990s is being envisioned as a decade of hope. Since the beginning of 1990, we have witnessed rapid and radical changes in economic and political structures in countries where democratic forces have long been suppressed. These events have forcefully reminded us that people are capable of shaping their own destinies.

People, in the final analysis, are fundamental to all development processes. In the past, the causes of human welfare and social development were argued with timidity, since they were perceived to be in competition with much-needed technological and economic development. In this context, promoting human health was considered secondary in the allocation of the limited resources available. In many instances, the needs of people were reduced to mere economic factors. Many development planners have realized the results of this approach and now consider it grossly shortsighted.

Much suffering could have been avoided if countries had realized that investment in human development provides the highest rate of economic

1. Address of the Director-General of the World Health Organization to the Regional Committee meeting of the European Region, Sept. 1990.

return and that this return is enormously increased when one is dealing with an educated population. The sustainability of economic and social transformation depends, to a great extent, on investment in people that enables their capabilities to expand and to be fully productive in all domains.

The recent importance accorded to human development by development organizations and agencies is most encouraging. The United Nations Development Program's recent report, entitled *Human Development Report 1990*, points out the inadequacies of previous development strategies that are still predominant in many countries. The report illustrates the inadequacy of considering income as the best basis for all human choices, since according to that argument, access to income permits exercise of every other option. The shortcomings of this assumption are as follows:

1. Income is a means, not an end. Although it can be used for purchasing essential medicines, it may, by contrast, be used to purchase addictive drugs. The well-being of a society depends on the uses to which income is put, not on the level of income itself.

2. Examples from several countries illustrate that high ratings of human development exist with modest income levels, in contrast to other countries, which have poor ratings of human development despite relatively high income levels.

3. The present income of a country may offer little insight into its future growth prospects. If a nation has already invested in its people, future growth may be much higher than

current income levels indicate, and where a nation has not invested in its people, future growth may end up being lower than current levels indicate.

4. The multiplication of human problems in many industrialized, affluent nations illustrates that high income by itself is no guarantee of human progress.[2]

The United Nations Development Program's 1990 report brings out the difference between a human development approach and conventional approaches to economic growth, human capital formation, human resource development, and human welfare or basic human needs. In contrast to these latter strategies, the human development approach brings together the production and distribution of material resources, as well as the expansion and use of human resources. It also focuses on "choices—[involving] what people should have, be and do [in order] to be able to ensure their own livelihood."[3] The key terms understood here include "to be," "to do," and "to be able to." When we carefully analyze this mandate for choice, we discover that functional literacy has a major role to play in self-determination, through building capacities, developing attitudes, and helping people to master skills.

In this article, we will address two aspects of functional literacy: first, the vital role of education as an essential factor in preparing people to lead healthy, socially rewarding, and economically productive lives; and

2. United Nations Development Program, *Human Development Report 1990* (New York: Oxford University Press, 1990), p. 10.
    3. Ibid.

second, the relevance of functional literacy to the improvement of health status, especially that of women.

EDUCATION AND
HEALTH STATUS

It is widely accepted that formal education is decisive in improving health and reducing mortality, especially in developing countries. Just a few years of schooling can provide the basic skills necessary for continued learning, which can make a vital difference in an individual's ability to handle life situations and cope with a changing environment. This capacity, however rudimentary, can have far-reaching implications for healthy behavior and further learning about health.

Poor countries that have given priority to investment in education have mortality levels that are far below those of countries with less educated populations, yet with much higher incomes per capita. The comparative analysis of mortality, per capita income, and educational level in a group of developing countries (see Figures 1 and 2) highlights the close relationship between education and health. Figure 1 shows that countries that give priority to primary schooling have high rankings for infant survival. Even though all but three of these nations have per capita incomes of under US$1100, only one has an infant mortality rate as high as 100 per 1000 births, and four have rates below 50 per 1000. Half of these countries have a life expectancy at birth of over 60 years.

In contrast, Figure 2 shows 13 countries that have infant survival

FIGURE 1

THIRTEEN COUNTRIES WHERE INFANT SURVIVAL RANKINGS EXCEED INCOME RANKINGS

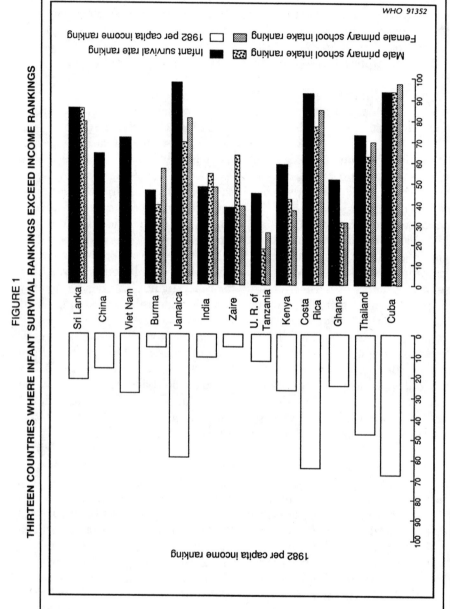

SOURCE: World Health Organization, Intersectoral Action for Health: The Role of Intersectoral Cooperation in National Strategies for Health for All (Geneva: World Health Organization, 1986), p. 76.

FIGURE 2

THIRTEEN COUNTRIES WHERE INCOME RANKINGS EXCEED INFANT SURVIVAL RANKINGS

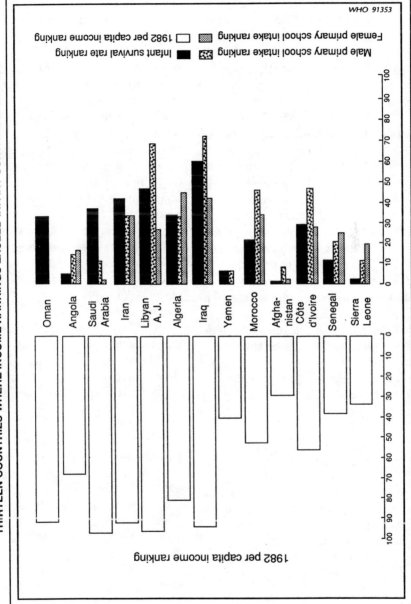

SOURCE: World Health Organization, *Intersectoral Action for Health*, p. 76.

107

rate rankings that are significantly lower than their income rankings. In every one of these nations the infant mortality rate is at least 25 ranks below that of per capita income. With only a single exception, the same relationship holds for child survival and life expectancy at birth.[4]

Survival rankings are also compared with the level of participation in primary schooling. It is interesting to note that survival ranking corresponds most closely to female participation in primary education. Furthermore, female school enrollment in 1960 is the key variable, and it comes closest to the survival ranking in 1983. The impact of primary education of females in the 1960s was thus manifested as the women entered child-bearing age in the 1980s.[5] It is clear in both figures that past—or parental—education is thus a better predictor than income level for infant mortality and, surprisingly, an equally good indicator of life expectancy at birth.

THE RELEVANCE OF FUNCTIONAL LITERACY

There is growing concern that, despite participation in formal educational systems, many children still graduate functionally illiterate. That is, these children will not have the ability and knowledge to perform literacy tasks in everyday life and to make adequate choices related to

themselves, their families, and their environment.[6]

It has been found that many functionally illiterate children drop out of school in search of more satisfying work and life experiences. Others complete their education only to find, to their distress, that their limited skills are not marketable. Many of these young adults quickly become part of the unemployment statistics. In life-styles in the industrialized countries, and increasingly in life-styles in the nonindustrialized ones, we find that overconsumption, smoking, and drug abuse are on the rise. The following question emerges: to what extent do our educational programs adequately prepare individuals to become functional and productive members of society?

In order to respond to the challenge of school curricula that are failing to prepare children for life, there should be consultation and dialogue between the education, social, and economic sectors in order to ensure that school curricula are shaped according to the real needs of both individuals and society. Relevant and functional education is the most important factor in the preparation of people who are able to articulate their needs and to make choices that lead to better health and a higher quality of life.

Education about health is as essential as learning to count. Knowledge of disease transmission, diet, and health problems that exist in one's community is as important as

4. World Health Organization, *Intersectoral Action for Health: The Role of Intersectoral Cooperation in National Strategies for Health for All* (Geneva: World Health Organization, 1986), pp. 76-77.

5. Ibid., p. 77.

6. Daniel A. Wagner, "Literacy Assessment in the Third World: An Overview and Proposed Schema for Survey Use," *Comparative Education Review*, 34(1):112-38 (Feb. 1990).

history and should be accorded equal importance in school curricula. There are positive experiences in some countries where schools have introduced health as a required subject. For example, Uganda's recent education policy made health mandatory alongside other subject matter in the school curriculum. Other countries have developed storybooks about health for primary school children. These books are based on their cultural beliefs and build on these beliefs to introduce scientific facts on disease transmission and prevention in their homes and communities.[7] Investment in early education for health as a means of disease prevention yields a high social dividend and is more cost effective than the treatment of preventable diseases, rehabilitative drug programs, and the distribution of medicine to combat the effects of unhealthy human practices.

During the 1960s and 1970s developing countries looked at the necessity of providing their populations with basic services including education and health. However, even after such historical meetings as the Alma Ata Conference in 1978, in which countries pledged their commitment to provide primary health care as the principal strategy for reducing inequities in health, measurable progress in achieving the goal of "health for all by the year 2000" has often proven difficult to achieve. Much of this was due to the economic crisis of the late 1970s and 1980s, which was characterized by soaring interest rates, rising energy costs, inflation, and the uncertainty of prices for primary commodities.

Primary health care is more important in the 1990s than ever before. Economic constraints have led to the realization that the state alone cannot respond adequately to the needs of all its citizens. Governments cannot afford to cover the cost of health care, which has become increasingly expensive as a result of the use of sophisticated technologies, the increasing incidence of diseases related to urbanization and industrialization, and the demands of an aging population. People themselves must develop a new self-reliance that will empower them to reduce the causes of mortality and morbidity and exert the necessary pressure for policy reform when this is vital to their safety and well-being.

We believe that functional literacy is pivotal to this process. Functional literacy is an empowerment process that enables people to acquire the economic skills and health knowledge needed to improve their health status and quality of life.

FUNCTIONAL LITERACY, HEALTH, AND QUALITY OF LIFE

In recent years, there has been tremendous documentation of the condition of women around the world. This documentation has brought into focus the powerlessness and discrimination that characterize the condition of the majority of women.

It is a startling fact that half a billion rural women have witnessed very little change in their situation

7. Silvio Pampiglione, *As Doencas Infecciosas: A que Sao, como Sao Transmitidas, como se Devem Combater* (Bologna: Graficoop, 1977).

over the last thirty years.[8] Despite women's shouldering much of the responsibility for development, they rarely reap the full benefits. Women throughout the world continue to be one of the most disadvantaged groups who fail to break out of the vicious cycle of poverty and inequity. On all continents, women seek paid work outside the home to fully support themselves and their families or to add to an insufficient household income, and yet they lack the educational opportunities that would prepare them for this role, they have poor or no access to credit, and they often lack the technology that would facilitate their tasks and ameliorate their quality of life. In times of economic hardship and rising unemployment, women are the first to lose their jobs outside the home and, within the home, they are the ones who must make a little go just a bit further.

A large part of this situation could be reversed if emphasis was put on (1) recognizing the contribution that women are making to the development process and (2) investing in the potential of women. The key to this process is functional literacy. Functional literacy for women is associated with low infant and child mortality, better family nutrition, and lower population growth rates. It has been shown that education improves a woman's skills for survival and her capacity for self-care and maintenance of good health during pregnancy. It enables her to acquire greater knowledge and skills, which can be applied in all spheres of her life from economic activities to better child-care practices.

Functional literacy is a process that empowers people, leads to an evolution in attitudes, sets the value system required for this process to develop, restores the inner worth and confidence of people, and develops their self-reliance and their ability to act and exercise choice. For the process to be firmly anchored, functional literacy skills that have relevance in the everyday life of the people, and that will be put to use, are essential. These will include, for example, the literacy and numeracy skills required for carrying out health and economic activities.

Some examples will serve to illustrate the way in which women's functional literacy is an important basis for improvement in health status. In Bangladesh it was found that child mortality was five times higher for children whose mothers were uneducated than for those whose mothers had received seven or more years of schooling.[9]

In Costa Rica the emphasis placed on education by successive administrations has resulted in a very low illiteracy rate with a high proportion of the population having completed at least grammar school, regardless of sex.[10] The most important change, however, has been seen in the level of schooling of the young population, especially women. In 1950 only 22.1

8. United Nations Development Program, *Human Development Report 1990*, p. 31.

9. Ibid., p. 32.

10. Leonardo Mata and Luis Rosero, *National Health and Social Development in Costa Rica: A Case Study of Intersectoral Action* (Washington, DC: Pan American Health Organization, World Health Organization, 1988), p. 35.

FIGURE 3
MALNUTRITION AND INFECTION CYCLE

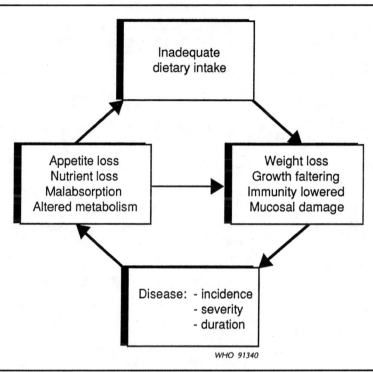

WHO 91340

SOURCE: Andrew Tomkins and Fiona Watson, *Malnutrition and Infection: A Review* (Geneva: United Nations Administrative Committee on Coordination, Subcommittee on Nutrition, Oct. 1989), p. 2.

percent of women aged 20-34 years completed grammar school. This percentage rose significantly, especially after 1965, to reach 70 percent in 1982.[11]

An extensive study carried out in Costa Rica shows how maternal education can play an important role in breaking the cycle of illness and death from preventable causes among infants and children. The communicable disease cycle is shown in Figure 3. The hygienic practices undertaken by mothers can make a significant contribution to diminishing the inci-

dence of infection and malabsorption, thereby breaking the communicable disease cycle in the home.[12]

From successive studies we can see that there was a significant improvement in the nutritional status of children, particularly after 1975 (Table 1). This occurred in spite of the fact that the consumption pattern from 1978 to 1982 did not change and real purchasing capacity did not increase.

11. Ibid.

12. Andrew Tomkins and Fiona Watson, *Malnutrition and Infection: A Review* (Geneva: United Nations Administrative Committee on Coordination, Subcommittee on Nutrition, Oct. 1989), p. 2.

TABLE 1

ADEQUACY OF THE DIET OF PRESCHOOL CHILDREN IN COSTA RICA

| Number of Children | Quality | Percentage of the Diets | | Study |
		Protein	Calories	
—*	Adequate	77	49	INCAP/OIR/MH (1969)[‡]
	Deficient	23	51	
151	Adequate	100(75)[†]	68(24)[†]	Valverde et al. (1975)[§]
	Deficient	0	32	
47	Adequate	100(83)[†]	60(17)[†]	Brenes and Mata (1978)[∥]
	Deficient	0	40	
24	Adequate	100	0	Murillo and Mata (1980)[#]
	Deficient	0	100	
155	Adequate	100	56	Whiteford (1981)**
	Deficient	0	44	

SOURCE: Leonardo Mata and Luis Rosero, *National Health and Social Development in Costa Rica: A Case Study of Intersectoral Action* (Washington, DC: Pan American Health Organization, World Health Organization, 1988), p. 49.

*Data not available.

[†]In parentheses, percentage of diets with more than 110 percent adequacy.

[‡]INCAP/OIR/MH, *Evaluación nutricional de la población de Centro América y Panamá* (Guatemala: INCAP, 1969).

[§]V. Valverde et al., "La deficiencia calórica en pre-escolares del área rural de Costa Rica," *Archivos latinoamericanos de nutrición*, 25:351-61 (1975).

[∥]H. Brenes and L. Mata, "Consumo de alimentos en niños menores de 5 años de comunidades rurales de Costa Rica," *Revista de biología tropical*, 26:467-83 (1978).

[#]S. Murillo and L. Mata, "¿Existe un efecto nutricional en el Centro de Educación y Nutrición (CEN) de Costa Rica?" *Revista médica del Hospital Nacional de Niños* (Costa Rica), 15:59-68 (1980).

**M. Whiteford, *The Socio-cultural Etiologies of Nutritional Status in Rural Costa Rica* (Ames: Iowa State University, Department of Sociology and Anthropology, 1981).

This nutritional improvement coincides with dramatic decreases in the incidence of diarrhea and intestinal parasites (Figure 4 and Table 2). The decrease in the prevalence of parasites was related to a number of factors among which we find both service elements—a steady increase in the availability of latrines and water toilets, and improved water supplies—as well as behavioral elements, including the wearing of shoes by the majority of the population, intensive health education programs, and systematic deworming in health centers and hospitals and by the population itself. All of these elements combined to enable the little food that was being taken to be fully and efficiently absorbed by the system, rather than being lost in bouts of diarrhea and other infections.[13]

While the provision of services such as latrines and improved water supplies certainly has a role to play, it is important to note that the attitudinal and behavioral changes are fundamental factors in breaking

13. Mata and Rosero, *National Health*, p. 46.

FIGURE 4
CRUDE DIARRHEAL DISEASE DEATH RATE AND
INFANT MORTALITY RATE IN COSTA RICA, 1926-1982

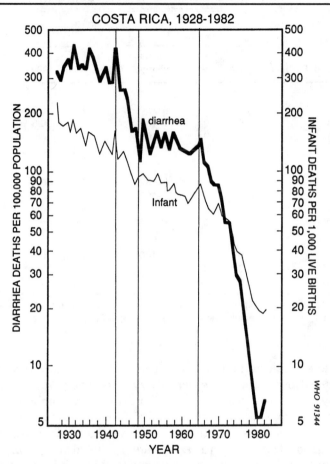

FIGURE 4
CRUDE DIARRHEAL DISEASE DEATH RATE AND
INFANT MORTALITY RATE IN COSTA RICA, 1926-1982

SOURCE: Mata and Rosero, *National Health*, p. 71.

NOTE: Note that all peaks, depressions, and plateaus of both mortality curves coincide. Mata and Rosero, "Estancamiento y tambaleo de la mortalidad infantil."

the infection and malnutrition cycle and are the result of action taken by an informed population, particularly by the women, who are the ones who encourage the wearing of shoes and proper clothing, treat diarrhea in their children, gather and treat water, and pass on proper hygienic practices.

These dramatic decreases in Costa Rica would not have been possible in the absence of a concurrent emphasis on increasing the literacy rates of Costa Rican girls and women. Figure 5 shows the evolution in the percentage of young women aged 20-34 years who attained primary schooling and the corresponding decrease in infant

TABLE 2
REDUCTION IN INTENSITY OF INFECTION
BY INTESTINAL HELMINTHS, 1966-82, COSTA RICA

| | Age (years) | | | | | |
| | Less than 1 | | | 5-9 | | |
Eggs per Gram of Feces	1966	1982	Percentage change	1966	1982	Percentage change
Ascaris						
100-900	4.1	3.1	−24	13.4	3.2	−76
1,000-9,900	6.1	0	−100	23.0	6.5	−71
10,000-49,000	1.2	0	−100	6.8	0	−100
50,000+	0	0		1.7	0	−100
Trichuris						
100-900	8.2	3.1	−62	48.6	16.1	−67
1,000-1,900	2	0	−100	10.8	0	−100
2,000-4,900	0	0		6.2	0	−100
5,000+	0	0		3.4	0	−100
Hookworm						
100-900	6.1	0	−100	15.3	0	−100
1,000-9,900	0	0		1.4	0	−100
10,000+	0	0		0.9	0	−100

SOURCE: L. Mata and L. Rosero, "Estancamiento y tambaleo de la mortalidad infantil en Costa Rica" (Document, INISA, Universidad de Costa Rica, 1985), as cited in Mata and Rosero, *National Health*, p. 112.

mortality. The break in the infection and malnutrition cycle, in which women play a vital role through their actions and examples, has led to important improvements in nutrient digestion, absorption, and utilization, thereby resulting in dramatic improvements in lowering infant mortality rates at constant levels of consumption.

Even with little income, educated mothers exercise their wisdom in choosing the most nutritious foods that are available and affordable, and in observing appropriate methods for cooking and storing food.

In addition to playing a key role in encouraging good health practices in the home, educated mothers are able to adhere to medical advice and ap-

propriately seek care when necessary. They also have smaller families. For example, Colombian women with a higher education have four fewer children than Colombian women who had completed only their primary education.[14] In spite of the fact that the use of birth control increases with higher rates of female literacy, most family-planning programs neglect this important fact and start with the assumption that if acceptable contraceptives are made available and are inexpensive, all women will automatically use them and that there will be a subsequent fall in the birth rate.

There have been many debates about the social dimensions of con-

14. United Nations Development Program, *Human Development Report 1990*, p. 32.

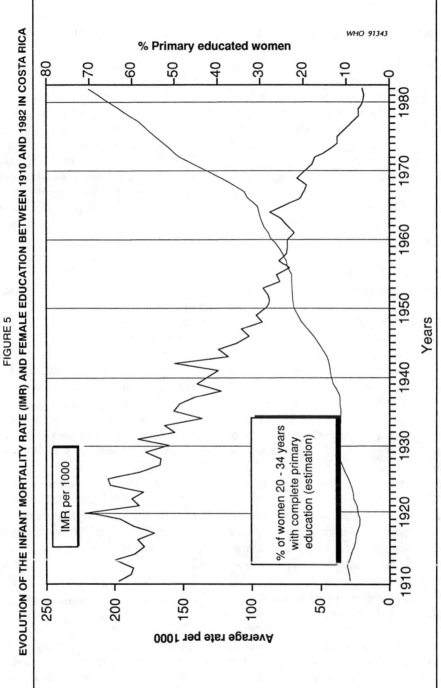

FIGURE 5

EVOLUTION OF THE INFANT MORTALITY RATE (IMR) AND FEMALE EDUCATION BETWEEN 1910 AND 1982 IN COSTA RICA

WHO 91343

% Primary educated women

IMR per 1000

% of women 20 - 34 years with complete primary education (estimation)

Average rate per 1000

Years

SOURCE: Data from Mata and Rosero, *National Health.*

115

traceptive use, especially when proposing family-planning programs. The economic plight of many families whose members are frequently unemployed or underemployed, lack social security, and yet have to cope with the high cost of living, causes the families to consider children as a valuable source of income since, under conditions of growing industrialization, they are increasingly used as a cheap source of labor. In this context, distributing contraceptives first, before investigating the root causes of the need for large families, accounts for the many failures of family-planning programs.

In this situation of despair, even the health argument as a plausible reason for limiting repeated pregnancies does not receive a sympathetic hearing. For many, choosing whether or not to increase one's family is similar to choosing between a risky job and no job at all. Having many children is an important source of revenue and is seen by many as better than facing economic hardship, even at the risk of losing one's life.

Another social dimension that has an impact on contraceptive use concerns the social security that children provide to their parents. In many societies children are counted on to take care of their parents in their old age. In situations where there are no social provisions or insurance schemes, and with the increasing cost of living, expenses incurred in caring for parents are much less of a burden when shared by numerous children.

The situation is even more dramatic for women who depend on their families or husbands for support and have no legal rights or income when their family situation does not work out. It is not surprising to find that in some situations many women have accepted polygamy rather than face loneliness, hopelessness, poverty, and very little chance of earning a living. In short, one can state that women count, but are not counted.

It is only when the cycle of dependency is broken, and people are empowered to take charge of their own lives, that the technologies available for choosing if and when to have children, with all the implications that this has for women's health, become really relevant as part of the choices that are now open to them and that they can exercise freely.

Investing in women's functional literacy not only allows women to improve the quality of their lives, and that of their families, but it also creates options for women to earn and control their own incomes. This reduces their dependency on literate family members and enables them to overcome many problems in their day-to-day existence that require basic literacy and numeracy skills. It also diminishes their dependency on offspring to provide for them in their old age.

THE ESSENTIAL ELEMENTS OF FUNCTIONAL LITERACY

Education that is functional and relevant to the problems faced by women in their everyday lives is clearly an essential element in the examples of the improvements in health status and quality of life that have been cited. Nevertheless, functional literacy should not be viewed as a panacea. The children in the Costa Rican example may have been breast-fed for six to nine months and then weaned in a healthy happy environment where there were all the amenities, such as clean water, access to health services for immunizations, deworming, and so forth, and where there was a mother whose education prepared her to correctly diagnose and treat simple health conditions, to use the health center for more serious problems, and generally to take good care of herself and her family.

Unfortunately, this is often not the situation for mothers in developing countries. It is not uncommon to find that, despite numerous health education programs, children are fed only once a day for nine months of the year. This is not because there is a lack of knowledge, but because there is no food and no money to buy more. No amount of health services will remedy the situation when the problem is one of economic hardship, which is precisely the situation that women are facing in many countries in which we are working. Health, education, and economics are inextricably linked to each other. It would be futile, and indeed wrong, to concentrate exclusively on one of these elements and forget the others, as has been done so many times in the past. Mosley refers to this interlinking and interdependence as "social synergy," "that is, a single social determinant, such as the level of education of women, can operate to influence the risk of death through several intermediate variables simultaneously." Our argument is precisely this: tech-

nical health interventions, such as the use of oral rehydration therapy by the mother, may decrease infant mortality due to dehydration from diarrhea, but they will not ensure that more food will be available to the surviving child.[15] So, too, narrowly based literacy projects and so-called income-generation efforts alone are unlikely to solve health problems or provide real solutions to economic needs.

The challenge is to find the unique combination of elements that will contribute to improving the health status and quality of life of the most disadvantaged groups, such as women. Innovative approaches must be explored and effective interventions introduced in such a way that they raise awareness, improve self-worth, increase self-confidence, and empower people to improve their lives. The most important liberating process, which will help the most vulnerable women both to increase and control their income and to adopt positive health behavior, is, in our opinion, functional literacy. It is this conviction that has led us to utilize functional literacy as the principal means for improving health status, increasing healthy behavior, and increasing the income of the most vulnerable women in five African countries.

The process of improving health status and quality of life through

15. W. H. Mosley, "Will Primary Health Care Reduce Infant and Child Mortality? A Critique of Some Current Strategies with a Special Reference to Africa and Asia" (Paper delivered at the International Union for the Scientific Study of Populations, Seminar on Social Policy and Mortality Prospects, Paris, 1983).

functional literacy comprises three components:

— acquiring knowledge of the causes of key health problems and learning how to manage these in the community;
— equipping people with the attitudes and skills necessary for improving their health and their quality of life; and
— enabling learners to acquire the skills, materials, and information necessary for improving their occupations and, through this increase in income, for improving their standard of living.

The uniqueness of the approach stems from the fact that it is based on a distinctive triad of three vital and interlinking elements, which are illustrated in Figures 6 and 7. Figure 6 interprets our objective, which is to improve the health status of vulnerable women through functional literacy and economic activities. In the first triangle, the focus is clearly on women and their functional learning needs. This process of education and empowerment leads to the second triangle, where the focus is on better health status, which results from an increase in income from viable economic activities and acquisition of new functional skills.

Figure 7 presents the strategic approach to linking the different elements of the triad and sums up how projects go about anchoring improvement of health status and use of increased income for health and educational activities in the process of acquiring functional literacy.[16]

The success of the program is judged according to the positive changes scored in each of the three elements. Through the functional literacy program, it is hoped that women will become engaged in economically viable activities that can be sustained over time. The functional literacy program is used as a springboard to initiate these activities and provide women with the required knowledge and skills. At the same time, health and other services available at the community level are strengthened. This combination enables women to improve their own condition, supported by the necessary knowledge, skills, and services.

Outcomes of the activities are assessed in terms of increased income levels, decreased malnutrition, and evidence that women are competent to keep accounts of their productive activities and the growth of their children by keeping growth charts. Furthermore, program success can be measured by the elimination of dehydration due to diarrhea through women's use of oral rehydration—an outcome of functional literacy—and by the reduction of maternal anemia through the prevention of maternal malnutrition.

Our commitment to focusing on functional literacy for women stems from our belief that, as beautifully stated by Mikhail Gorbachev, "women [can] prevent the threads of life from being broken." It is our belief and hope that this interlinking three-

16. World Health Organization, "Promoting Health through Women's Functional Literacy and Intersectoral Activities" (Unpublished report on an intercountry meeting held 12-16 Nov. 1990, Lusaka, Zambia).

FIGURE 6
**IMPROVING WOMEN'S HEALTH THROUGH
FUNCTIONAL LITERACY AND ECONOMIC ACTIVITY**

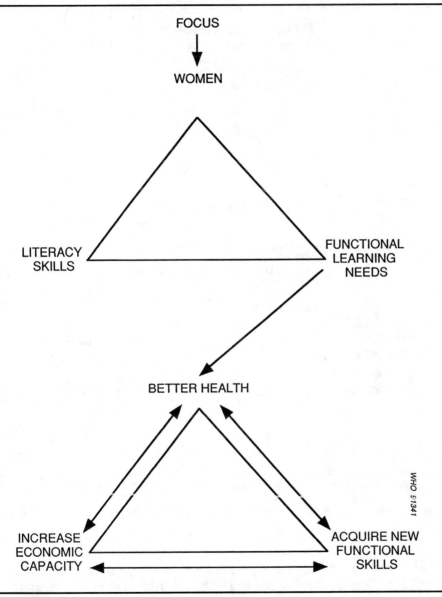

SOURCE: World Health Organization, unpublished report of the annual intercountry meeting "Promoting Health through Women's Functional Literacy and Intersectoral Action," Lusaka, Zambia, 12-16 Nov. 1990.

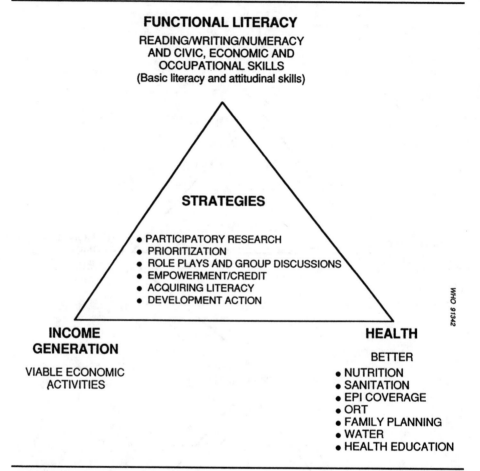

FIGURE 7
STRATEGIC APPROACH TO LINKING
FUNCTIONAL LITERACY, INCOME GENERATION, AND HEALTH

FUNCTIONAL LITERACY
READING/WRITING/NUMERACY
AND CIVIC, ECONOMIC AND
OCCUPATIONAL SKILLS
(Basic literacy and attitudinal skills)

STRATEGIES

- PARTICIPATORY RESEARCH
- PRIORITIZATION
- ROLE PLAYS AND GROUP DISCUSSIONS
- EMPOWERMENT/CREDIT
- ACQUIRING LITERACY
- DEVELOPMENT ACTION

INCOME GENERATION

VIABLE ECONOMIC
ACTIVITIES

HEALTH

BETTER
- NUTRITION
- SANITATION
- EPI COVERAGE
- ORT
- FAMILY PLANNING
- WATER
- HEALTH EDUCATION

WHO 91342

SOURCE: World Health Organization, unpublished report of "Promoting Health through Women's Functional Literacy and Intersectoral Action."

NOTE: "EPI" stands for "expanded program immunization"; "ORT" stands for "oral rehydration therapy."

pronged approach to addressing the complex problems affecting life and health will signal a turning point in development planning and processes that will break the vicious cycle of poverty and inequity.

ANNALS, *AAPSS*, 520, March 1992

Women and Literacy in Morocco

By JENNIFER E. SPRATT

ABSTRACT: This article examines the gender gap in literacy and education in Morocco, presenting the distribution of education and literacy by gender, its relation to labor force participation and family health, and the implications for literacy efforts that these factors suggest. Morocco's literacy and educational participation rates for both genders, while improving, remain among the lowest in the region, and a large gender gap—22 points for adult literacy—persists. Like men, women with a relatively high degree of education benefit in the urban labor market. In the rural labor market, postprimary education appears to be a liability, especially for females, although females with only a primary certificate may fare better than males. As elsewhere, literate and educated Moroccan women tend to have fewer children, lose fewer children to disease, and use more modern health care practices. More effective literacy work in this context demands improved statistics, targeted research, and attention to societal expectations.

Jennifer E. Spratt is a researcher in educational development at the Center for International Development, Research Triangle Institute. She received her Ph.D. in 1988 from the University of Pennsylvania, where she was assistant director of the Morocco Literacy Project. Her specializations include literacy assessment, participation and internal efficiency in educational systems, gender issues in education, and research design and methodologies. In addition to long-term work in Morocco, recent assignments have taken her to Egypt, Haiti, Jordan, Malawi, and South Africa.

THE existence of a gender gap in literacy skills and education is a phenomenon found in many countries. It is not a problem of equity or human rights only, but one with potentially important economic, demographic, and family health ramifications as well. Numerous studies, for example, have shown important, positive relationships of women's literacy and education to employment, reduced fertility rates, and infant and child survival. This article examines specific features of this phenomenon in one country, Morocco. It presents the distribution of education and literacy in Morocco by gender, its relation to socioeconomic outcomes of labor force participation and family health, and the implications for literacy efforts that these factors suggest.

Morocco has a long history of literacy through the strength of its Islamic educational institutions. The number of individuals capable of using literacy for everyday economic functions, however, was historically limited to a small proportion of the male population.

That pattern has changed markedly with the advent of secular public schooling, adult and nonformal educational opportunities, and increasing female enrollments in Koranic preschools. In 1990, the World Bank reported estimates of adult illiteracy in Morocco for the year 1985 at 78 percent of females and about 56 percent of males.[1] When compared with census data from 1960, which reported illiteracy rates of 96 percent

for females and 78 percent for males over age 10, these figures reflect appreciable reductions in illiteracy. But in Morocco, as in many developing countries, there is still a long distance to be traveled toward universal literacy, and a gender gap of about 20 points persists.

At this point, I offer some caution concerning the data. Current statistics on literacy in Morocco, as in most other countries, tend to be based on self-report or even third-person-report census information on literacy ability and educational level. They are presented as dichotomous, despite the great range of skills and definitions that have been described as constituting literacy. Existing statistics typically contain the assumptions, for example, that those who have attended school are literate—with no adjustment for attrition of skills—and that those who have not attended school are illiterate; these assumptions result in unknown distortions. There may also be little comparability across countries, due to employment of different definitions, school systems, and age-group denominators. While acknowledging their shortcomings, however, one is obliged to use such literacy statistics until means of information collection on literacy improve.

Educational enrollment figures, frequently used as proxies for determining literacy rates, may obscure the real level of participation in a number of ways. In a system with substantial grade repetition and many overage children, gross enrollment rates—total numbers of students divided by population of school age—say little about the real degree

1. World Bank, *World Development Report 1990* (New York: Oxford University Press, 1990), p. 178.

of educational participation of school-age children. Second, educational enrollment figures do not typically indicate actual school attendance. Observations suggest, for example, that school attendance rates can differ greatly across population subgroups, sometimes resulting in very different amounts of actual time spent in school despite similar or identical gross participation rates.

MOROCCAN LITERACY AND EDUCATION INDICATORS IN REGIONAL PERSPECTIVE

Examining recent statistics on Moroccan education and literacy by gender in the context of the Mideast and North Africa (MENA) region and for countries of lower-middle income (LMI) generally, Morocco's rates of educational participation are generally lower overall than those of its MENA neighbors. Morocco's reported adult illiteracy rates are among the highest within this group, with the exception of North Yemen (Table 1). The difference between female and total illiteracy rates shows a remarkable consistency of about 11 to 13 percentage points for most of these lower- and middle-income MENA countries—with the notable exceptions of Libya and Syria, at 17 points each—indicating a gender gap of roughly 22 to 25 points. This gap in the MENA region is considerably larger than the overall LMI average of a 5-point difference between female and total illiteracy rates, or a 10-point gender gap, lending support to the argument that cultural factors are at work.

The number of girls as a proportion of the number of boys in school is also lower generally for MENA countries than in LMI countries as a whole. Morocco's ranking in 1987, at 63 girls per 100 boys enrolled in primary school, was poor even among its North African and Mideast neighbors, with the exception of Yemen.

CURRENT LITERACY AND EDUCATIONAL PARTICIPATION RATES

Morocco has made clear progress, however, in extending literacy and education to greater portions of the population in recent decades. Total primary school enrollments have increased from about 1 million children in the early 1960s to a relatively stable level of 2.1 million in the mid-1980s, representing approximately 72 percent of the primary-school-age population in 1988. In the decades following independence, girls in urban areas have gained rough parity in enrollment in primary schooling, constituting 46 percent of all urban primary enrollments in 1988. In rural areas, however, boys still outnumber girls in school at a rate of over 2 to 1: boys at 71 percent, girls at 29 percent.[2] The southern eco-

2. One factor that has been implicated in the lower rate of girls' participation in rural primary schools is the low proportion of female teachers in such schools: while 50 percent of urban primary school teachers were female, only 18 percent of rural teachers were female. Efforts to improve this ratio with incentive programs are hoped to reduce the reluctance of some traditional rural parents to send their daughters to schools and classrooms presided over by single male teachers.

TABLE 1

LITERACY AND EDUCATION INDICATORS FOR MOROCCO AND NEIGHBORING COUNTRIES

Country	Adult Illiteracy, 1985 (percentage)		Females per 100 Males in School				Persistence to Fourth Year of Schooling, 1987 (percentage)	
			Primary school		Secondary school			
	Female	Total	1970	1987	1970	1987	Female	Male
Morocco	78	67	51	63	40	66	77	79
Tunisia	59	46	64	81	38	75	90	94
Algeria	63	50	60	79	40	73	90*	95*
Libya	50	33	59	—	21	—	92*	95*
Egypt	70	56	61	75	48	68	85*	93*
Yemen Arab Republic	97	86	10	29	3	12	71	76
Jordan	37	25	78	96	53	95	99	92*
Syria	57	40	57	87	36	70	96	97
Turkey	38	26	73	89	37	60	97	98
MENA average	53	41	70	82	86	104	88	94
LMI average	32	27	85	88	85	94	82	86

SOURCE: World Bank, *World Development Report 1990* (New York: Oxford University Press, 1990), pp. 178-79.

NOTE: "Persistence to fourth year of schooling" was estimated as the ratio of students in year 4 to new entrants in grade 1 three years earlier. All countries listed are rated as lower-middle income by the World Bank with the exception of Algeria and Libya, which are rated upper-middle income. "MENA average" includes lower- and middle-income countries in the Middle East and North Africa region.

*Indicates 1973 figures; 1987 figures not available.

nomic region in particular is marked by a relatively low proportion of both female enrollments and female teaching staff. Vocational and technical education, similarly, shows an overall female enrollment that seldom exceeds one-third of all enrollments and is as low as 25 percent in rural areas.[3]

Educational attainment of the adult population is also on the rise, although the gap between men and women persists. As of 1988, 28 percent of all adults had received some form of formal education. According to 1985 World Bank estimates, 78 percent of the adult female population was reported to be illiterate, in contrast to about 56 percent of males, representing no reduction in the gender gap over the past thirty years. The gap remains greatest in rural areas.

EXISTING LITERACY PROGRAMS

Literacy instruction is available in Morocco through basic formal education, some vocational education programs, and nonformal efforts offered by the Ministry of Artisanry and Social Affairs and the Ministry of Youth and Sports.

The current organization of Moroccan public education is derived from the French system introduced during the protectorate (1912-56). The present system, under the jurisdiction of the Ministry of Education, consists of a five-year primary cycle, a four-year junior secondary cycle,

and a three-year senior secondary cycle, with general and technical branches. Tertiary education is also available; in addition to the public university system run by the Ministry of Education, a number of specialized training institutes are maintained by other ministries. Preschool education in Morocco, while nominally required for primary school registration, reaches roughly half of the preschool-age population. About 713,000 preschool-age children—28 percent of whom are girls—attended Koranic preschools in 1987-88; 33,282 —47 percent girls—attended non-Koranic kindergartens—in lieu of or in addition to Koranic preschool— provided by Youth and Sports and Entr'aide Nationale Ministries and a few private institutions.[4]

The Ministry of Artisanry and Social Affairs conducts adult basic literacy programs, which as of 1987 had enrolled approximately 120,000 persons since 1981 and currently reaches about 40,000 persons annually.[5] About half of all enrollees are women; as elsewhere—for example, Malawi—women tend to enter these programs in higher proportions than anticipated by the organizers, indicating a need for program-planning efforts to better examine and assess the demand for literacy among women. The program consists of three contact hours per week over a period of 50 weeks, and the curriculum includes basic literacy and numeracy skills. As is typical in most campaigns of this

3. Morocco, Ministry of National Education, *Statistiques de l'enseignement primaire 1987-1988* (Rabat: Ministry of National Education, 1988).

4. Ibid., p. 1.

5. Morocco, Ministry of Artisanry and Social Affairs, *Le programme de'alphabetisation des adultes* (Rabat: Ministry of Artisanry and Social Affairs, 1988).

kind, there is virtually no information available to assess the effectiveness of the program in actually providing needed skills; it is not clear from available statistics what percentage of enrollees even complete the program. The literacy curriculum and materials are designed for use with both male and female learners; however, a cursory look at such materials indicates substantial gender stereotyping in the activities and occupations of the men and women depicted in the stories.

The Ministry of Youth and Sports runs *les Foyers Feminins*, popular centers for women across the country that provide opportunities for social gathering and offer knitting, sewing, embroidery, and other courses. Rudimentary literacy skills are also taught, for no more than six hours a week. For urban and rural poor women, training in literacy and traditional crafts is also available through the Ministry of Artisanry and Social Affairs' *Centres d'Education et de Travail*. While half of each day is given to literacy training, few participants attain more than rudimentary literacy skills.

Varying amounts of literacy training are also offered through other vocational and technical training programs, which typically absorb school leavers with some level of education rather than those with no literacy skills to begin with. These programs are administered through vocational training sections of several government offices as well as some private institutions. As of 1986, existing vocational training centers were capable of absorbing about half of all school leavers.

LANGUAGE, LITERACY, AND GENDER IN MOROCCO

Language is an important factor implicated in gender disparities as well as regional disparities in literacy and educational outcomes in Morocco. While the majority of the population of Morocco speaks a variety of Arabic, a substantial minority still speaks Berber—in one of three dialects—as a native language. Among Berber speakers, it is estimated that women are much more likely to be monolingual, while men have more opportunities through market and business activities to acquire Arabic as a second language. Any Arabic literacy-training efforts—Berber is not currently utilized in written form—with this predominantly female group of monolingual Berber speakers would have to assess and address the special needs for basic language training as well as literacy training. Seckinger has pointed out that even Moroccan Arabic radio and television programming on health and other development information topics, promoted as a short-term solution to the delivery of development messages and training to the illiterate, has effectively excluded monolingual Berbers—especially women—from receiving such messages.[6]

The shape of an effective adult language-and-literacy program has yet to be determined, for Morocco or elsewhere. While there is evidence that Berber-speaking children catch up in Arabic reading skills with their Ara-

6. Beverly Seckinger, "The Communication Gap: Language, Literacy, and Moroccan Women Excluded from Development" (Manuscript, 1988).

bic-speaking peers in the de facto total-immersion setting of the primary school classroom,[7] the prognosis for nonliterate adult literacy learners in a second-language setting is virtually unknown.

GENDER, EDUCATION,
AND FORMAL LABOR
MARKET ACTIVITY

Meaningful research on the relationship of education to labor force structure and participation requires special attention to gender-specific patterns. Whether or not a more educated female population is more likely to be employed is clearly a function of the structure of the labor market and the types of employment opportunities within it.[8]

Internationally, formal education has been found to be positively associated with women's participation in wage labor or salaried labor, typically the only type of labor represented in published figures. To the extent that it exposes them to nontraditional attitudes, values, and information and to a bureaucratic, worklike public institution, in addition to imparting specific marketable skills such as literacy or bilingualism, the education of females in particular appears to affect not only their earnings but their entrance into the formal labor market to begin with.[9]

Such patterns of increased labor force participation are evident in recent statistics for urban Moroccan women with postprimary education, although the distribution of participation exhibits a U-shaped curve, with relatively high rates of labor force participation among those with no formal educational degree (see Table 2). For urban men, the pattern is similar but flatter, with relatively low labor force participation except at the extreme ends of the educational distribution, although always higher than for women with similar educational levels. What is striking is the gap in unemployment rates between urban men and women, at any level of education: with equivalent educational credentials and at every education level, urban women active in the labor force are twice as likely to be unemployed than urban men, belying employment patterns that go beyond credentials and smack of discrimination against women. Such patterns demand investigation.

In the rural setting, educational degrees would appear to depress the likelihood of participation in the for-

7. Abdelkader Ezzaki, Jennifer E. Spratt, and Daniel A. Wagner, "Childhood Literacy Acquisition among Children in Rural Morocco: Effects of Language Differences and Preschool Experience," in *The Future of Literacy in a Changing World*, ed. Daniel A. Wagner (London: Pergamon Press, 1987), pp. 159-73; Daniel A. Wagner, Jennifer E. Spratt, and Abdelkader Ezzaki, "Does Learning to Read in a Second Language Always Put the Child at a Disadvantage? Some Counter-Evidence from Morocco," *Applied Psycholinguistics*, 10:31-48 (1989).

8. Thomas O. Eisemon, *The Consequences of Schooling: A Review of Research on the Outcomes of Primary Schooling in Developing Countries*, BRIDGES Educational Development Discussion Paper no. 3 (Cambridge, MA: Harvard Institute for International Development, 1988).

9. Ibid.; George Psacharopoulos, "The Contribution of Education to Economic Growth: International Comparisons," in *International Comparisons of Productivity and Causes of the Slowdown*, ed. J. W. Kendrick (Cambridge, MA: Ballinger, 1984), pp. 335-55.

TABLE 2

EDUCATION AND LABOR FORCE PARTICIPATION BY GENDER, URBAN MOROCCO, 1986

Employment Rates	None	Highest Educational Certificate				
		Primary certificate (CEP)	Junior secondary certificate (CES)	Senior secondary degree (Bac)	University or professional degree	Other
Female						
Percentage of population aged 15 and older	72.8	10.8	7.1	2.0	1.7	5.6
Labor force participation rate (percentage)	20.5	15.2	18.9	26.5	86.4	
Unemployment (percentage)	16.2	34.7	44.0	41.3	10.4	
Male						
Percentage of population aged 15 and older	56.5	17.0	12.2	4.1	4.4	5.8
Labor force participation rate (percentage)	84.5	52.7	43.1	39.3	93.2	
Unemployment (percentage)	12.4	18.2	24.5	22.0	5.0	

SOURCE: Morocco, Centre d'Études et de Recherches Démographiques, *Relation entre l'éducation et l'activité* (Rabat: Ministère du Plan, Direction de la Statistique, 1988).

TABLE 3
EDUCATION AND LABOR FORCE
PARTICIPATION BY GENDER, RURAL MOROCCO, 1986

Employment Rates	Highest Educational Certificate		
	None	Primary certificate (CEP)	Postprimary degree
Female			
Percentage of population aged 15 and older	98.6	1.0	0.3
Labor force participation rate (percentage)	53.5	20.8	19.6
Unemployment (percentage)	1.4	12.7	42.9
Male			
Percentage of population aged 15 and older	92.6	5.2	2.2
Labor force participation rate (percentage)	88.8	56.2	46.1
Unemployment (percentage)	7.8	19.9	27.2

SOURCE: Morocco, Centre d'Études et de Recherches Démographiques, *Relation entre l'éducation et l'activité.*

mal labor market for both men and women, or the data may reflect the fact that the most ambitious educated rural youths are likely to try to migrate to cities (see Table 3). According to the data, the less educated one is, the more employable one is in the rural setting. Rural girls with primary education only, when they do seek work, are more successful than their male counterparts, although the unemployment pattern reverses dramatically with postprimary education.

WOMEN'S EDUCATION,
FERTILITY, AND FAMILY HEALTH

Important positive effects of education, particularly education of females, on health indicators such as infant and child survival have been documented through cross-national and intracountry findings for a number of developing countries.[10] It has been hypothesized that both the

10. John C. Caldwell, "Routes to Low Mortality in Poor Countries," *Population and Development Review*, 12:171-214 (1986); S. H.

knowledge imparted and the increased earnings potential gained through education enable parents to provide a health-enhancing environment for their families, although the processes or mechanisms by which school-learned knowledge is translated into better health behaviors are still unclear.[11] Education may also have a more direct effect on child health and survival, to the extent that schools provide children with informal health care, immunizations, and dietary supplements.

Population research, furthermore, has consistently provided compelling

Cochrane, J. Leslie, and D. J. O'Hara, "Parental Education and Child Health: Intracountry Evidence," *Health Policy and Education*, 2:213-50 (1982); J. N. Hobcraft, J. W. McDonald, and S. O. Rutstein, "Socioeconomic Factors in Infant and Child Mortality: A Cross-Country Comparison," *Population Studies*, 38:193-223 (1984); Robert A. LeVine, "Women's Schooling, Patterns of Fertility, and Child Survival," *Educational Researcher*, 16:21-27 (1987).

11. Eisemon, *Consequences of Schooling*; LeVine, "Women's Schooling," pp. 21-27.

evidence of an effect of the schooling and literacy of women on overall reductions in fertility.[12] In explanation of such findings, it has been argued that education of women improves understanding of biology, enhances acceptance and correct application of birth control methods, and delays marriage, all of which may be expected to reduce fertility rates. In addition, because educational participation in general tends to extend the length of the child's economic dependency on the family, it may result in an attitude shift toward reduced family size.[13] On the other hand, educated working women are more likely to breast-feed each child for fewer months, a practice that may contribute to shorter spacing between births and a potential increase in fertility.

As elsewhere, Moroccan women with higher levels of education tend to have fewer children, lose fewer children to disease in infancy and childhood, and are more likely to use modern health care facilities and vaccinations. Based on 1986 estimates by the Centre d'Études et de Recherches Démographiques in Morocco's Ministry of Planning, the fertility rate for women aged 45-49 who had no education was 7 births per woman, while the rate decreased dramatically with increasing levels of education: for those with primary education, the rate dropped to 6 births per woman; for junior secondary education, 4.6; for senior secondary, 3.3; and for higher education, 2.8.[14]

Rates of utilization of prenatal care and vaccination facilities by Moroccan women also show striking differences by educational level. While only 24 percent of surveyed women with no formal education sought prenatal care, 62 percent of primary-school-educated and 89 percent of those with education beyond the primary level sought such care. As educational level is also associated with urban residence—and greater accessibility of health services—and higher socioeconomic status, inferences of direct causality from these figures may not be made without detailed and controlled tests of the strength of the relationship. Survey efforts examining the information sources and decision processes of women who seek and those who do not seek health care are also to be encouraged; they would provide valuable information to planners of health care programs.

CONCLUSION: LITERACY ACTIONS IN THE INTERESTS OF MOROCCAN WOMEN

As in many countries, Moroccan women continue to reach lower levels of literacy and educational attainment than do men. To help reduce

12. Caldwell, "Routes to Low Mortality in Poor Countries," pp. 171-214; S. H. Cochrane, *Fertility and Education: What Do We Really Know?* World Bank Staff Occasional Paper no. 26 (Washington, DC: World Bank, 1979); LeVine, "Women's Schooling," pp. 21-27; R. S. Moreland, "Population, Internal Migration, and Economic Growth: An Empirical Analysis," *Research in Population Economics,* 4:173-216 (1982); J.-P. Tan and M. Haines, *Schooling and Demand for Children: Historical Perspectives,* World Bank Staff Working Paper no. 697 (Washington, DC: World Bank, 1984).

13. Cochrane, *Fertility and Education.*

14. Morocco, Centre d'Études et de Recherches Démographiques, *Effets de l'éducation sur la mortalité* (Rabat: Ministry of Planning, 1988).

this gender gap in literacy skills and education, and to bring to more Moroccan women the clear benefits that literacy can offer in the domains of family health and urban employment, I conclude with a series of recommendations for action.

Improve the literacy statistic: Knowing where we are

Improving the information base on literacy is important for development efforts. First, there is the accuracy of the statistic itself, which may fluctuate wildly from one year to the next. Second, the positive relationship often found between education and a number of development outcomes requires more detailed analysis. To what extent is this relationship due to the socialization that education provides? Is it due to the reading and writing skills imparted by the school? To numeracy? Or something else? Conducting such analyses requires the separate measurement of each skill area.

Accurate, reliable, and meaningful literacy statistics are also essential to successful literacy campaigns, for targeting communities and subpopulations in need, for targeting skill areas in need of development, and for evaluating the results of campaigns. Sound literacy statistics are critical to the planning of effective development programs and the judicious use of literacy materials in health and family planning; agricultural extension; small-business development; and credit activities.

Properly designed, direct-assessment techniques can be employed to collect information on literacy skills that addresses all these needs. The National Assessment of Educational Progress and the United Nations' National Household Survey Capability Programme provide examples of such techniques.[15] Direct assessment can be used to estimate the accuracy of existing self-report measures of literacy. It can be designed to provide more information on types and levels of skill than is typically gathered and to identify or estimate, through the periodic reassessment of the same individuals, the attrition of skills. Direct assessment also offers opportunities for independent evaluation of the outcomes of education or literacy training.

This approach to literacy information entails special implementation and analysis considerations that differ from the self-report survey or census approach. The individual assessment of multiple household members tends to take more time per family than the typical head-of-household survey. It also requires special training of the interviewer and special sensitivity to the ease and comfort of the respondent. In multilingual settings, the comparability of assessment performance across languages must also be determined. In cross-national analy-

15. See Irwin S. Kirsch and Ann Jungeblut, *Literacy: Profiles of America's Young Adults, Final Report* (Princeton, NJ: Educational Testing Service, September 1986), for a full description of the National Assessment of Educational Progress literacy assessments and results; United Nations, *Measuring Literacy through Household Surveys* (New York: United Nations, 1989), produced as a volume in the United Nations' National Household Survey Capability Programme.

ses using direct-assessment data, comparability will depend on the equivalency of assessments and a certain coordination of efforts across countries.

Target research to inform the design of literacy efforts

There are a number of basic and policy research topics with special implications for the design of literacy programs for women. The need for research on the processes of adult literacy learning in a second-language context has already been noted, and it has special importance for women. Research into the frequently observed difference between literacy program planners' expectations for female enrollments and the often much larger numbers of women who actually enroll in programs could suggest ways to improve planning estimations of demand. Study of the value and implementation of promoting the literate household may be especially valuable in contexts where individual literacy programs are too costly or culturally impracticable. Information on communities' and individuals' perceived needs for literacy should be collected as well, for the design of appropriate programs and the targeting of groups.

Improve the effectiveness of literacy training for Moroccan women

Better statistics and better, directed research should enhance these efforts. Cost sharing or coordination across multiple ministries offering literacy programs in the development of these programs should be encour-

aged. Because employability gains through education and literacy for women are far from clear, as stressed by Stromquist,[16] societal expectations and structures for economic activity must first be rendered gender equitable; literacy programs may be one place to begin this process. Better targeting of groups in need—by language, gender, urban versus rural location, as well as specific regions—and of the specific skills desired by these groups will also facilitate the design of tailored, more efficient programs. Literacy-training modules could also be developed for integration into other Women in Development efforts.

Recent developments in Morocco

It would appear that interest in broad-scale survey utilization of direct literacy assessment is increasing, in part as a response to growing dissatisfaction with the crudity of current methods and statistics on literacy. The Ministry of Planning, with World Bank assistance, has recently appended a direct-assessment literacy module to its National Survey of Living Standards. Recent efforts to revise the literacy curriculum and textbooks by the Ministry of Artisanry and Social Affairs are also promising. Materials are currently being developed that present literacy lessons around broad development themes such as health and nutrition, agricultural extension services, banking, and credit.

16. Nelly P. Stromquist, "Women and Literacy: Promises and Constraints," this issue of *The Annals* of the American Academy of Political and Social Science.

ANNALS, *AAPSS*, 520, March 1992

Raising Literacy under Fragile State Institutions

By BRUCE FULLER

ABSTRACT: Governments and educators are digging more deeply into the question of how to make Third World classrooms more stimulating settings in which to learn. Interventions emphasize making more complex the skills of teachers and the social organization of classrooms. But are fragile political institutions and education agencies equipped to move teachers toward more complex, more invigorating forms of instruction?

Bruce Fuller is associate professor of education at Harvard University. His work focuses on the social rules of classrooms and how these patterns are influenced by, or insulated from, the earnest efforts of central governments. His recent book, Growing-Up Modern, *describes the state's motivations, methods, and frustrations as it struggles to expand mass schooling and to deepen its effects on children.*

NOTE: The research reported in this article is sponsored largely by the U.S. Agency for International Development.

POLITICAL leaders often express concern over persisting, especially rising levels of, illiteracy. But are central governments organizationally equipped to effectively reduce illiteracy? What are the institutional constraints that limit political actors' efficacy in boosting popular demand for official forms of literacy? What factors limit government's capacity to supply more effective primary school teachers—the principal means for boosting literacy over time? I focus on these issues in this article.[1]

The best remedy for illiteracy—during most of the postwar period—was assumed to be rapid expansion of basic schooling. Many governments, especially revolutionary ones, experimented with literacy campaigns. The empirical evidence that these efforts made a significant difference is not convincing. In the poorest developing countries, rapid school expansion was impressive and certainly signaled government concern with broadening mass opportunity. But the thinning-out of educational quality through unbridled expansion has eroded the primary school's capacity to impart literacy that sticks in the minds of the masses.

Over the 1980s, two major shifts occurred in how public strategies were constructed for truly boosting literacy. First, both governments and parents in the Third World became more attentive to eroding levels of school quality. The relentless spread of mediocre schooling is no longer a remedy that goes unquestioned. Of course, elite parents in developing countries quickly figured this out after independence. Recent work by the World Bank and discourse among government leaders reveal that political agencies are questioning how much literacy children actually acquire in the classroom and are debating how to best adjust policies and institutions to provide incentives for classroom and school-level improvements.[2]

Second, Western donors' own thinking about how to improve school quality has widened and deepened. Increasingly, the focus is on a bundle of deeper questions about the character of Third World schooling: What are teachers actually doing in classrooms? Do teachers effectively motivate children? What are the social rules and technical skills that children should learn? How do these learning objectives vary across countries and cultural conditions?

A decade ago, the debate was whether to buy more textbooks or desks, whether to lengthen teacher training or install radios in class-

1. I do not assume that primary schooling is the only way of raising literacy levels. But at least we have a great amount of empirical knowledge about literacy acquisition in formal classrooms in Third World countries. For review, see Bruce Fuller and Stephen Heyneman, "Third World School Quality: Current Collapse, Future Potential," *Educational Researcher*, 18:12-19 (Mar. 1989).

2. For important examples of this conceptual shift, see World Bank, *Primary Education in Developing Countries: A Policy Paper* (Washington DC: World Bank, 1990); Marlaine Lockheed et al., *Improving Primary Schools in Developing Countries: A Review of Policy Options* (New York: Oxford University Press, 1991); World Conference on Education for All, *World Declaration on Education for All* (Jomtien, Thailand: World Conference Secretariat, 1990); United States Agency for International Development, "U.S. Assistance for Africa: The Development Fund for Africa," 1989.

rooms. Today, the focus is on broader, contextual issues related to the action of teachers, as well as the social norms and forms of literacy that children are or are not acquiring. Empirical research should continue on which discrete medicines and tools will more likely boost children's literacy, but the move to place these instructional inputs into the classroom's social rules and teaching practices is a major step forward.[3]

ROUTINIZED CLASSROOMS AND FRAGILE STATES

This story begins inside classrooms in southern Africa. I will first summarize findings from our three-year study, sponsored by the U.S. Agency for International Development, of 350 teachers and classrooms in Botswana. Then, once pedagogical constraints and social rules of classrooms are revealed, it is necessary to move up organizational levels to discover how to remedy or enliven life in classrooms. Here the common litany of constraints facing Third World governments is quickly encountered: limited fiscal resources, limited political will to recognize pluralistic community priorities, limited know-how regarding how to sustainably change teachers' roles and behaviors, and limited capacity to coordinate the action of central-government actors, as exemplified by, inter alia, disparate offices overseeing curricula, teacher training, personnel systems, materials production, and national examinations.[4]

In short, this article emphasizes that political actors often live within fragile state organizations. Even when education ministers or influential bureaucrats do recognize the importance of improving school quality, they are constrained by common features of the fragile state: relentless popular pressure to expand basic schooling, as a crisp symbol of mass opportunity; scarce public resources; centrifugal cultural pluralism, leading to calls for central authority and secular uniformity in schools, curricula, and language of instruction; and a desire to construct so-called modern management in the public sector, which usually implies hierarchical control and routinized forms of local administration.[5] These pressures on state actors often discourage effective responses by government to the local weaknesses of teachers and teaching.

I certainly do not want to detract from this renewed focus on school

---

3. International agencies may be catching up with Third World governments. Since independence, many developing countries have debated which language of instruction should dominate schools. Many education ministry officials decry pedagogical remnants of colonial or mission schooling. From Eastern Europe to East Asia to southern Africa, new governments debate how schooling can pursue authoritarian, democratic-individualistic, or more collective social rules—in the classroom. For instance, see Patrick Molutsi, "The School System: Is It Teaching Democracy?" in *Democracy in Botswana*, ed. John Holm and Patrick Molutsi (London: Macmillan, 1989), pp. 89-92.

4. Due to its small size and its tradition of democratic openness, these limitations are present less in Botswana than in most developing countries.

5. For more detailed description of the fragile state and implications for education, see Bruce Fuller, *Growing-Up Modern: The Western State Builds Third World Schools* (New York: Routledge, 1991).

quality and, in particular, an unprecedented desire to understand life inside schools and classrooms. If we engage in "backward mapping"— starting with a clearer grasp of the constraints facing teachers—we are more likely to construct policy adjustments that make a difference within local schools.[6] But current enthusiasm will be short-lived unless we recognize the institutional rigidities that characterize different levels of educational organizations, from the ritualized roles of many teachers to the complexities of central governments.

BOTSWANA TEACHER AND CLASSROOM STUDY

In 1988 the education ministry initiated the Botswana Teacher, Classroom, and Achievement study. This research effort aims to evaluate the ministry's effort to redesign the curriculum and to improve teaching practices. Yet the study also will provide a wealth of longitudinal data on teachers, teaching practices, classroom organization, and student achievement.

The study's full sample, drawn in 1989, includes 350 teachers and 9000 students located in 44 junior secondary schools. Our research team has observed these teachers four times over two years, 1989 and 1990. The literacy and numeracy skills of students also were assessed four times over the two-year period.

Determining what types of teacher behavior or classroom organization

6. On the idea of "backward mapping," see Richard Elmore, ed., *Restructuring Schools: The Next Generation of Educational Reform* (San Francisco: Jossey-Bass, 1990).

should be observed, then devising a reliable protocol for recording these facets of classroom life, are not simple tasks. We were guided by two basic objectives. First, we wanted to learn how teachers actually use instructional inputs. Second, we hoped to better understand the basic social rules of the classroom, including the intensity of the teacher's authority, his or her form of interaction with pupils, and the cognitive demands placed on students. Eventually, we related these aspects of teachers and classrooms to measures of learning gains.

Each teacher observation was for a 40-minute class period. Overall, the observation instrument provided data in the following areas: (1) availability of basic instructional materials; (2) the frequency with which different materials are mobilized by the teacher and pupils; (3) different ways in which class time is utilized by the teacher, including academic and administrative-control behaviors; (4) the degree to which the teacher dominates the instructional process, versus organizing individual exercises, small work groups, or discussions between pupils; (5) task demands placed on pupils, particularly reading and writing exercises in class; (6) principal actions of observed target pupils, including academic work and off-task behavior; (7) the propensity of the teacher to ask questions of students and whether these questions require high levels of cognition or simple recall of discrete pieces of information and facts; (8) teachers' language of instruction; and (9) both the teacher's and the pupils' level of engagement and affect within the classroom.[7]

In this article I will summarize certain salient findings from early analysis of our 1989 data. Other recent papers contain detailed discussion of findings from our 1988 pilot study, as well as the method and measurement properties of our teacher-observation instrument.[8]

CLASSROOM STRUCTURE AND INSTITUTIONALLY CONSTRUCTED LITERACIES

Four basic findings emerge from our study of Botswana classrooms:

1. Teachers spend an enormous proportion of class time talking at pupils—communicating simple bits of information, maintaining order, and reinforcing their basic authority. It is interesting that John Goodlad's extensive study of North American classrooms reveals this same basic pattern.[9]

2. Few instructional tools are mobilized by teachers during the course of routinized lessons. This is not due to lack of supply—of textbooks, teacher guides, or writing materials—in Botswana's well-endowed secondary schools.

3. The range of cognitive demands placed on pupils is highly constrained. Less than three questions were asked by the average teacher during the ten-minute segment in which we recorded the number and types of questions posed by the teacher. In just one-fifth of all class periods observed did the teacher assign any written task to students.

---

7. The classroom-observation instrument contains six segments, completed consecutively by the researcher. During the first segment, which is 10 minutes long, the researcher records basic information about the classroom: the number of children in attendance, when instruction actually starts, and availability of textbooks, exercise books, and other basic materials. Segments 2 and 3 involve checklists of actions by the teacher and a target group of four pupils, respectively. Each segment contains a matrix defined by type of action and type of instructional material utilized with this action. A teacher, for instance, may be lecturing to the entire class while using the chalkboard; the appropriate cell in the matrix is simply checked if this combination occurs. Segments 2 and 3 each run for 7 minutes. This matrix structure was adapted from Jane Stallings's observation instrument, extensively pilot-tested, and further adjusted. See Jane Stallings and H. Jerome Freiberg, "Observation for the Improvement of Teaching," in *Effective Teaching: Current Research*, ed. Hersholt Waxman and Herbert Walberg (Berkeley, CA: McCutchan, 1991), pp. 107-31. Segment 4 focuses on the frequency and type of questions asked by the teacher. This includes queries directed to the entire class and to individual pupils over the 10-minute duration of this segment. Segment 5 includes the researcher's estimate of how the teacher spent class time, percentage of teacher talk in English or Setswana, and additional summary items. This segment is completed during the final 5 minutes of the 40-minute period.

8. Pilot study findings are reported in Bruce Fuller and Conrad W. Snyder, Jr., "Silent Pupils, Vocal Teachers? Life in Botswana Classrooms," *Comparative Education Review*, 35(2):274-94 (May 1991); Conrad W. Snyder, Jr., and Philemon Ramatsui, *Curriculum in the Classroom* (London: Macmillan, 1990). Measurement information and other details regarding our observation instrument appear in Bruce Fuller and Conrad W. Snyder, Jr., "Teacher Productivity in Sticky Institutions: Curricular and Gender Variations," in *Strategies for Enhancing Educational Productivity*, ed. David Chapman and Herbert Walberg (Greenwich, CT: JAI Press, 1992).

9. John Goodlad, *A Place Called School* (New York: McGraw-Hill, 1984).

4. Teachers almost always speak in English during class periods, despite the fact that in the home children grow up speaking Setswana, the tongue of the Tswana people, who compose the vast majority of Botswana residents. By the junior secondary level, Setswana has become a discrete subject.

We found, of course, that teachers do vary somewhat in how they organize lessons and interact with children. We are trying to figure out the underlying patterns and antecedents to this variation. The subject matter being taught explained, significantly, some differences in teacher behavior. Mathematics teachers mobilized more instructional materials—textbooks, the chalkboard, exercise books, for example—than did teachers of other subjects. Social studies teachers tended to ask slightly more open-ended questions and assign fewer written exercises. These findings match recent contrasts found between subject areas in the United States.[10] The organizational similarities of classrooms across vastly different cultural settings is remarkable.

Notwithstanding the variation between teachers, the typical Botswana classroom displays rather simple pedagogical scripts. Most teachers rely on lecturing, choral recitation, a few closed-ended questions, and perhaps a round of written exercises toward the end of the 40-minute period. This routinized way of structuring classrooms may be quite functional, given the forms of knowledge and

10. Susan Stodolsky, *The Subject Matters* (Chicago: University of Chicago Press, 1988).

literacy that are assessed and reinforced by Botswana's national examination. This exam, linked to a uniform syllabus, primarily assesses knowledge of facts and arithmetic skills. Indeed, the ways in which teachers typically construct the classroom's social rules and their own pedagogical practices fit well into how the broader institution defines becoming educated, how one should demonstrate a certain form of literacy. The process of becoming schooled is synonymous with learning to conform to these classroom rules and the forms of authority, knowledge, and social interaction or passivity implied therein.

INSTITUTIONAL
CONSTRAINTS ON RAISING
OR REDEFINING LITERACY

Critics push for the introduction of greater complexity into such highly routinized classrooms. Students must become more active in the classroom; learning should involve articulation of one's own position, not just memorizing sacred facts and figures; the teacher must assume the role of facilitator and leave the image of learned expert behind. So the argument goes.

But many teachers dedicate themselves, as they have been thoroughly trained, to limiting uncertainty and complexity. Traditional ways of training teachers—introduced by colonial authorities—involve making sure that young teachers know the one and only curriculum, page by page. International agencies, recognizing the apparently limited skills of Third World teachers, advocate installing unambiguous tools—from programmed instruction to radio receivers—aimed at reducing knowledge into bits and pieces that the teacher cannot disassemble. This institutionalized attraction of routinizing teaching and learning, of course, defines a particular form of literacy.

Recasting or altering the organization of literacy in the classroom may involve earnest attempts at making the classroom's social rules more complex. The teaching of science topics in Botswana, for example, often involves memorizing in English the parts of different organisms, such as common plants or crops. Recasting the definition of "scientific literacy" to include understanding biological processes or interactions with soils found in Botswana requires more complexity in the instructional process. Teaching social studies in ways that encourage critical discourse, or even an analytical edge, similarly requires greater pedagogical versatility on the teacher's part.

In both Botswana and neighboring South Africa, one intervention requiring greater complexity is the Breakthrough to Literacy program. Learning centers and activities are organized in different areas of the classroom. Over time, some students learn how to engage in different tasks over the course of an hour. The teacher may concentrate on facilitating certain activities, such as the reading corner. Students are clearly more active in these classrooms. But will such interventions help construct more useful forms of literacy? Will more complex classroom rules conflict with narrow conceptions of literacy that are reinforced by national exams?

Some educators and project designers remain optimistic that teacher behavior can be changed, altered in ways that will boost levels of acquired literacy. Unfortunately, this optimism often leads to remedies that focus on the individual teacher, not on the contextual forces that implicitly define a certain role and normative set of pedagogical behaviors. The teacher who is a little too innovative—encouraging student participation, demystifying set curricula and sacred facts, or allowing individual children to articulate their own views—comes to be viewed as not serious or as simply a little crazy. Teachers must follow institutionalized expectations of what credible teaching practices look like.

Institutional forces help reproduce these routinized forms of pedagogy and classroom structure. Parents are concerned over whether their children will pass the national exam. National syllabi and curricular materials legitimate certain forms of knowledge, particularly languages of instruction. Teacher training and licensing agencies construct a normative role and behavior set to which new teachers must express loyalty.[11]

MOVING UP THE
ORGANIZATION: DELINEATING
INSTITUTIONAL CONSTRAINTS

To improve the context within which teachers work, those institu-

11. For a conceptual overview, see John W. Meyer and Brian Rowan, "Institutionalized Organizations: Formal Structure as Myth and

TABLE 1
REDEFINING OR RAISING LITERACY IN CLASSROOMS: POLITICAL AND ECONOMIC CONSTRAINTS

	Low-Income Nations	Middle-Income Nations
Political and social organization		
Fragility of the central state	Major constraint	Moderate constraint
Clarity of and consensus around schooling goals (definition of literacy)	Minor	Moderate
Normative form(s) of modern organization	Minor	Moderate
Strength and rights of school constituencies	Minor	Major
Institutional hosts of diverse literacies	Major	Mixed
Public sector resources*		
Government spending on the education sector	Major	Moderate
Supply of inputs directly linked to achievement	Major	Minor
Competition with access or equity objectives	Major	Moderate

*Investment in children's literacy by nongovernment institutions—churches, families, village authorities, and firms—is often important within, although variable across, nations. We know very little about what policy levers can boost private investment or whether such commitments lead to differences in school quality and the distribution of educational opportunity.

tional factors that most strongly constrain organizational change must first be identified. Again, the end objective is to redefine or simply raise levels of achieved literacy within classrooms. By "redefine" I mean alter the form of literacy that is advanced, given dominant teacher behavior and social rules found within the classroom. This may involve change in the language of instruction, or it may relate to whether literacy acquisition occurs in an active, participatory way or through more passive forms of learning. Language and literacy-related skills are embedded within the classroom's situational social rules.

Table 1 outlines a first set of institutional constraints, those operating at high levels of social organization.

Ceremony," *American Journal of Sociology*, 83:340-63 (1977).

The severity of each constraint is likely to vary according to general levels of national wealth. For instance, within the poorest Third World countries, the fluid character of political power and technical stability represents a major constraint on altering the definition of, or even exploring innovative ways of raising, literacy in classrooms. In so-called middle-income Third World countries, state organizations are usually more stable; political fragility is less of a constraint.

By "normative form(s) of modern organization" (in Table 1), I refer to classic bureaucratic forms of school administration. These pseudosystems—involving apparent centralization, local inspectors, and regulatory roles for headmasters—are often so weak in low-income countries that they do not present much of a constraint. In middle-income countries this form of

TABLE 2
REDEFINING OR RAISING LITERACY IN CLASSROOMS:
INSTITUTIONAL CONSTRAINTS WITHIN THE EDUCATION SECTOR

Organizational Source of the Constraint	Strong Central States	Weak Central States
Education ministry and central government		
Uniformity of sanctioned literacy forms	Major constraint	Moderate constraint
Specificity and routinization of teaching practices	Moderate	Moderate
Mechanical versus professional organization of the teaching occupation	Major	Moderate
Qualities of new teacher trainees	Moderate	Moderate
District education offices and headmasters		
Forms of teacher behavior that are sanctioned	Moderate	Minor
Distribution of instructional materials	Moderate	Moderate
Classrooms		
Class size and availability of basic materials	Moderate	Moderate
Institutionalized authority of the teacher	Moderate	Mixed
Professional associations and knowledge/curricular constituencies		
Organized conception of curricula, knowledge, and legitimate literacies	Moderate	Mixed

management may be more effective and squeeze out inventive forms of school management or pedagogy. The countervailing force here is that teachers may be pushing for a more professional, less mechanical definition of their role.

Levels of government support for education obviously influence the extent to which teachers are held in line or encouraged to innovate and reflect on their own practice. If central states must first attend to signals of mass opportunity and equity—via highly visible school expansion—the likelihood is low that serious efforts will be mounted to raise school quality or to rethink the form of literacy being reproduced in local schools.

Table 2 takes us into the education sector, delineating major constraints on accomplishing real change in classrooms. In this table, to illustrate systematic variation in different types of nations, I have contrasted strong and weak central states with respect to the probable severity of the constraints found in educational institutions that operate in those states. The uniformity of sanctioned literacy—for example, permitting only one language in the classroom—represents a strict constraint but only under a strong central state.

I argue that a mechanical and narrow role for teachers will more often be observed under strong central states. Indeed, central political strength is manifest, in part, through careful specification and control of teaching practices and curricula—the idealized French model. Where the central state is weaker, alternative roles and pedagogical practices are more likely to flourish.

It is difficult to generalize about the severity of some constraints. For example, one might argue that larger class size or scarce instructional materials militate against inventive forms of literacy or pedagogy. This tendency is likely, but some strong states and effective education ministries can equip teachers to adjust to these conditions. The social authority and status of teachers may vary within a country, especially under weak central states. The important task is to assess which of these constraints are operating within a particular situation.

CONCLUSION

We are entering an exciting period. Civic leaders, political actors, and international agencies—major players in Third World countries—are asking penetrating questions: How much are children actually learning in classrooms? Are the dominant social rules and literacy forms found in classrooms really the ones intended? Can teachers become more effective and motivating? Should the social norms and values advanced in classrooms be adjusted to advance economic or cultural ideals?

I hope the optimism in tackling these questions is not short-lived. For this new wave of issues presents a myriad array of institutional constraints. Most of these center on the school organization's capacity to introduce greater complexity into the teaching process. Pressures are very strong to routinize, to control simplified facets of teaching, to sanction impoverished forms of knowledge and learning.

Two steps can help loosen at least a few of these organizational rigidities. First, we must learn what teachers actually do in classrooms. Second, those institutional forces that reinforce and sanctify the normative roles and behaviors to which teachers must conform should be identified. Once life inside classrooms—or the lack thereof—is better understood, the incentives and meanings enacted by headmasters, education ministries, and political actors can be observed. Until these contextual forces become clear, earnest reformers risk simply attacking the hearts and minds of teachers while ignoring the forces that surround and shape them.

ANNALS, *AAPSS*, **520**, March 1992

Children's Literacy and Public Schools in Latin America

By EMILIA FERREIRO

ABSTRACT: Illiteracy problems in Latin America cannot be faced successfully without taking into account what actually happens at the beginning of primary school. Almost all children enter primary school, but those from marginal sectors of the population repeat the first grades one or more times and leave school before completion. Nonpromotion and low retention constitute the evidence of a deeper problem. Traditional school practices make the beginning of literacy more difficult precisely for those children who are more dependent on school help. The present situation may be overcome on the basis of research results generated in Latin America as well as innovative pedagogical experiences to improve literacy acquisition. If failure at the beginning of primary school continues as it is, the children of today will become the low-literate adults of tomorrow.

Emilia Ferreiro, born in Argentina, earned her Ph.D. in Geneva, Switzerland, with Professor Jean Piaget. A specialist in psycholinguistics, she received a Guggenheim fellowship and started research in her native country on the psychogenesis of written language. Her first book on this subject (1979) was translated into English, Italian, and Portuguese. Since 1980 she has been full professor at the Center for Research and Advanced Studies, Mexico. She often lectures at universities in Latin America, the United States, and Europe.

THE 1979 meeting of ministers of education from the Latin America and Caribbean region that took place in Mexico City under the auspices of the United Nations Educational, Scientific, and Cultural Organization was a very special meeting. The participants agreed on a global plan for the region, aimed at overcoming inequalities in the literacy situation. This plan was called "Proyecto Principal de Educación." The final document established three main objectives: (1) to attain literacy for the entire adult population before the year 2000, (2) to offer to all children a minimum of 8 to 10 years of schooling, (3) to improve the quality and efficiency of the educational systems. In order to achieve those objectives, the participants committed themselves to assigning at least 7 percent of the gross national product of their countries to education.

Today, the Latin America region is as far from accomplishing those objectives as it was at the time of the foregoing declaration, more than ten years ago. The weight of the foreign debt has severely depressed public investment in the social sector. A reduction of 25 percent is the figure estimated by the Economic Commission for Latin America.

Illiteracy among adults—that is, among people aged 15 years and older—in absolute figures, is a stationary problem in Latin America. There were 44 million illiterates in 1970 and the same in 1980 and 1985. The more optimistic estimates project 38 million adult illiterates for the year 2000.

Getting all children to enter primary school seems to be a feasible goal for most or all of the countries in Latin America; the principal difficulty lies in promotion from one grade to the next and retention. Latin American children who succeed in finishing primary school, as well as those who quit before completion, repeat one or more grades one or more times. Repetition is found mainly in the first three grades of primary school. Children repeat the first or second grade several times because they do not succeed in obtaining a minimum of literacy skills. Of course, those children who fail always fall in the same categories: children of the marginal sectors, such as those who live in the slums that surround the big cities, those who live in poor rural areas, and those who speak one of the many native languages of the region.

It is too easy to blame this failure on the fact that these children lack many basic human needs: good nutrition, good health, social security, and family stimulation. The problem is how to achieve universal literacy given such conditions. Can we continue to say, year after year, that literacy and democracy go hand in hand, without being able to overcome this situation? Whose failure is it? The children's? The school system's? Or is it a question of government policy? How can we hope to remedy the situation of adult illiteracy without taking into account what goes on during the early years of primary school? Children who interrupt their schooling after three or four years of attendance are usually far from having completed the third or fourth grade. As repetition at the beginning of primary school is so frequent, they may leave school with very low levels of literacy. It is not surprising, therefore, to find them joining the group of illiterate adults some years later. For this reason, it is very important to consider illiteracy as a problem affecting a wide range of ages. Remedial actions are directed at the adult population, but preventive actions need to be taken with children six or seven years old. These preventive actions should have a clear objective: to attain a successful literacy level in the early years of primary school.

Let us now look at the feasibility of such a goal. I will present my position on this question in two steps. First, I will argue that traditional school practices found all over Latin America make the beginning of literacy more difficult precisely for those children who are more dependent on school help—those belonging to marginal sectors. Second, I will claim that our present knowledge of literacy development provides us with powerful conceptual tools that point to a major challenge for our educational practices. In addition, we already have pedagogical experiences in Latin America that show what ought to be done so that school practices can be designed to take into account the conceptual difficulties all children face on their way to literacy.

TRADITIONAL SCHOOL PRACTICES AND CHILDREN OF MARGINAL SECTORS

I will refer mainly to urban slum children, because our knowledge about literacy development in poor rural areas in Latin America is still fragmentary.[1]

It is now widely recognized that literacy acquisition starts well before the beginning of primary school.[2] Children who live in urban settings— even those from very poor sectors— grow up surrounded by print. The mere presence of written marks in urban environments allows the children to start asking themselves some sound questions about the nature and purposes of such marks. The differentiation between the two basic types of written marks—drawing and writing—can be carried out even before knowing that the written marks are related to oral language. In order to grasp this link, it is necessary to participate in literacy events, those social events in which literate people use these marks for a given purpose. Such events include, for instance, reading a newspaper searching for particular information, or writing a message to someone, reading the instructions for the use of a

1. At present we are conducting a three-year follow-up study in small, poor, rural communities in Mexico where a particular type of school service—pertaining to an agency of the Ministry of Education called CONAFE (National Council for Promoting Education)—has been in operation throughout the country since 1973.
2. A great number of works are relevant, including: Hillel Goelman, Antoinette Oberg, and Frank Smith, eds., *Awakening to Literacy* (Portsmouth, NH: Heinemann Educational Books, 1984); David Olson, Nancy Torrance, and Angela Hildyard, eds., *Literacy, Language and Learning* (New York: Cambridge University Press, 1985); Yetta Goodman, ed., *How Children Construct Literacy* (Newark, DE: International Reading Association, 1990).

medicine, searching for a telephone number in a directory, or writing something down that needs to be remembered later on. Even when these literacy events are not conceived as learning experiences, they offer children meaningful information about the social functions of the written marks. Still more valuable information can be obtained if the children participate in literacy events directed at them—having a book read to them, for example—and particularly when they can ask questions about the written marks. None of these experiences is available to children surrounded by illiterate or low-literate adults. As a consequence, many children start primary school without much knowledge about the meaning and purposes of written marks. They know that they are important, but they do not know exactly why they are important.

In contemporary Latin American schools, a first-grade teacher does not read in order to obtain or to provide information but only to teach how to read; she or he does not write in order to keep or to send information but only to teach how to write. The social purposes of reading and writing remain outside the school setting. This is not a big handicap for middle-class children, who usually have had multiple occasions at home to learn about the social functions of this particular behavior. But it is a great handicap for children whose parents are illiterate or low-literate, because these children do not have similar learning opportunities outside the school. It is not surprising, then, that after a year at school, disadvantaged children learn that the main purpose of learning to read and write is promotion to the next grade. That is, they have learned a school function of a purely school activity.

Furthermore, a first-grade teacher teaches that every letter or combination of letters stands for a given speech sound or combination of sounds. Then, in order to learn how to read, it is necessary to learn how to pronounce the letters or letter sequences. As teachers usually think that the only way to read correctly is to read with the standard pronunciation, they start rejecting the ways of speaking of children who belong to the poorest sectors of the society and who do not use the standard pronunciation.

Linguistic rejection of this sort is one of the discriminative mechanisms with the deepest negative consequences for a child's future. As the primary school teachers are given little or no linguistic information or training, they are ignorant of the fact that in Latin America one may find at least as many officially recognized versions of standard Spanish as there are countries. There is no country in Latin America that can be considered as having a spoken dialectal variation more closely related to the standard way of writing than any other. In each of the countries the same situation can be found: children who speak the dialectal variation that is socially validated as being the right one have less difficulty becoming literate. At the same time, those very children are the ones that belong to groups with social prestige.[3]

3. The same happens in Brazil with respect to the many varieties of Brazilian Portuguese that are spoken. Cf. Luiz Carlos Cagliari,

To sum up, regardless of the purely linguistic characteristics of their social dialect, some children are allowed to read as they speak while others are obliged to abandon their way of speaking in order to have access to written material as it is presented at school. In focusing on one standard pronunciation, the teachers make the children think that they, the children, must use that pronunciation in order to be able to read.[4]

The preceding are only two examples of many practices linked to traditional teaching that introduce additional difficulties into the literacy development of children of poor sectors. In using these practices, the school implicitly introduces mechanisms of rejection and discrimination. The practices are difficult to eradicate because they are not dependent on a given methodology of teaching but are rooted in deep and often unconscious presuppositions about the link between oral and written language. Let us now turn to these presuppositions.

THE LINK BETWEEN ORAL AND WRITTEN LANGUAGE

In what follows I will refer only to alphabetical writing systems, as there are no other writing systems currently used in Latin America.[5]

The main principle underlying any phonographic writing system—be it syllabic or alphabetical—is the following: the written symbol represents similarities and differences between sequences of speech sounds—a signifier or segments of it—regardless of similarities or differences in meaning. Nonetheless, meaning must not be forgotten, otherwise the written marks will lose their connection with language as such.

What are the conditions that allow the learner to grasp such a general principle? A naive empiricist answer would be to be informed of such a type of correspondence between letters and sound sequences. Such a simplistic answer—well rooted in so-called common sense—is based on some strong presuppositions. The main assumption is that the translation from oral to written language is only a matter of ciphering. For a highly literate person, writing does in fact look like "a fairly simple mapping of units of the phonological representation—morphemes or phonemes or syllables—into written symbols."[6] It does not necessarily follow, however, that writing looks the same way to an illiterate person, whether that person is an adult or a child. Instead of assuming that what seems natural for a highly literate person is natural everywhere and for everyone, it is advisable to question this assumption and look for empirical evidence.

Alfabetizacão & Lingüística (São Paulo: Editora Scipione, 1989).

4. Emilia Ferreiro and Ana Teberosky, *Literacy before Schooling* (Portsmouth, NH: Heinemann Educational Books, 1982), chap. 7. For the original Spanish version, see idem *Los sistemas de escritura en el desarrollo del niño* (Mexico: Siglo XXI Editores, 1979).

5. A very interesting linguistic analysis of writing systems can be found in Geoffrey Sampson, *Writing Systems* (London: Hutchinson, 1985).

6. Ignatius Mattingly, "Reading, the Linguistic Process, and Linguistic Awareness," in *Language by Ear and by Eye*, ed. James Kavanagh and I. Mattingly (Cambridge: MIT Press, 1972), p. 138.

When children start to realize that the written marks have the strange property of eliciting language, they begin to search for the nature of the link between oral language and written marks. One dimension of these explorations concerns the comprehension of the specific terms that refer to our relationships with the written marks: "to read" and "to write." Unfortunately, many metaphorical expressions are in use that do not help to clarify this issue for the child. For instance, adults point to the written marks saying, "Here it says . . . ." In fact, the letters themselves do not "say" anything, but they allow the reader to "say" something that was not elaborated by him or her. In addition, it is easier to understand what is meant by "to write" than to understand what is meant by "to read." The act of writing introduces specific modifications on a surface; after such an act, the surface will present some marks that are not like drawings. These marks are permanent, unless another act—erasing—destroys them. Since it is an action that results in a product leading to a permanent modification on the object, "to write" is an action understood very early on. On the contrary, "to read" has none of these properties, as the object of the action remains as it was before. In addition, reading can be done aloud or silently, and a page that was read and one that was only observed, for instance, do not bear any specific marks that differentiate them.

Even when the nature of the specific actions denoted by the verbs "to read" and "to write" start to be understood, the main question still needs

to be answered: if the written marks represent what we are able to say, what are the properties of the language that are retained in the representation?

The actual orthography of a given alphabetical system, including Spanish, is a historical construction that departs in many respects from the simplicity of the main principle of alphabetical writing systems. Children living in urban environments deal spontaneously with written language in all its graphic complexity, because they deal with environmental print, where all the letters appear, in many different types, as do numbers, punctuation marks, and many other graphic devices. Children who grow up in urban settings do not wait until some skilled teacher presents them with a simplified version of the written language, easy to learn but applicable only inside a school setting.

The complexities of the actual spelling do not prevent children from searching for regularities. As in all other domains of cognitive development, children start on their way to literacy by trying to make sense of a mass of rather chaotic information. They will be at a loss if they try to add one bit of information onto another. What they do instead is to construct tentative theories that help them to absorb but also to reject information, that help them to produce changes in the object in order to understand it.[7]

After many years of careful research we can now say that the successive theories constructed by chil-

7. Emilia Ferreiro, "The Interplay between Information and Assimilation in Beginning Literacy," in *Emergent Literacy*, ed. W. Teale and E. Sulzby (Norwood, NJ: Ablex, 1986).

dren are not attempts that the children must reject in order to understand what the school will teach them. On the contrary, what they construct before schooling—or even at school, if lack of opportunity has prevented them from doing so before—are the solid bases for making further constructions.[8]

RECENT PEDAGOGICAL EXPERIENCES IN LATIN AMERICA

While research findings lead to the conclusion that children are actively engaged in understanding the writing system—treated by them as an object of knowledge embedded in social contexts—traditional school practices reduce the child to someone who is not able to think and who can only receive, associate, and repeat. It also reduces the object of the learning process—the writing system—to a school object, divorced from its social purposes and functions.

During the decade 1981-90, many pedagogical initiatives were conducted in the region—particularly in Brazil, Mexico, Venezuela, and Argentina—taking into account the research findings on literacy development. All were carried out with children belonging to marginal urban sectors, but the experiences varied from small-scale projects to state-level and national-level ones. Some were with preschool children, others with primary school children; some took place in regular public schools and some in special services for children who have repeated grades in school.[9]

One of the main results of these experiences was to make the objectives of literacy more ambitious at the beginning. Literacy acquisition based on mechanical exercises and memorization as opposed to conceptual comprehension does not lead to functional literacy and permanent literacy acquisition. Many factors that distort the conceptual process need to be eliminated. For instance, effective literacy acquisition is hampered when

— the social functions of the written marks are hidden;
— mechanical exercises, based on reproduction alone, are presented as if they were writing activities;
— the sounding out of letters, without comprehension, is presented as reading;
— the range of reading materials is restricted to school-type material;
— a standard pronunciation is required for the child to be recognized by the teacher as being able to read; and
— real text-production activities are delayed until the child has proved to be a good "copier."

On the contrary, the literacy-acquisition process in children from the marginal sectors is helped when

8. Emilia Ferreiro, "L'écriture avant la lettre," in *La Production de Notations chez le Jeune Enfant*, ed. Hermine Sinclair (Paris: Presses Universitaires de France, 1988).

9. For more information, see Emilia Ferreiro, ed., *Los Hijos del Analfabetismo: Propuestas para la Alfabetización Escolar en América Latina* (Mexico: Siglo XXI Editores, 1989). For the Portuguese version, see idem, *Os filhos do analfabetismo* (Porto Alegre: Artes Médicas, 1990).

— the teacher understands the conceptual problems that children face in learning to understand the written marks as a system that represents only some properties of oral language;

— children are allowed to read and to write from the very beginning, each one at his or her level of conceptualization;

— everything that can be read outside the school becomes readable inside the school;

— children are stimulated to engage in small-group activities to discuss the best way to produce a piece of writing or to interpret a text;

— to copy is not forbidden but becomes only one type of activity among many others related to writing; and

— children are encouraged to think aloud, to guess, to discuss, to request, to try, and to revise.

Children who participate in such literacy experiences show us that they are not afraid of written marks because they can interact with them, transform them, and re-create them. In so doing, they become the owners of their culture's writing system. They can read but they can also write what they want to express, and they start to know that to write is the best way of speaking aloud.

ANNALS, *AAPSS,* 520, March 1992

Literacy Efforts in India

By ANIL BORDIA and ANITA KAUL

ABSTRACT: This article highlights literacy efforts in India over the past few decades. Failure to universalize primary education, grounded as it is in complex socioeconomic issues, has had serious implications for planning universal literacy. Program delivery hitherto rested with the official hierarchy and included limited participation from the general population. Where such participation did occur, the programs failed due to insufficient learning levels or insufficient facilities for continuing education. Through use of new strategies, such as microplanning and minimum levels of learning, India is attempting to universalize access, participation, and achievement at the primary level. Simultaneously, the National Literacy Mission is adopting a systematically planned campaign approach to literacy through mass mobilization and innovative learning techniques that emphasizes predetermined learning levels. The value of literacy can be truly harnessed only if literacy skills are retained and applied and if literacy contributes to social change. India has learned from past trials, is conscious of the gravity of the problem, and is moving ahead with new vision.

Anil Bordia, a member of the Indian Administrative Service, has held important positions in education administration. Currently secretary of the Department of Education, Government of India, he is also president of the International Bureau of Education, Geneva. He has written several books and scholarly papers. He has also taught at the University of Toronto's Ontario Institute for Studies in Education and the International Institute for Educational Planning, Paris.

Anita Kaul, also a member of the Indian Administrative Service, is involved with the Adult Education Programme in India.

ACCORDING to estimates of the United Nations Educational, Scientific, and Cultural Organization, India contributes to a large percentage of the world's illiterate population. This, plus the fact that India is a very diverse nation, makes the task of achieving universal literacy in India an immense and difficult one. Literacy education has been and is a priority of the Indian government, however, and various adult literacy efforts are currently being explored throughout the country. This article looks at past literacy efforts, current barriers to literacy, and different components of the approaches currently under way. In order to set the scene and to provide an initial understanding of literacy education in India, the article begins with case studies involving three villages in rural India: Rohana, Birmalu, and Shaklet.

ROHANA

Rohana, a village with a population of 1400, is situated in the West Champaran district of Bihar. A primary school has been in existence in the village for twenty years. Practically all the children of the higher castes—Brahmins, Bhumihars, Kayasthas—regularly attend school. Of late, the agriculturist communities—Yadavas, Kurmis, Ahirs—have also started sending their children to school. But half the population of the village comprises tribal people, brought as indented labor from South Bihar by the British indigo planters, and the scheduled castes, which include Chamars, Bhangis, Julahas,

and others. Children of the tribal and scheduled castes in the village rarely benefit from the school system. Of 150 children aged 6 to 14 years, 60 to 65 either never went to school or dropped out after one or two years of study. These children work as domestic servants with the families of higher-caste people, assist their parents on the farm, or tend cattle; most of the girls stay home looking after their siblings. Whenever government officials put pressure on teachers to secure the enrollment of all village children, teachers persuade the parents to allow them to enroll the children, but the children are soon withdrawn because the families perceive it as more beneficial for their children to work outside of school.[1]

Failure to universalize primary education has serious implications for planning for universal literacy in India. To the extent that this failure is grounded in complex social and economic issues, the task becomes all the more complicated.

BIRMALU

Birmalu is a small village with a population of about 600, located in the Jaipur district of Rajasthan. Birmalu, like several other villages in this region, has a family of sculptors who can make beautiful stone carvings; a rich tradition of folk theater, which comes alive during the numerous festivals and fairs in the

1. J. P. Naik, *Equality, Quality, and Quantity—The Elusive Triangle in Indian Education* (Bombay: Allied, 1975), pp. 109-10; Moninder Singh, *The Depressed Classes* (Bombay: Hind Kitabs, 1947), pp. 145-46.

area; and a family of *kathakars* ("storytellers") who can hold large audiences spellbound with their recitation of epics and ballads dating back several centuries. When the green revolution was ushered into rural India—along with high-yielding varieties of seeds, fertilizers, and plant-protection chemicals—an integrated adult education program called the Farmers Functional Literacy Project was started. A composite package of literacy, farmers' training, and information on new technologies through transistor radio was envisaged; however, the integration never materialized.

In Birmalu, an adult education center was set up for 30 learners under the charge of a volunteer instructor who was paid an honorarium of Rs 50, or $3, per month. Special textual material was prepared, and training included information on new farm inputs. In 1978, however, when the National Adult Education Programme (NAEP) was launched throughout India, the literacy rate of Birmalu was only marginally better than that of the villages that did not have an adult education center. To create a balance, a women's center was also established under NAEP, and in addition to literacy and functional knowledge, the component of awareness building was added. Although adult education centers have existed in the small village of Birmalu for 22 years, the literacy rate in the village is not much higher than the literacy rates of other villages without an adult education center.[2]

2. N. R. Sanskaria, "Khedai Rapat" (in Hindi), *Lok Sahitya Pratisahan* (Bikaner, India: Kalu, 1984).

The adult education program in India has relied on the establishment of adult education centers that are run through government machinery or voluntary agencies. Little attention is paid to forms of learning and recreation. Although functional aspects of education are emphasized along with simple literacy, neither of the goals is achieved to any significant degree.

SHAKLET

Shaklet is a large village in the Satara district of Maharashtra, with prosperous agriculture and a population of 2300. Good-quality sugarcane is grown in Shaklet, and the village takes pride in having a boys' high school and a separate primary school for girls. It is also the headquarters of the *panchayat* union, whose leaders have succeeded in establishing a small cooperative sugar mill, which has created work opportunities for many people. In 1960, 60 percent of Shaklet's population was still illiterate. When a large movement called Gram Shikshan Mohim (Village Literacy Campaign) was started at the headquarters of the Satara district, the village leaders of Shaklet, comprising large landowners and persons with political influence, came together determined to eradicate illiteracy in one year. All educated men and women showed enthusiasm. The local leaders pointed out that the definition of a literate person was one who can read and write a simple sentence; hence all that was required was to teach the alphabet, that is, the manner in which letters are constructed into words, and words into sentences. Very often it was considered enough if adults were able to write their name, the name of their spouse, and the name of the village. Within this definition, the people of Shaklet became literate in one year.

This achievement was followed by a much publicized celebration of total literacy. Several volunteer instructors were honored with small gifts and meek villagers who became literate were called on the microphone to pronounce how proud they were at having acquired literacy skills. A small library was also set up, but the villagers were expected to contribute money for it. Enthusiasm for literacy waned soon after the celebration, and the library remained nonfunctional. At the time of the census of 1971, a majority of literate persons had relapsed into illiteracy, and literacy had made no difference in their lives. Nonetheless, the current literacy rate in Shaklet is 70 percent, much higher than that of many other villages of the district.[3]

As exemplified by Shaklet, the creation of local enthusiasm, particularly harnessing the support of influential local leaders, can result in the launching of a literacy campaign. Unless, however, the level of literacy achieved is sufficient, learning material is provided to neoliterates, and facilities for continuing education are available, a majority of literate persons can relapse into illiteracy.[4]

3. India, Planning Commission, *Report on Gram Shikshan Mohim in Maharashra*, 1964, pp. 14-15.

4. Homer Kempfer, "Guidelines for an Attack on Illiteracy," in *Adult Education in India*, ed. Anil Bordia, J. R. Kidd, and J. A. Draper (Bombay: Nachiketa, 1973), pp. 219-22.

FACING THE CHALLENGE OF UNIVERSAL PRIMARY EDUCATION

As is evident from the foregoing case studies, many obstacles need to be overcome in order to achieve the goal of universal literacy in India. Provision of basic services—education, health services, drinking water, and so forth—for the people in rural India has followed a pattern comprising the creation of a supply system and its supervision by a hierarchy of officials. The results are obvious. Even where facilities are available, they are, in fact, not accessible, particularly to those people who need them most.[5] The situation with regard to primary education has been reviewed in the last couple of years, and altogether new strategies have now been elaborated for achieving the goal of universal primary education.[6] These are

1. Universal access. This presupposes that a primary school or a nonformal education center is available and within walking distance of all children.

2. Universal participation. Access by itself does not ensure participation; universal participation implies not only that all children who start primary education continue until the

5. Education and National Development, *Report of the Education Commission*, vol. 1, *1964-66* (New Delhi: National Council of Educational Research and Training Publication Unit, 1966), pp. 198-203.

6. Government of India, "The Eight Plan—Strategies and Programmes: Report of the Working Group on Early Childhood Education and Elementary Education," mimeographed, pp. 11-13.

end of the stage but also that their participation is active and regular.

3. Universal achievement. Achievement in a vast majority of schools in India is far lower than the curricular expectations; it is necessary to lay down a minimal level of learning and to ensure that all children have mastered that level when they complete their primary education or the corresponding stage of nonformal education.

Microlevel planning is the instrument for providing access and for securing primary school participation by all children. This is to be done through village education committees, to whom the primary school becomes accountable. Microplanning envisages a survey of each family to identify eligible children and to see whether they can benefit from existing schools. If they reside far from school or have other difficulties, an alternate mode of providing primary education has to be planned. The members of the village education committee and teachers need to hold discussions with the parents and monitor the children's participation and the regularity of their attendance.[7]

For a number of reasons, a large percentage of children in India cannot benefit from primary schools. They are working for wages, assisting their family in agriculture, or looking after their younger brothers and sisters at home. For these children, as well as for those in small habitations where schools cannot be set up, the only alternative available is to set up nonformal education centers. Such centers, which are an essential part of the strategy of universal access and universal participation, are run at times that are convenient for the children. The responsibility for running such centers is assigned to a local youth, who is paid remuneration in keeping with the number of hours put in. Special learning material, particularly in language and mathematics, is designed to ensure that the scholastic achievement of the children participating in nonformal education programs is comparable to the achievement of children who attend schools.[8]

The problem of achievement of a minimum level of learning by all children is complex. Nationally acceptable minimum levels of learning have been laid down by the National Council of Educational Research and Training. These levels, naturally, correspond to the desirable level, rather than to the actual levels obtained in an average primary school in the country. Currently, the National Council of Educational Research and Training and State Councils are engaged in developing techniques that would enable groups of teachers to make an assessment of current levels of learning, again particularly in language and mathematics, and to design their own minimum levels of learning that may be attainable within the following couple of years.

7. India, Department of Education, "Operationalizing Microplanning," mimeographed, 1991, pp. 5-6.

8. Anil Bordia, "Child Labour in India: Implications for Educational Planning" (Working paper delivered at the Asian Regional Triparite Workshop on Practical Measures to Combat Child Labour, Bangkok, 22-30 Sept. 1986).

Educational administrators are also involved in this exercise so that they can plan the inputs—such as instructional facilities and retraining of teachers—to enable the teachers to achieve these levels.[9]

A major problem in achieving the goals of universal primary education is the dearth of financial resources. Improvement of school facilities, appointment of additional teachers to cope with the increase in the number of school-going children, establishment of a credible nonformal education system, and other measures for quality improvement call for a massive investment of resources. The government of India has decided to increase the allocation of resources for primary education substantially and to supplement these resources by seeking external aid from bilateral and multilateral sources. Significant new programs being launched include a large basic education project in the state of Bihar with support from the United Nations Children's Fund, another in Rajasthan with financial assistance from the Swedish International Development Agency, and a project for basic education in Uttar Pradesh assisted by the World Bank.

These efforts at the primary school level will, it is hoped, reduce the illiteracy rates of the next generation of Indian adults. The next section of this article will look, by contrast, at past and present efforts at improving adult literacy education.

FROM INSTITUTIONALIZED CENTERS TO MASS CAMPAIGNS

The Farmers Functional Literacy Project, begun in 1967, envisaged the establishment of projects with a fixed number of adult education centers where learners would learn about new agricultural practices along with literacy. This represented a systematic literacy effort on a large scale and did succeed in developing skills and disseminating knowledge of improved agricultural practices. It was unsuccessful, however, in that it was mainly relatively well-off farmers who took advantage of the program, especially those who wanted to introduce new agricultural practices. Thus, as in the case of the green revolution, this revolution in ideas touched only the fringe of the problem, leaving the mass of the illiterates—exploited marginal farmers and landless agricultural workers—outside its scope. Moreover, this was, and was seen as, a purely governmental program, with the community and the voluntary agencies playing only a nominal role.[10]

A decade later, in 1978, the NAEP was launched, heralded as a program that would not be confined to the government machinery but that would draw in all voluntary agencies, youth organizations, and universities and colleges.[11] It was a multipronged program aimed at the acquisition of literacy skills, social awareness, and

9. Government of India, *Minimum Levels of Learning at Primary State* (New Delhi: National Council of Educational Research and Training Publication Unit, n.d.), pp. 61-67.

10. United Nations Development Program, "India County Profile," in *The Experimental World Literacy Programmes—Critical Assessment* (Paris: UNESCO Press, 1976), pp. 48-54.

11. India, Ministry of Education and Social Welfare, *National Adult Education Programme—An Outline*, 1979.

functional development by the participants. As it consciously tried to move away from being identified as a government program, it provided for greater participation of voluntary agencies in a host of activities, ranging from the running of centers to the development of learning materials, training, research, and evaluation.

This program should have led to a more flexible structure. In actual fact, however, programs of various agencies, governmental and nongovernmental, tended to be entirely center based and to follow rigid patterns. At the center, an instructor, who received a small honorarium, ran the program by enrolling 30 learners. For every 30 centers, there was a supervisor; each cluster of 300 centers was under the charge of a project officer; and a district adult education officer coordinated the program at the district level. Financial patterns and inflexible administrative structures deflected the focus from the acquisition of literacy skills for the development of the individual and the community to running x number of centers, appointing y number of instructors, and enrolling z number of learners. With the program's excessive emphasis on enrollment and target setting, a situation arose whereby achievement was seen as a game of multiplication with the number 30. Thus, if there were 300 centers operating in a given area, achievement was computed as being 9000 students, and scant attention was paid to actual individual learning achievements or outcomes. Often, interest in perpetuating the centers at the ground level existed solely because functionaries felt that if the center closed, or if a project was

shifted elsewhere because full literacy had been achieved, their honorarium would be lost.

The long duration of the program was also seen as an impediment. The teaching-learning program is spread over 300 hours during a 10-month period. Evaluations carried out by external evaluation agencies of programs in Bihar, Gujarat, Maharashtra, Rajasthan, Orissa, and Tamil Nadu indicate that in the initial 3- to 4-month period, the response to learning is generally good. Interest tends to waver after the initial spurt of enthusiasm, however, resulting in a high dropout rate.[12]

In summary, inherent structural deficiencies, coupled with inflexibilities of all kinds and at all levels—in the timing of the centers, in the numbers enrolled in the provision of funds, and in the bureaucratized, hierarchical attitudes—led to a situation where the NAEP, which had had a promising start, became another ineffective government program.

12. Madras Institute of Development Studies, "National Adult Education Programme: An Appraisal of the Role of the Voluntary Agencies in Tamil Nadu," mimeographed, 1980, pp. 81-82; J. Aikar and J. Henriques, "Achievement of the Adult Education Programme: A Triple Stage Study of Adult Learner in Maharashtra," mimeographed (Bombay: Tata Institute of Social Sciences, 1983), pp. 22-25; D. M. Pestonjee, S. N. Laharia, and Deepti Dixit, *National Adult Education Programme in Rajasthan: A Second Appraisal* (Ahmedabad: Indian Institute of Management, 1981), pp. 40-43; K. R. Shah, "Adult Education Programme in Gujarath, Third Evaluation," mimeographed (Ahmedabad: Sardar Patel Institute of Economic and Social Research, 1963), pp. 515-16; *Evaluation of an Adult Education Project* (Jaipur: Jana Kalyana Samithi; Jamshedpur: Xavier Labour Relation Institute, 1980).

After the launching of the National Policy on Education in 1986, a thorough review of the strengths and shortcomings of past programs was undertaken and wide-ranging consultations organized. As a result, the government initiated a move to start a number of "missions," most of them for application of modern science and technology to developmental issues affecting the disadvantaged social groups. The National Literacy Mission, started in 1988, was one such mission. It was described as a societal mission, with the aim of imparting functional literacy to 80 million adults, aged 15-35 years, by 1995.[13]

In the last two years, the National Literacy Mission has made it possible for the country to adopt a systematically planned campaign approach, characterized by large-scale mobilization and the creation of an atmosphere in which educated youths, students, and community volunteers take on the challenge of illiteracy. This approach has brought a fresh excitement to the entire literacy scene.

In the most exciting experiment in recent years, the Ernakulam district of Kerala State in South India has achieved 100 percent literacy and is thus the first district to become fully literate in the country. More than 185,000 persons aged 6 to 60 years were involved in a literacy program through the mobilization of 20,000 volunteers. The Ernakulam campaign was based on the following premises: (1) to succeed, a literacy campaign has to be time-bound and

area-bound; (2) it has to be a total and one-time effort; (3) a demand has to be generated among the illiterate to acquire literacy, along with enthusiasm among the educated to impart it; and (4) it has to be voluntary effort.

The Ernakulam campaign was one year long. Enhanced mobilization efforts through local troupes created a social pressure and an environment where everybody worked to participate in the program. The Ernakulam success story is the story of people from different walks of life joining hands for the purpose of eradicating illiteracy with a spirit of determination and urgency.[14]

As a result of the Ernakulam success, there is today an air of excitement among literacy workers, and programs more challenging in size and complexity are being initiated on the Ernakulam pattern elsewhere in the country. A mass campaign for achieving the twin objectives of immunization and literacy has been started in Midnapore District of West Bengal, for example. Midnapore, whose population of 8 million makes it one of the largest districts of the country, has 2 million illiterates. The campaign seeks to enroll a volunteer army of 200,000 to take on the teaching and learning activity. Similar efforts have started that cover the states of Kerala, Goa, and Pondicherry and several districts of other states.

One approach currently being explored is the area approach, which

13. India, Ministry of Human Resources Development, *National Literacy Mission*, Jan. 1988, pp. 14-16.

14. P. K. Michael Tarakhan, "The Ernakulam District Total Literacy Programme: Report of the Evaluation," mimeographed (Trivandrum: Centre for Development Studies, May 1990), pp. 14-25.

looks at adult education and primary education for children together in a holistic fashion. Using this approach, planning focuses on all groups in a given area, whether participants are adults, children, women, or members of certain ethnic and tribal groups, so that education is available to all. This concentrated effort at basic literacy should be followed up with suitable post-literacy structures to complement the adult education activities and to provide a suitable forum for continuing education. Above all, the area approach comprises identification of positive elements and agencies within the area who will support and guide the entire educational program.

Another new approach is the Improved Pace and Content of Learning. Evaluation studies have pointed to three crucial factors in literacy learning: program duration, program content, and visibility of results. The Improved Pace and Content of Learning is an innovative technique of learning that envisages a reduced duration of learning, improved motivation of learners and functionaries, and a built-in mechanism for evaluation. A three-level primer ensures that, through a number of simple tests, the learner achieves the expected levels of learning. From the earlier 300 hours and a course of 10 months, the learning period has been reduced to 200 hours spread over 5 to 6 months. The new technique introduces a process of self-directed learning and self-evaluation by the learners, and it is hoped that, with heightened motivation, the dropout rate will fall.

These experiments have shown the need for and subsequent trend toward a move from traditionally administered adult education to more holistic approaches. The transition from an established, institutionalized, and traditionally administered system of adult education to a people-oriented mass campaign is not easy, however, due to several factors. First of all, the center-based adult education program conforms very well to the Brahmanic system of education to which India has been accustomed for centuries. The main features of the Brahmanic system are dependence on professional teachers, who during ancient times came to constitute a caste; rigid hours and course duration; distancing from the community; and nonuse of the spoken language of the people as medium of instruction. Over the years, the instructor of adult education has come to acquire the trappings of a formal education teacher. There has been excessive rigidity regarding learning material, instructional timing, and duration of the literacy course. By and large, involvement of the community has been more token in nature, rather than genuine participation, and the organizers are seldom conscious of the difference between the standard language used in the primers and the spoken language of the learners.

Moreover, several vested interests have grown over the years around the traditional adult education program. One involves the instructors, who are not willing to forgo their honorarium, paltry though the amount is. Also, the entire supervisory and administrative machinery has become accustomed to a nonproductive style, the casual pace of the adult education centers, and even corruption. Some voluntary agencies have adapted to the well-carved area of activity and influence in the centers where they have a number of workers with a steady source of funding. Also, field-level workers of practically all political parties have protégés among adult education workers and voluntary agencies.

Finally, the traditional literacy program fits very well with the formal education system, which itself is not amenable to change. Added to this is the sheer logistical problem of absorption, or redeployment of thousands of employees working in adult education who cannot be removed from service. The switch-over, therefore, from the center-based program to a volunteer-based mass campaign will have to be organized with tact and determination.

HARNESSING THE VALUE OF LITERACY

Protagonists of literacy assert that an illiterate person lives in a world of darkness and ignorance, that literacy is a basic human right, and that literacy is indispensable for the development of an individual and a nation. But are these assertions really so? We have seen literate persons living their lives in a manner no different from that of people who have not had the privilege of literacy learning. One example comes from Maharashtra, where the Gram Shikshan Mohim was claimed to have made three districts and 5000 villages fully literate.

An assessment of the way in which people lived there before and after Mohim did not show any significant difference in the lives of the people.

The fact is that there are some conditions that have to be fulfilled if literacy is to influence the living conditions of the people significantly. Major prerequisites for literacy learning to be worthwhile are the following: (1) literacy programs should be preceded, accompanied, and followed by mass mobilization; (2) literacy learning should go side by side with a coming together of the learners to understand their predicament and to acquire necessary skills for their survival; (3) the level of alphabetization should be sufficient for a person, should he or she so desire, to continue his or her learning in a self-reliant manner; and (4) the problem of retention and application of literacy should be considered in a comprehensive fashion.

In the preceding section we made reference to the manner in which mass mobilization has been instrumental in the transformation of adult education programs from the adult-education-center approach to the mass-campaign approach. To achieve mass mobilization, thousands of workers in voluntary agencies, members of the people's science movement, political cadres, and cultural activists trudged from village to village talking with people, presenting plays and songs, and showing films to arouse interest in teaching and learning. As a result, in some districts the peasantry, known for its passivity and fatalism, has come to demand literacy programs and books. If properly organized, then, mobilization activities can make literacy a weapon in the hands of the poor.[15]

As an integral part of literacy activity, dialogue and discussion enable learners to systematize their thoughts, relate learning to their own situation, and articulate their views. This is of particular importance in the case of women because they have been accustomed to a culture of silence in a fashion that the males of their own families are not. It is also important that women acquire a solidarity based on commonality of experience.

India undertook mass campaigns for literacy in the 1930s and the 1960s. One significant aspect of these campaigns was the lack of attention to the levels of literacy and numeracy achieved. While neither of the campaigns involved much financial expenditure, they did involve great investment of human resources, such as the time of workers as well as the time of the learners. If, as seems likely, those campaigns did not change the living and working conditions of the people in any significant fashion, we have to make sure that those mistakes are not repeated.

A parallel is often drawn between the Indian literacy campaign and the campaigns launched in Tanzania and Ethiopia. Such comparisons are inappropriate. Tanzania and Ethiopia, whatever the limitations of their situation might be, have envisioned literacy campaigns as a part of fundamental socioeconomic and sociocultural transformation. The African

15. B. K. Roy Burman, "Formative and Summative Evaluation of Special Programme for Eradication of Illiteracy of Burdwan District, West Bengal," mimeographed, pp. 10-11.

campaigns were, moreover, organized in a single-party political system, which had the authority to compel all citizens to participate. The situation in India is quite different. We cannot always hold out the promise of a better future for literate people, for the simple reason that mass education is not accompanied by redistributive justice and a dismantling of age-old social, economic, and political power structures. If, therefore, young people in India are to pursue their literacy courses to a satisfactory level, it has to be out of a respect for learning, an assertion of personal will, and a motivational environment created by mass mobilization.

To help fulfill the current goals, the National Literacy Mission has laid down specific levels of literacy to be achieved by all learners. Even where campaigns of short duration are being launched and workers as well as learners are impatient to conclude the literacy campaign as early as possible, an insistence is being made on the achievement of the prescribed levels of reading, writing, and arithmetic. There is constantly a danger that rhetoric and euphoria will get the better of the literacy campaign and that the importance of systematic application of teaching and learning processes will be disregarded.

It is necessary to plan comprehensively to ensure the retention and the application of literacy. Even in the best of circumstances, relapse into illiteracy cannot be prevented in a certain percentage of neoliterates. The critical question is how many people relapse into illiteracy and how many retain their literacy knowledge. While it is futile to venture any norms in this area, it is obvious that there are no simple or cheap solutions to the problem. Approaches currently under way to assure literacy retention include the creation of reading-room networks, post-literacy training programs, vocational training programs with a literacy component, the production and distribution of books and journals, and the use of radio and television.

CONCLUSION

Learning is an ancient tradition in India and, since times lost in the dawn of history, Indian people have developed various types of means and institutions to pass on to the next generation the knowledge and wisdom gained by their predecessors.

A person may have much ancient wisdom and perspicacity and still need to read and write and work figures so that he or she can take part in modern economic pursuits and civic life. Indeed, the bafflement of Gova[16]—in Rabindranath Tagore's novel of this name—at seeing widespread illiteracy in the village of his

16. Rabindranath Tagore, "The Heart-Rending Reality, Extract from 'Gova'" in *Adult Education in India*, ed. Bordia, Kidd, and Draper, pp. 165-68.

nativity and the stress laid by Tagore on the spread of literacy and education in rural areas stand as an ideal and challenge for us all. As we move in India from one crisis to another, to new programs after others have gone sour, our determination becomes only stronger, our perception clearer, and our struggle better planned.

In this article three issues have been referred to: ensuring that primary education be made available to all children, so that the fresh flow of illiterates is arrested; recognizing that literacy is an inherent need and right of the masses, so that the responsibility for its delivery can be transferred from the hierarchy of officialdom to mass organizations; and shifting the emphasis from one-time literacy learning to life-long education that would improve the condition of life of the learners. The issues have only been raised, and some of the answers that are being explored in different parts of India have been reported on. The message we want to convey is that people in India have concern for the literacy situation, that the gravity and urgency of the task is understood, and that although our country does not yet have final answers, progress is being made to find them.

ANNALS, *AAPSS*, 520, March 1992

Sociolinguistic Minorities and Scholastic Difficulties in France

By GENEVIÈVE VERMES and MICHÈLE KASTENBAUM

ABSTRACT: In France, 6-17 percent of the adult population can be categorized as functionally illiterate. Most of the illiterate population comprises young adults of immigrant origin from sociolinguistic minorities and has at least six years of schooling in French. Efforts have been made to reduce functional illiteracy, in particular through native-language (NL) courses given in the schools or in community associations. The study described here reports on possible links between these NL courses and students' attitudes toward academic achievement, scholastic activities, and classroom adjustment. The focus is on Arabic NL students. These students evaluated themselves more negatively regarding scholastic achievement than did the rest of the sample; however, they expressed more interest in scholastic activities than the others. However, no differences were observed between students enrolled in Arabic NL courses and those who were not. The discussion centers on a comparison with Portuguese NL pupils, where a difference was observed between pupils enrolled in NL courses and pupils not enrolled in them.

Dr. Geneviève Vermes is maître de conférences of cognitive psychology and developmental psychology. Her research has focused on literacy in bilingualism and sociolinguistic minorities. She is coeditor of volumes on minorities' languages in France and current president of the Association pour la Recherche Interculturelle (ARIC).

Dr. Michèle Kastenbaum is maître de conférences of differential psychology and educational psychology. She has evaluated pedagogical media and teaching programs and written many articles in scientific journals.

NOTE: This study was carried out due to the generous cooperation of a large network of associated researchers: Le Comité de Liaison pour l'Alphabétisation et la Promotion. We also thank Claire Bazin and the team of social workers who helped in the realization of this study.

ALTHOUGH the problem of functional illiteracy in France has only recently become highly visible in the society at large, its importance is becoming increasingly clear. In 1984, the French government asked for the first official report on the literacy situation in France.[1] Defining functional illiteracy as "great difficulty in speaking, reading, writing and understanding French," recent surveys estimate that illiteracy affects between 6 and 17 percent of the adult population living on French soil.[2] Another source of information, but one that involves only men who are of French nationality, is the French army, whose tests reveal that at the legal age of military service, 18 years, 0.8 percent of young men of French nationality are illiterate and 4.7 percent functionally illiterate.[3]

In France, illiteracy is commonly associated with the complete lack of schooling. As it is seen to affect in this case only those groups who have not been able to attend school, such as the handicapped, adult immigrants, the aged, and those living in overseas territories, it is therefore not considered a real problem. The relatively recent discovery that young adults who had received 6, 8, and up to 10 years of schooling were functionally illiterate came as a great shock, however, and functional illiteracy is now considered a veritable challenge for society—a challenge highlighted by the difficulty that these young individuals have in entering the work force.

A certain number of attempts at solutions to the problem have been put into action to help prevent functional illiteracy in these young people, who typically come from suburban zones, from underprivileged environments and are often of immigrant origin. Efforts include widespread availability of nursery school at the age of three years; attempts to fill in the gap between nursery school and the first two years of compulsory schooling; installation of a collège structure linking primary and secondary schooling;[4] different teaching methods; identification of geographic zones needing educational priority, and the endowment of these zones with more teachers, extracurricular activities, and orientational counseling; special classes in French for non-French-speaking children of school age (CLIN); help and training for teachers of classes receiving large proportions of immigrant children; and courses in the language of origin—native language (NL)—whether within the school or within subsidized associations. It is this last initiative that we intend to address here.

The NL classes were established with several aims. First, the courses were conceived to give students a means for acquiring a positive atti-

---

1. Véronique Esperandieu and A. Lion, *Des Illettrés en France* (Paris: Documentation Française, 1984).

2. Jean L. Borkowski, "Etudes des conditions de vie, une enquête sur le cumul des inégalités," *Courrier des Statistiques*, 40 (Oct. 1984).

3. *Service National en Chiffres* (Paris: Ministère de la Défense, 1987).

4. Primary school comprises the first five years of compulsory schooling; collège, the sixth, seventh, and eighth years of compulsory schooling; and lycée, the next three years of education after the period of collège.

tude toward school learning, to have self-confidence in learning situations, and to use and see as valuable characteristics and abilities directly related to their origin. In this way, the courses are integrated into a more general perspective of "intercultural pedagogy," in which learning is backed up by nonscholastic knowledge.

The NL courses were also created for political reasons (that is, to encourage immigrants to return to their own countries), ideological reasons (to give people the right to be different), social reasons (to structure the community), and socioemotional reasons (to encourage social integration and maintain family cohesion). They were instituted either under the aegis of official agreements between their nation of origin and the French nation, in the framework of the primary school, or outside the school under the responsibility of community associations. Whatever their form or institutional framework, they have been, and continue to be, the subject of much criticism. The difficult conditions surrounding their creation and functioning—insufficient training and follow-up of professors, poor educational facilities, and badly defined programs and relations with the schools—render this teaching very problematic. For example, the definition and the content of the courses are extremely vague, and there has not been sufficient analysis carried out to find teaching methodologies that lend themselves to the courses' goals of reevaluation of the identity of one's community and the development of self-esteem.

On arriving in France, if immigrant children have no knowledge whatsoever of the French language, they are taught in classes of total immersion—the CLIN mentioned earlier—that use a French-as-a-second-language pedagogy. If the children are not totally ignorant of French, they are taught with, and exactly the same as, the pupils of French origin, without any specific support. In spite of French being their second language, their spoken French generally shows no qualitative difference from that of their classmates of French origin from the same milieu and living under the same conditions, and their linguistic habits in the "other" language are ignored. Further, many surveys have noted that these children state that they speak the language of their parents very seldom and poorly.[5]

Statistically speaking, however, and paradoxically, these children have real difficulties in learning to write. These difficulties are commonly considered to be due to their bilingualism. Some researchers, however, believe that the analysis of their situation simply in terms of a direct effect of bilingualism is inadequate.[6] Rather, they see the situation of bilingualism as part of a complex, unfavorable situation, characterized by a low level of parental education, unfavorable sociocultural sta-

5. Louise Dabène and Jacqueline Billiez, "Le parler de jeunes issus de l'immigration," in France, Pays Multilingue, by Geneviève Vermes and Josiane Boutet, vol. 2, Pratiques des Langues en France (Paris: L'Harmattan, 1987).

6. Gérard Ludi and Bernard Py, Etre Bilingue (Berne: Peter Lang, 1985).

tus, and difficulty in integration and acculturation.[7]

Immigrants of North African origin constitute the largest portion of French immigrants. Taking into account the particular historical past that links France to North Africa and more particularly to Algeria, this group of immigrants lives in conditions of major sociocultural minorization and marginalization, conditions that are then added to the linguistic complexity inherent in the Arabic language. This linguistic complexity comes from the existence of several varieties of language: interlingual Arab-French, the Arabic of immigration, Arabic dialects, modern Arabic, and classical Arabic.[8]

Even if we cannot make a strict parallel between social integration and scholastic integration, and even if the children do not occupy the same position at school as their parents do in society, it is clear that these children have a harder road to travel than the others. Scholastic success is a product of multiple determinations that cannot simply be reduced to success in learning. Rather, one can properly analyze it only by taking into account adaptation in the classroom and the appropriation of scholastic values.[9] Thus, in our work, we examined the position of pupils of

7. Geneviève Vermes, ed., *Vingt-cinq Communautés Linguistiques de la France*, vol. 2, *Les Langues Immigrées* (Paris: L'Harmattan, 1988).

8. M. Falip and B. Deslandes, "Une langue un peu plus étrangère que les autres: L'enseignement de l'Arabe en France," *LIDIL*, 2:51-89 (1989).

9. R. Zazzo, *Les 10-13 Ans: Garçons et Filles en CM2 et en Sixième* (Paris: PUF, 1982).

North African origin in relation to their peers, looking not only at scholastic success but at the more general idea of integration in class and in the scholastic system as well.

In doing this, we sought a better understanding of the different aspects of school adaptation from the pupil's point of view. This includes scholastic results, as well as the subject's perception of them, his or her daily life, and his or her feelings about school and school activities. As we stated earlier, some of the pupils also take nonobligatory courses in their NL. We tried to find out if these courses had any link with scholastic performance, asking more specifically whether the systematic learning of the native language and the ability to write it helps the pupil to better penetrate the scholastic universe.

In this study, we set forth two hypotheses with which to guide our work; both pertain to the effectiveness of systematically teaching the native language in order to facilitate entrance into the world of the written word:

1. Joint, systematic learning of the native language and how to write it facilitates and encourages development of cognitive activities consistent with daily knowledge that the child works out orally with his or her parents in the parents' language.

2. These cognitive and intellectual activities practiced in the native language render the systematic analysis of speech in the school language more simple and thus facilitate initiation into writing and the acquisition of scholastic knowledge.

TABLE 1

BREAKDOWN OF SURVEY GROUPS

Group	N	NL	Study
1	27	Arabic	NL—with our associations
2	13	Arabic	NL—not with our associations
3	30	Arabic	NL—not studied
4	15	Other than Arabic	NLs
5	34	Other than Arabic	NLs—not studied
6	212	Only French language	

In order to find out what correlation, if any, taking a course in the student's NL has with overall school adjustment, we carried out a survey of schoolchildren in urban areas of France that have a large immigrant population. To find out whether the Arabophone pupils have scholastic difficulties in relation to other pupils—evident in grade repetition—whether they have specific attitudes toward scholastic activities, and whether those who take NL classes react differently from those who do not, we compared groups of Arabophone students with their peers.

The population concerned in this analysis comprises 331 pupils from 19 classes—from CE2, or third grade, to the Sixieme, or sixth grade. In each class we used the questionnaire responses of the pupil or pupils attending classes in Arabic, and 14 pupils chosen at random. Only 27 of the 331 pupils in the survey study Arabic with the associations we worked with and they formed Group 1. The group of peers itself is broken down into several subgroups: children who study Arabic elsewhere; children who speak Arabic as an NL but who do not study it; children who speak an NL other than Arabic and who study it; children who speak an NL other than Arabic and who do not study it; and children whose only language is French. See Table 1 for the breakdown of survey groups.

As an initial part of the survey, we gathered background information regarding usage of the NL by immigrant children's families. We discovered that 80 percent of the students had taken 3 or more years of NL classes. In addition, 50 percent of the students frequently speak the NL with their parents at home, and 75 percent of the parents frequently speak the NL with each other. Naturally, these last findings are related, as the more parents speak between themselves, the more the NL will be used between parents and children. We also found that the Arabophone population used their NL more than did the others; this is especially true for the children. Finally, there was no link between participation in NL courses and the frequency of use of the NL in the family.

A comparison of scholastic progress between the different groups revealed that problems with schoolwork are indeed present in our

TABLE 2
SCHOLASTIC PROGRESS

	Normal Progress	Grade Repetition	Total
Groups whose NL is Arabic	32 (46%)	38 (54%)	$N = 70$ (100%)
Groups with other NL	31 (63%)	18 (37%)	$N = 49$ (100%)
Group speaking only French	152 (72%)	60 (28%)	$N = 212$ (100%)

population. Table 2 is a chart presenting the distribution of children showing normal progress, or having fallen behind, for the Arabophone groups, for the groups with other NLs, and for the group speaking only French. As can be seen, the Arabophone children show a larger percentage of grade repetition. Although not indicated in the table, the survey showed that whether or not an NL course is taken does not affect school progress for any group.

In order to pursue the issue of school adaptation, we formulated two questionnaires about scholastic interest. We borrowed a great deal from two main research trends: one concerns the pupils' classroom adaptation, taken from the works of Zazzo;[10] the other involves levels of self-concept and is from American and French social psychology.[11]

Each pupil completed both questionnaires, one of which concerned interest in and adaptation to the schoolwork in French and one of which concerned scholastic material in general. The responses obtained in the two questionnaires were strongly linked. Following is a presentation of the information on responses regarding the questionnaire on interest in French only; interest in French, we found, represents interest in the class and the scholastic work in general. Each questionnaire was made up of about 20 questions and explored many areas, which can be summarized as follows:

— a self-evaluation of the scholastic level. Example: "In written French, I am: (a) a very good student, (b) a fairly good student, (c) an average student, (d) a below average student."

— expressing possible difficulties encountered. Example: "Some-

10. Ibid.

11. Ellen Piers and Dale Harris, *Manual for the Piers-Harris Children's Self Concept Scale* (Nashville, TN: Counselor Recordings and Tests, 1969); Richard J. Shavelson, Judith J. Hubner, and George C. Stanton, "Self-Concept: Validation of Construct, Interpretations," *Review of Education Research*, 46(3):407-41 (Summer 1976); Allen L. Shoemaker, "Construct of Area of Specific Self-Esteem: The Hare Self-Esteem Scale," *Education and Psy-*

chology Measurement, 40:495-501 (1980); Nicole Dubois, "Perception de la valeur sociale et norme d'internalité chez l'enfant," *Psychologie Française*, 36(1):13-23 (1991); Terry M. Honess, "Soi et identité: Analyse notionnelle et examen des courants de recherche actuels," ibid., 35(1):17-23 (1990).

TABLE 3
RESPONSES CONCERNING SELF-EVALUATION AND INTEREST IN SCHOOL

Quadrant 1	Quadrant 2
I am a good student. I participate in everything we do in French class (often).	What we do in French class interests me a lot. At home, I leaf through my French book, reading here and there (very often).

Quadrant 3	Quadrant 4
What we do in French class interests me little. At home, I leaf through my French book, reading here and there (almost never).	I am a below average student. I participate in everything we do in French class (a little).

times, even when I work very hard, I am not able to do well what is asked of me in French: (a) this is true, I am not able; (b) it is not true, I am able."
— whether or not these difficulties are attributable to the teacher. Example: "Sometimes, if I don't understand, it is because the teacher has not explained well: (a) almost always, (b) sometimes, (c) often, (d) very often."
— interest stated in scholastic work. Example: "The work we do in French class: (a) interests me a little, (b) is of average interest, (c) interests me very much, (d) interests me very very much."
— evidence of interest and follow-up of school activities at home, and participation in class. Examples: "At home, I leaf through my French book, reading here and there: (a) almost never, (b) sometimes, (c) often, (d) very often"; "I participate in everything we do in French class; for example, answering the teacher's questions or asking questions myself, or speaking out when I have something

to say: (a) hardly ever, (b) sometimes, (c) often, (d) very often."

RESULTS

Our analysis of the results[12] is based on an examination of tables of contingency between the responses, which highlights the association between the responses. The method permits the grouping of different categories of answers, allowing us to look at the relationship between the characteristics of the subjects—the language of the parents, taking courses in NL or not—and their responses. This analysis revealed two dichotomies: the first is good adaptation and good success in class, versus mediocre adaptation and mediocre success; and the second separates the responses of self-evaluation, good or bad, from those showing interest in school, positive or negative. Table 3 represents a schematic breakdown of the responses into four quadrants.

Two of the quadrants—quadrants 1 and 4—represent self-evaluation of success—a realistic self-evaluation of success, because it is linked with re-

12. Philippe Cibois, *L'Analyse des Données en Sociologie* (Paris: PUF, 1984).

tardation or absence of scholastic retardation—feelings of the presence or absence of problems, attribution or not of these problems to the teachers, and self-evaluation of comportment in class, that is to say, attention and participation in scholastic activities. The questions of these two quadrants, in other words, are concerned with the pupil's perceptions of the functioning of class activities. In quadrants 2 and 3, the questions express interest, positive or negative, in scholastic activities as well as in the manifestation of that interest in the home through nonobligatory activities that are an extension of scholastic activity.

We compared the responses of the small groups—Groups 1 to 5—to those of their French-NL peers—Group 6—which act here as a control group. A primary observation is that if we remove our 119 students with an NL other than French—Groups 1 to 5—from the ensemble of the population, the structuring of the responses remains identical, with the same sets forming in the same way. This signifies that our 119 pupils with a non-French NL organize their responses in the same way as do the 212 others and thus use the same logic in their system of answering. This indicates further that they understand and interpret the questions in the same way as do their classmates and that they see the reality of the scholastic system in the same way.

However, having an NL other than French, whatever language it is, and whether or not one takes courses in his or her NL, is related to some specific responses. We saw earlier that scholastic retardation was more frequent among students with an NL other than French than among the others. It is, therefore, not surprising to find that those whose NL is not French express having more problems during class activities and have less favorable self-evaluations. These students have a tendency, as well, and more than their peers, to attribute their problems to the teachers.

Furthermore, the groups for whom French is not the NL respond more positively to the statement "For my parents, it is important that I get good grades in French." The fact that they respond with "important" and "very important" more often than do their peers seems to indicate that they are aware of the importance of the stakes connected with surmounting the difficulties they have. In addition, having an NL other than French is connected to the expression of more interest in French, and more manifestation of that interest in home activities than is so for French children. This is especially true for those whose NL is Arabic.[13]

In terms of questions concerning interest in scholastic work or study of French, we found no differences in the responses of the 70 Arabophone students between those who take courses in Arabic and those who do

13. It is easier to discern specific traits characteristic of the Arabophone pupils in relation to the population in general than for the other groups whose NL is not French. This is not surprising, however, since the group with other NLs—the 49 students who speak Portuguese, Turkish, Tamil, among other languages—is probably very heterogeneous, which is likely to block the emergence of possible specific traits.

not. All of the Arabophone students position themselves, preferentially, in the zones of great interest and great difficulty: they have a marked interest in scholastic activity; they manifest it in activity at home rather than where it should be manifested, in class; they are also conscious of the existence of problems in class, which they attribute partially to the teacher.

We have brought to light the fact that Arabophone pupils, whose difficult situation as a sociocultural minority we have presented, see their situation in relation to schoolwork in a way different from their peers. This particular situation presents some negative aspects, such as a higher tendency toward failure and a negative self-evaluation. It can also be looked at positively, however, in that they take a greater interest than do the other pupils in school activities and in activities of a scholastic nature in the home.

We found no difference between the situation of the Arabophone students who take courses in Arabic and those who do not, at least on the points contained in the survey. The study of Arabic was not related in this case to having a better situation in the scholastic system, in spite of the advantages that these NL courses are said to offer: amelioration of self-image, more positive feeling in relation to the community of origin, and facilitation of learning to write in French by having been taught how to write in the NL.

To try to obtain some understanding of the reasons underlying the absence of a relationship between tak-

ing courses in Arabic and scholastic standing, we compared the survey results to those we obtained in a similar experiment involving Portuguese children. We found that Portuguese children who take courses in Portuguese do better in school than their Portuguese peers who do not.[14] The Portuguese and Arabophone samples were not completely comparable, as the Portuguese students are older—12 to 16 years old—and more advanced in the study of their NL than were the Arabophone students we studied. Nevertheless, we can advance some hypotheses in the hope of clarifying the contrasts between the two groups in terms of the effects of NL classes.

First, teaching Arabic poses specific problems that teaching Portuguese does not. We noted above that the situation of linguistic diglossia in social usage by the Arab immigrant population. A recent survey of ours indicates that the NL courses do not escape this diglossic employment and that there is, from one course to another, from one teacher to another, and even within each course, a very great heterogeneity of registers of language. These factors, we hypothesize, are manifested in great difficulty in the conception of practices of a scholarly order, such as in the practice of learning to write and doing lessons and homework.[15] Further, in

14. Michèle Kastenbaum, *Rapport No. 3* (Paris: Comité de Liaison pour l'Alphabétisation et la Promotion, 1990).

15. Geneviève Vermes and Alexandra Androussou, *Rapport No. 1* (Paris: Comité de Liaison pour l'Alphabétisation et la Promotion, 1989).

Arabic courses, oral expression and oral communication are much more greatly valued and practiced than is written communication. Portuguese, on the other hand, presents a very considerable linguistic homogeneity in and outside of Portugal, and the literary culture, as well as the teaching methods, are all done in the same language. The systematic instruction of Portuguese does not present, then, the same difficulties as the instruction in Arabic.

Second, the courses in Portuguese are based on a classic scholastic model, which in our view renders the transfer of competence provided by these courses easier. The courses in Portuguese, in other words, are largely made up of systematic instruction supported by determined progressions and are therefore more structurally similar to the French scholastic framework than are the Arabic NL classes. Furthermore, teachers of Portuguese consider themselves teachers. Those who teach Arabic are also teachers, but they define themselves more as animators. This additional element makes the courses in Portuguese more similar to those given in the French scholastic system and, therefore, more easily conveyers of transferable benefits.

A final possibility relates to a major assumption in the current interpretation of survey results: that nothing differentiates the Portuguese or Arabophone pupils who take courses in their NL from those who do not, at the outset. One could hypothesize that the students who take the NL courses have personal, familial, and other characteristics that distinguish them from the others. In this case, a scholastic advantage would precede the courses instead of following them. Indeed, since the courses in Portuguese are organized to prepare for the normal examinations of transition in the Portuguese scholastic system, it is possible that those who take Portuguese courses are self-selected on the basis of a desire to perform well in future studies in Portugal. These students obviously may have performed better on average in school than did the others.

Having shed some light on the dynamics of the problematic scholastic situation of children of Arabic origin, we conclude that Arabophone students fail more than their classmates, and they state a greater interest in the educational material; more than their friends, they state that they do homework, which testifies to their interest. This interest in education, although not associated with success in school, is most apparent in the home. We can understand this in relation to the fact that school is more difficult for these children than for their classmates, and the class probably makes demands on them that are inappropriate. In the home, they can conduct scholastic activities at their own rhythm and in their own way. This fact seems important to us: in effect, one too often associates failure with lack of interest.

It would be a mistake not to take advantage of this investment in scholastic interest in order to renew the dynamics of the desire for learning and education in school. At the ages considered here, between 8 and 12 years, falling behind in school rarely lasts more than two years, and students may catch up to their peers. One can be hopeful that continued research in this area will lead to more understanding of how to capitalize on the strong, early, positive aspects of Arabophone students' scholastic experience, so as to diminish the possibility of functional illiteracy as an outcome in later years.

ANNALS, *AAPSS*, 520, March 1992

Literacy Acquisition in Peru, Asia, and the United States

By HAROLD W. STEVENSON and CHUANSHENG CHEN

ABSTRACT: An important question in the study of literacy is the degree to which environmental conditions influence children's ability to learn to read. A comparison was made of the reading ability of schooled and nonschooled children in three locations in Peru: the city, the highlands, and the rain forest. Increased attendance resulted in improved reading ability, but the degree of improvement varied according to the environments in which the children resided. When the children were followed up nine years after the original testing, they showed continued improvement in reading ability, especially in the environment where economic conditions had improved. A comparison of the Peruvian children with children in three industrialized societies, Japan, Taiwan, and the United States, revealed little difference in the children's cognitive abilities but great differences in their reading ability. More stimulating environmental conditions and better schooling in the industrialized societies were presumably responsible for these differences.

Harold W. Stevenson is professor of psychology at the University of Michigan. He received his M.A. and Ph.D. at Stanford University. His primary areas of research are in children's learning and cognitive development and, in particular, the effect of cultural factors on children's academic achievement.

Chuansheng Chen, a native of China, is a doctoral candidate in Michigan's Department of Psychology. He received his B.S. from Hangzhou University and his M.A. from the University of Michigan. He has been involved in comparative study of children's academic achievement for the past several years.

RARELY are there occasions in industrialized societies when we can compare the reading achievement of children who do attend school and children who do not. Yet many questions concerning the acquisition of literacy depend on such comparisons. We know that the operations of mathematics can be acquired without going to school,[1] but we have little information about the degree to which children can also learn to read without formal academic instruction. Most urban children encounter written language every day in road signs, billboards, displays in stores, books, television, and newspapers. Do encounters with these stimuli serve to provide children with the fundamentals of literacy? How about children living in remote rural areas of developing countries, where children seldom, if ever, encounter written language in their everyday lives? Is formal schooling their only avenue to literacy?

The effects of schooling on children's academic achievement in industrialized societies have been studied in great detail, and from studies in developing countries we know something about the effects of such factors as the availability of textbooks, class size, and teachers' salaries on children's scholastic performance.[2] Seldom, however, have the studies in developing countries investigated how the effects of schooling are influenced by such potentially important variables as the experiences available in children's everyday environment, the cognitive stimulation provided by the home, and efforts by parents to teach their children to read. These factors are of special interest when one considers that children have opportunities out of school to acquire some of the information and skills taught in school and that the effects of schooling may be decreased when both schooled and nonschooled children live in stimulating and informative environments.

The questions we asked in our research concern the relationship of literacy to the environments in which children live. We chose several markedly different environmental settings to evaluate these effects. In an initial study, we compared the performance of schooled and nonschooled children in three regions of Peru: the city, remote villages in the Peruvian highlands, and isolated villages in the Peruvian rain forest. Nearly a decade later we returned to these locations in an effort to find out as much as possible about what changes had occurred in the lives of the individuals and how these changes might have influenced their level of literacy. Following our initial study, we conducted a study with children living in large cities in three highly industrialized societies: Japan, Taiwan, and the United States. A comparison of the performance of children in these societies with that of the Peruvian

1. Terezinha N. Carraher, David W. Carraher, and Annalucia D. Schliemann, "Mathematics in the Streets and in Schools," *British Journal of Developmental Psychology*, 3:21-29 (1985).

2. Bruce Fuller, "What School Factors Raise Achievement in the Third World?" *Review of Educational Research*, 57:255-92 (1987); Stephen P. Heyneman and William A. Loxley, "The Effect of Primary School Quality on Academic Achievement across Twenty-Nine High and Low Income Countries," *American Journal of Sociology*, 88:1162-94 (1983).

children offered us additional information about how environmental conditions may facilitate or limit the degree to which young children acquire literacy.

The diversity of environments and the opportunity to compare the achievement of schooled and non-schooled children make Peru an appealing country in which to study the acquisition of literacy. Peru is a developing country with a long and illustrious cultural history. The indigenous population of Quechua-speaking Indians is composed of descendants of the Incas, who once governed an empire of millions from their highland capital in Cuzco. As in many Latin American countries, however, life in Peru has been dominated by mestizos—persons of mixed Spanish and Indian heritage—for over four centuries.

The population of the highlands is still predominantly Quechua speaking, but the number of Quechua speakers in the capital city of Lima has increased during the past several decades due to the migration of many families from the highlands. Squatter settlements housing millions of people now cover the outskirts of the city. As might be expected in a country that has faced intractable economic problems, many families in Peru are unable to send their children to school. At the time of our study, only 53 percent of the general population of Peru enrolled their children in school at the appropriate age, despite the fact that elementary education is compulsory. The per-

centage of Quechua children attending school is undoubtedly even lower.

We selected three locations in Peru for our study of Quechua children and their families: the highlands, Lima, and the *selva* (rain forest) area of northeast Peru.

Highlands

In the highlands we chose the region of Andahuaylas, an area from which residents have migrated to both the city and the *selva*. Families have lived in Andahuaylas for many centuries, and they have maintained their traditional cultural values, the Quechua language, and their own style of dress. Because it has become increasingly difficult in recent years to make even a subsistence living, many families from this region have migrated to Independencia, one of the squatter settlements in Lima that we selected as our second research site.

Lima

Inhabitants of the *pueblos jóvenes*, the "new cities" of the squatter settlements, live under very difficult conditions. Neighborhoods are relatively stable near the roadways, but as one climbs the rocky hills of Independencia, the construction of the homes becomes more flimsy, the population becomes more transient, and living conditions become more primitive. Migrants to the city must adapt to the urban mestizo culture. This means that they must abandon Quechua and learn Spanish, and replace their traditional garments with Western clothing.

Selva

Hundreds of kilometers northeast of Cuzco is Lamas, a region of the *selva* to which descendants of a group of Chancas migrated from the highlands over 500 years ago after their defeat in a battle with the Incas. Chancas have not intermarried with mestizos or other Amazonian Indian groups. They are farmers, and, in this mestizo-dominated region, they have been forced to establish their plots of land for farming deep within the rain forests. This means that they must leave their villages during the week, returning only on weekends. Children typically remain in the villages, tended by their older siblings and a few village elders.

All of the Quechua are poor, but poverty is most severe in the *selva*. The modern world is immediately available to anyone who takes the bus from the squatter settlements to downtown Lima, but Quechua homes of the *selva* have no electricity, and few persons in Lamas have ever seen a television set or a motion picture. Children in the *selva* suffer from poor nutrition, for in the barter economy of the region the more desirable foodstuffs are exchanged for clothing and implements. Similarly, the poverty of the region has resulted in schools that are housed in small, crowded buildings often lacking a blackboard or sufficient desks for the students. In Lima, schools in the *pueblos jóvenes* may have broken windows and some classrooms may lack a roof, but the supplies and equipment are superior to those in Lamas. Andahuaylas stands between Lima and Lamas in the quality of the physical environment provided for children.

The children

We studied over a thousand children: 387 from Lima, 428 from Andahuaylas, and 336 from Lamas. There were 6- to 8-year-olds—"younger children"—who had not attended school or who were enrolled in first grade, and 9- to 12-year-olds—"older children"—who had not attended school or who were enrolled in first, second, or third grade. In each location, the two groups—nonschooled and enrolled in first grade—of younger children had approximately the same chronological age, as did the four groups—nonschooled and enrolled in first, second, or third grade—of older children.

We tested children from all of the schools we could find in each location. Our procedure for locating children who did not attend school was to send a person to the neighborhoods or villages. This scout sought out families with a child of the proper age and attempted to arrange for the child's participation in the study.

Practically no children refused to cooperate or wanted to leave once testing began. They had never participated in an experience like the one we provided. They were fascinated by the bright and interesting materials that had been constructed for the study, and they enjoyed interacting with an attentive and responsive adult. Their interest was also maintained by the trinkets and snacks given during the testing.

READING ACHIEVEMENT

We had to devise our own test of reading achievement. Although there was a movement about twenty years ago to introduce Quechua as the language of instruction in the highlands, none of the textbooks or teaching materials used in the schools we visited were in Quechua. Because the textbooks and reading instructions were in Spanish, the reading test was written in Spanish. We based our test on an analysis of the content of the textbooks used in Peruvian elementary schools, our own experience in Peru, and on discussions with Peruvian colleagues.

The test required children to read letters and words, to select pictures described by words, and to answer questions about what they had read. The words ranged from easy ones, such as *dos*, *sol*, and *día*, to more complex ones such as *maestro*, *hermano*, and *horizonte*. Our test of reading comprehension had two parts. In the first, the children were asked to read a word or words aloud and to select one of three pictures that best described what had been read. For example, an easy item included the word "girl" and three line drawings depicting a boy, a girl, and a knot. The most difficult item included the phrase "two people dancing while the children watch"; three drawings depicted adults dancing with children watching, adults dancing without children watching, and adults working while children watched. In a final part of the test, children read short paragraphs about which they later were asked several questions.

We found that the younger non-schooled children in Andahuaylas and Lamas were illiterate. They apparently had little opportunity either within or outside their homes to learn even a few letters of the alphabet. In Lima, the younger nonschooled children had learned a few letters and the older nonschooled children knew many letters and a few words. Only in Lima, therefore, had nonschooled children—even those as old as 12—acquired the fundamental components of reading.

Attending school had vastly different effects, depending upon where the children lived. Children who were enrolled in the first grade in Lamas and Andahuaylas showed very little benefit from their instruction. They were able to answer fewer than 15 percent of the questions asked on the test. Schooling had a much greater effect in Lima, where both younger and older first-graders were able to read and understand some of the words on the test.

The children's reading skill improved with increased attendance at school, but the increase was not equivalent in the three locations. Children in Andahuaylas were consistently one year behind the children in Lima in their reading skill, and children in Lamas were about two years behind. In other words, third-graders in Lamas and second-graders in Andahuaylas were reading little better than Lima first-graders.

The finding that very few of the nonschooled children were able to read reflects the fact that reading skill requires more than facility with the spoken language. In fact, whether or not the children were able to speak Spanish had no relation to their reading scores. If reading skill were strongly dependent upon the language spoken at home, the schooled children of Lamas, who speak Spanish at home, should have shown less difficulty in learning to read Spanish words than the children from the Quechua-speaking families of Andahuaylas. This was not the case.

In addition to the general environmental differences in the three locations, there were also indications that the home life of the children in the three locations differed greatly. We obtained information about the children's everyday home environments from interviews with the children's parents.

Most of the parents had little education. Fathers in Lima had attended school an average of 4.9 years; the average was 2.7 in Andahuaylas and 1.9 in Lamas. The corresponding values for the mothers were 2.2, 0.7, and 0.1 years, respectively. Thus it is doubtful that most parents provided their children with a highly literate environment at home.

A direct index of the stimulation offered by the home was based on a question in which we asked about what the parents had attempted to teach their children. We asked about 8 activities: numbers, colors, letters, money, the seasons, riddles, Spanish, and games. We also asked whether they read to their child and whether they told their child stories. The mean number of positive responses was 6.5 in Lima, 4.5 in Andahuaylas, and 5.5 in Lamas.

The quality of a home environment depends, in part, on the material wealth of the family, such as books or toys. We asked about 10 items of material wealth: electricity, radio, television, newspapers or magazines, books, machines, children's books, pictures, toys, and portraits. Each family was given a value between zero and 10, depending on how many of these items they possessed. According to this index, homes in Lima provided children with the greatest opportunities to encounter items that might be helpful to them in learning how to read, and the homes in Lamas, the fewest. The mean number of items in the Lima homes was 4.7; in Andahuaylas, 3.8; and in Lamas, 1.9.

Except for the data related to parental involvement in teaching, these data support the impression that children in Lamas experience a much more severely deprived environment than do children in Andahuaylas or Lima. Their remoteness from cultural activities that might help them in learning how to read, the lack of physical resources in the home, and the low levels of education of their parents were likely contributors to their poor reading skill.

FOLLOW-UP STUDY

Our experiences in Peru did not end with the completion of the original study. Nine years after the testing was completed, we decided to initiate a follow-up study to evaluate the ultimate educational outcomes for these three groups of Quechua children. We returned to Independencia, Andahuaylas, and Lamas and attempted to locate our original subjects. In view of the high mobility of these families, we were reasonably successful; we were able to interview and test approximately one-third of the subjects in each location: 141 in Lima, 165 in Andahuaylas, and 89 in Lamas.

There is always a worry in follow-up studies that the persons who can be located are not representative of the original sample. We were able to test this possibility by comparing the reading scores from the original testing of the subjects we were able to locate with those of the remainder of the original sample. The average score for the two groups differed by only 0.8 of a point. Parental educational level and quality of the home environment did not differ significantly between members of the follow-up sample and the remaining subjects.

We increased the difficulty of the reading test for the follow-up sample by adding more difficult words to the test and by increasing the length and complexity of the text material. The most difficult items on the test were ones that an average fifth-grader should be able to read and understand.

As might be expected, reading scores improved over the nine-year period that separated the original and follow-up testing. Scores for the three locations did not differ greatly from each other on the second testing; they ranged from 85 percent to 92 percent correct response to the original test items, and from 77 percent to 83 percent correct response to the items on the total test. There was no indication of a loss in literacy after leaving school, a finding in line with similar results reported by Wagner

and his colleagues for children in Morocco.[3]

The residents of Lamas made the greatest gains between the two testing periods. We believe that the large improvement reflects the remarkable changes during the past decade in the economy of the *selva*. The highly profitable cocaine trade is centered in the northeast section of Peru. Tobacco fields have been replaced by coca plants, and residents of Lamas have benefited from the flourishing business of processing of cocaine. The gain in the economic status of residents of Lamas is reflected in the increased attendance at school. The individuals we followed up in Lamas had attained an average of 5.3 years of education. This is a remarkable gain for Lamas, for the difference between the levels of education of the children and of their fathers was 3.4 years. The improvement in the economy of Lamas was also evident in the increased number of material possessions in the Lamas households. For example, in the original study, only 27 percent of the Lamas households possessed a radio; nine years later, 73 percent owned a radio. This percentage compares favorably with the 99 percent of the families in Lima and the 71 percent in Andahuaylas who owned a radio. Similarly, half of the families in Lamas visited in the follow-up study owned books, compared to 30 percent in Lima and 21 percent in Andahuaylas. The earlier deficiencies of the children of Lamas were

3. Daniel A. Wagner et al., "The Myth of Literacy Relapse: Literacy Retention among Moroccan Primary School Leavers," *International Journal of Educational Development*, 9:307-15 (1989).

lessened, therefore, by their greater opportunities to attend school and by marked improvements in their daily environments.

COMPARISONS WITH CHINESE, JAPANESE, AND AMERICAN CHILDREN

Shortly after we completed our first study in Peru, we began a study in Japan, Taiwan, and the United States that also included a test of reading ability. Regardless of the language being read, a reading test must include an evaluation of children's knowledge about the fundamental components of the written language and the children's comprehension of text. The test that we constructed for this later study was very similar to the one used in Peru. It contained sections that required the child to read letters of the alphabet in English (hiragana, in Japanese, and zhuyin fuhao, in Chinese) and words in English and characters in Chinese and Japanese. As in the Peruvian test, children were given words or short phrases that described the appropriate choice of one of three accompanying pictures.

The reading tests were given to 240 children randomly selected from 20 representative first-grade classrooms in each of three cities: Minneapolis, Minnesota; Sendai, Japan; and Taipei, Taiwan.

Differences between the reading skill of the first-graders in Peru and those in the three other locations were very great. Nearly every child in Taipei, Sendai, and Minneapolis knew all of the letters (hiragana, zhuyin fuhao); none of the three groups of Quechua children had learned even half of them (see Figure 1). Differences were equally dramatic for the portion of the test requiring the child to read words and to demonstrate comprehension of their meaning.

American and Asian children's scores for comprehension were higher than those for reading words. This may indicate that they were aided in reading by the presence of pictures depicting what was described in the word or phrase. For example, seeing a rainbow in one of the drawings may be of help in recognizing the word "rainbow." Quechua children apparently found these cues to be of little help.

We can suggest two hypotheses to account for these startling differences in children's achievement. The first suggests that environmental conditions, both at home and at school, facilitate learning how to read to a much greater extent in the three industrialized societies than in the Quechua societies. The second suggests that Quechua children simply may not have attained the level of cognitive development necessary to benefit readily from the kinds of opportunities they are provided.

The close interaction between environmental conditions and intellectual functioning makes it impossible to isolate the independent contribution of each. Nevertheless, it would be of interest to compare the cognitive functioning of young children in these diverse environments. Fortunately, information was available from the two sets of studies to make several comparisons possible.

In addition to the reading test, each Quechua child was given a bat-

FIGURE 1
DIFFERENCES IN READING SKILLS

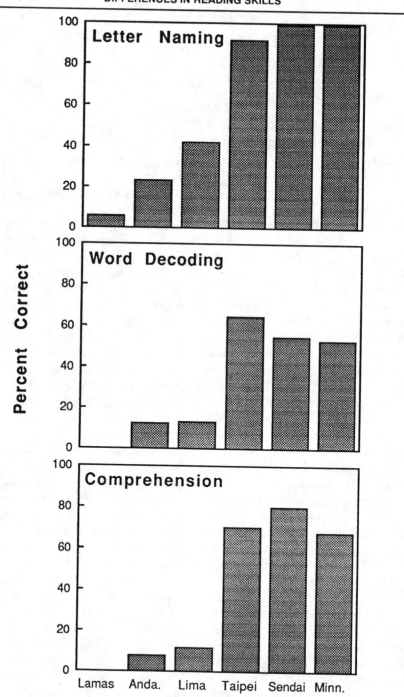

tery of cognitive tasks that contained tasks of the types typically found in tests of intelligence. Among these were tests of general information, story memory, and auditory memory. The general-information tests contained questions whose answers are not directly taught in school but are part of common knowledge. Easy items involved telling how many paws a dog has; more complicated ones required naming things a plant needs in order to grow and explaining why people cannot live under water. In the story-memory test, the children listened to a brief story and then were asked questions about its content. In the auditory-memory test, the children were asked to repeat a pattern of taps separated by short (S) and long (L) pauses. The patterns ranged from simple ones consisting of a sequence of two taps, such as SL, to much more complex ones, such as SSLSLSS.

Children were tested by examiners who were fluent in the child's preferred language, Quechua or Spanish. Over 75 percent of the children in Andahuaylas were tested in Quechua, and nearly every child in Lima was tested in Spanish. In Lamas, the language of testing depended on the child's status in regard to schooling; nearly all of the children who attended school were tested in Spanish, but approximately half of the children who did not attend school were tested in Quechua.

The results were surprising. Children of Andahuaylas and Lima demonstrated no deficiencies in cognitive functioning (see Figure 2). They generally obtained scores on the cognitive tasks that were equivalent to those of the Chinese, Japanese, and American children. Children in Lamas received somewhat lower scores than the other groups on general information and story memory, the two tasks requiring verbal response, but even on these tasks the departure of their scores from those of the Chinese, Japanese, and American children was much less dramatic than was the case for the reading scores. Children in Minneapolis received higher scores than the other groups on the two verbal tasks. We believe that the Minneapolis first-graders did well on these tasks because of the greater tendency of the American than of the Chinese and Japanese mothers to read to their young children, engage them in social conversation, and take them on excursions.[4] All of these activities are ones that would help the children develop verbal skills and build up a fund of general information.

There is little evidence, therefore, that the slower acquisition of reading skills by the first-graders in Peru was a consequence of deficits in intellectual functioning. Rather, it seems likely that the slowness with which they progressed in learning how to read was due to the inability of their parents and teachers to provide them with an environment conducive to learning how to read and with instruction that was comparable to that experienced by children in the industrialized societies of Japan, Taiwan, and the United States.

4. Harold W. Stevenson et al., "Contexts of Achievement: A Study of American, Chinese, and Japanese Children," *Monographs of the Society for Research in Child Development*, 55(1-2) serial no. 221 (1990).

FIGURE 2
DIFFERENCES IN COGNITIVE SKILLS

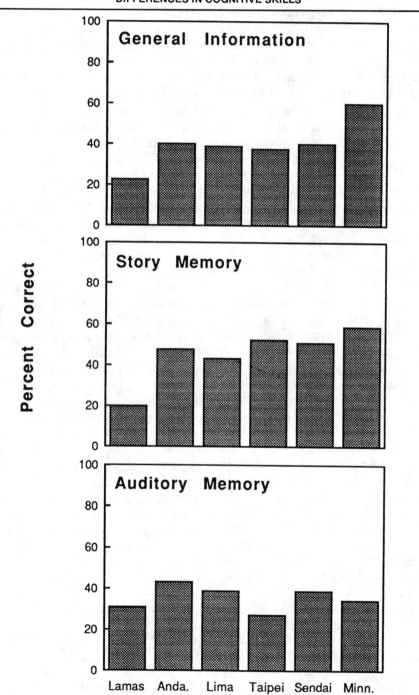

CONCLUSION

Literacy depends on education; it is not something that is readily acquired outside of school. Unlike the skill in mathematics demonstrated by many uneducated persons,[5] we have found little indication that children learn to read more than some of the alphabet and a few words when they are poor, live in families with low levels of education, and spend their days in disadvantaged environments.

Parents were correct in assuming that opportunities in the city for learning would be greater than in their native villages. Whether or not the children went to school, their reading ability benefited by the city environment. Even in the city's impoverished *pueblos jóvenes* it was possible to attract better teachers and to provide better conditions for learning than in the villages of the highlands or the *selva*. The worst conditions existed in the *selva*, where there were fewer opportunities in the home, in the everyday environment, and in school to encounter circumstances that would be helpful in gaining literacy.

Children in all three locations gained in their reading ability over the nine-year period between the original and final testing, but the most notable gains were made by the children in the *selva*. These children demonstrated that with an improved environment, presumably better teachers, and a longer time in school, they could attain reading scores equivalent to those of the children in the city. Results from the cognitive tests reinforced the assumption that the poor performance of children in the original testing was due to the situations in which the children lived, rather than to cognitive inadequacies.

Conditions in Peru are similar to those in many developing countries of the world: poverty, bilingualism, and an indigenous and an imposed culture. All of these factors have combined to make the recent decades among the most tumultuous since the time of the Spanish conquest. The large migration to the city has been motivated by the poor economic conditions in the highlands but also by the desire of parents to improve their children's opportunities for education.

To the degree that parents in the countryside are motivated to move to the city because of educational opportunities for their children, an improvement in schools in the countryside should stem such migration. It seems unlikely, however, that there will be advances in either urban or rural schools of developing countries without a strengthening of the economic conditions of these countries.

5. Carraher, Carraher, and Schliemann, "Mathematics in the Streets and in Schools."

Book Department

INTERNATIONAL RELATIONS AND POLITICS

BROWN, FREDERICK Z. *Second Chance: The United States and Indochina in the 1990s.* Pp. xvii, 163. New York: Council on Foreign Relations Press, 1989. $14.95.

LeBOUTILLIER, JOHN. *Vietnam Now: A Case for Normalizing Relations with Hanoi.* Pp. xix, 115. New York: Praeger, 1989. $18.95.

These two books appear just as the United States finds itself in transition in its Southeast Asian policy, moving from opposition and hostility to Vietnam and its client state in Cambodia to cautious groping toward a more accommodating position. In many ways, the steps advocated by John LeBoutillier and Frederick Brown are in the initial stages of being played out. That is, the United States has begun talking to the Vietnamese again and, at the time of this writing, has established a liaison office in Hanoi to facilitate the accounting of soldiers missing in action. Moreover, the United States has stated that it does not want the Khmer Rouge to return to power in Cambodia—a position shared by Vietnam. That both books were written before these steps toward rapprochement were begun demonstrates the prescience of the two authors.

The books have several similarities. One is that they are primarily volumes advocating a change in direction in American policy. Both agree that the United States should regain the initiative in Southeast Asia by normalizing relations with Vietnam and no longer allowing the Association of Southeast Asian Nations (ASEAN) to take the lead. Both say that not doing so cedes preponderant political influence there to the Soviet Union and, Brown would add, China, while economically Japan and ASEAN, LeBoutillier would say, would gain a march on us. They differ in that *Vietnam Now* is more narrowly focused on Vietnam while *Second Chance* looks more broadly at Southeast Asia and especially the Cambodian issue.

Brown's *Second Chance* delves into the history of the post-unification period, when the first chance for normalization occurred. After this failed and the United States sided with China and Vietnam sided with the Soviet Union, the players were seemingly frozen. Now, the time is right for another or second chance—hence the title of the book. Brown emphasizes the changes in Cambodia, specifically the International Conference on Cambodia in 1989 and the Vietnamese pledge to leave (at this writing, Vietnamese troops have indeed departed from Cambodia), as the key to this new opportunity. How to deal with the Khmer Rouge and a possible settlement in Cambodia occupy much of his attention. He brings to his analysis experience as a Foreign Service officer in Thailand and Vietnam and as a member of the staff of the Senate Foreign Relations Committee.

LeBoutillier clearly states his thesis at the outset: the United States should normalize relations with Vietnam unilaterally, without any quid pro quo. While Brown stresses changing Vietnamese policy in Cambodia, LeBoutillier's argument is based upon the assumption that Vietnam's new quasi-capitalist, pro-Western leadership, installed in 1986, is prepared to become independent of Moscow. Moreover, he argues, if the United States can utilize constructive engagement in South Africa, it can do the same for Vietnam. In many respects, this was the rationale for Richard Nixon's rapprochement with China in the early 1970s. Indeed, Nixon writes the introduction to the book. Like Nixon, LeBoutillier is a conservative, served in the United States House of Representatives, and asserts that the Soviet Union still represents the biggest threat to the United States. He is probably best known as the founder and president of Account for POW/MIAs, Inc.

One can question some of LeBoutillier's assertions. For example, he argues that the Soviets are pursuing expansionism throughout the Pacific. He further argues that Vietnam would offer us bases if we lost Clark and Subic in the Philippines. By claiming that Moscow pressured Vietnam to invade Cambodia in the late 1970s, he does not give the Vietnamese much credit for being able to decide things like that for themselves. In somewhat contradictory fashion, he argues at one point that Vietnam would not have invaded Cambodia had the United States recognized it, but, at another, he says that Vietnam had no choice but to invade. In addition, and quite naturally, given his position, he assumes that American prisoners of war are still being held in Vietnam. Finally, he takes a swipe at American foreign policy decision-making processes in charging that a small group within the National Security Council dominated our policymaking in Vietnam.

In the final analysis, Brown's *Second Chance* represents a more balanced and more comprehensive treatment than LeBoutillier's *Vietnam Now*, is somewhat less polemical in nature, and deals in detail with the Cambodian problem in a more satisfactory way.

WAYNE PATTERSON

St. Norbert College
De Pere
Wisconsin

[Editor's note: The preceding review was written in May 1991, before the breakup of the Soviet Union.]

MILLS, RICHARD M. *As Moscow Sees Us: American Politics and Society in the Soviet Mindset.* Pp. xi, 308. New York: Oxford University Press, 1990. No price.

TUCH, HANS N. *Communicating with the World: U.S. Public Diplomacy Overseas.* Pp. xvi, 224. New York: St. Martin's Press, 1990. $39.95.

The sole commonality of these two books is that their titles refer nominally to American international relations. Mills's is essentially a dense scholarly exercise in applied epistemology, combined with an interesting exploration of methodology and flavored with a bit of comparative politics. Tuch's is a relatively simple catalogue of the United States Information Agency (USIA), drawn from his 35 years of activity as a career officer with the agency and including some interesting anecdotes.

Mills is really concerned with how selected Soviet scholars describe and analyze politics, economics, and society in the United States, given the constraints imposed by historical communist ideology and authoritarian discipline. The link to the Soviet government—the question inferred by the title—is hardly demonstrated by his text: how the writers' work influences decision makers is never satisfactorily explained. Mills's bibliography suggests that he knows the views of other scholars, but he does not offer his own.

Mills makes it clear throughout that the Soviet mind-set—he is reluctant to use the term "ideology" too broadly—as applied largely by the writers themselves, has forced them to handle American facts with caution and some cant. He feels it requires rare intellectual and—implicitly—some physical courage for a Soviet writer to break new ground or to make use of the Western social science methods that Soviets have learned to remark since the 1950s. Whether this intellectual constraint is reinforced by official repression is not fully addressed. The point is reinforced by his references to Gorbachev's views circa late 1989 and their influence on Soviet writing.

The writers themselves are virtually dismembered by Mills's technique of topical discussion in chapters 2-4. Only in later chapters does Mills focus on the intellectual schools that have grown from the mind-set. From these he then ranks the writers within a typology of approaches to the study of the American system. The appearance of this latter material sooner in the book would tend to remedy the complexity and discontinuity of the early chapters. The work concludes

with two useful chapters, one of them presenting Mills's reconsideration of analysis and methodology.

Tuch served principally in Germany, with periods as public affairs officer in the Soviet Union and Brazil. His discussion of USIA's intent, charter, structure, and activity is annotated from heavily to lightly, with illustrations from these three countries.

"Public diplomacy" is an amorphous concept, a support for the more conventional diplomacy of the Department of State. Its purpose is to persuade "gatekeepers" of another country of the correctness and truthfulness of American policy goals and acts, while simultaneously persuading American decision makers of the characteristics and needs of that country so their words and acts can be better understood and accepted. USIA is thus charged with being the middleman in any exchange. How widely it casts its net within the other country is circumstantial; youths, as future leaders, may be as much a target as the head of government of the moment.

Two chapters are devoted to defining public diplomacy, and Jimmy Carter's 1978 directive to his USIA director is quoted at length to suggest what it should be. Professional USIA personnel must always be on guard against political hackery imposed by elected officials, and they can easily lose a skirmish. Although Tuch is a team player even in retirement, he leaves little doubt of his distress at these travails and the shallowness that caused them, from the era of Joe McCarthy through Lyndon Johnson and Ronald Reagan.

I was often dismayed by Tuch's work. On the whole, it is impersonal, and it is diffuse to the point of being uninformative. The uninformed reader is not likely to become more informed, despite exposure to much detail, for there is very little critical analysis of the application of principles. The reader who has seen some of USIA's work will be left with exasperation, for Tuch too often indulges in generalization, bureaucratic detail, or even jargon.

Tuch's anecdotes and many illustrations break new ground, as indeed they should, for they reflect reminiscences of a lifetime of hard work. But the discussion of the most deserving topic raised—if we accept the inferences of Tuch's treatment—namely, USIA's role during the German-American policy process of the 1980s, when intermediate-range nuclear weapon deployment was most debated, is not well organized and lacks conclusion. Some of the material offered, especially on Colombia and Brazil, is virtually a throwaway.

I cannot usefully compare these two books, for they are in entirely different conceptual arenas. The Mills work is interesting, if not distinguished, but his techniques make the work difficult to all but the most intent reader.

PHILIP B. TAYLOR, Jr.

Gualala
California

SMOLANSKY, OLES and B. SMOLANSKY. *The USSR and Iraq: The Soviet Quest for Influence.* Pp. xi, 346. Durham, NC: Duke University Press, 1991. $55.00. Paperbound, $24.95.

Based on scholarly analysis of Arab and Soviet sources, *The USSR and Iraq* examines Iraq's relations with the Soviet Union and others during the Cold War era of 1958-88. The focus is on Iraq and its relations with Moscow, not, as the title may suggest, the other way around. Drawing upon significant case studies and domestic and regional developments, the book examines the following historic events as they relate to Iraq's quest to

achieve political autonomy through economic independence: the nationalization of the Iraqi oil industry, the Kurdish question, the Iraqi Communist Party, the security of the Persian Gulf, and the Iran-Iraq war. Some readers may find the long-winded discourse on the dynamics of power politics in chapter 1 to be self-evident. At the same time, others may feel that certain dramatic regional events affecting Saddam Hussein's future behavior in the international arena could have received more attention; these include Israel's 1981 bombing of Iraq's nuclear reactor, its 1982 invasion of Lebanon, and the 1987 Palestinian *intifada*.

This meticulously researched and thoroughly documented work shows that during the Cold War, Iraq was neither Communist nor a client state of the USSR, as often believed in the West. Even as a superpower, there were limits to Moscow's influence over Iraq. At no time did Moscow succeed in imposing its will on Baghdad. This is made clear since, especially during the Cold War, the use of military force was not a viable option for either superpower. The Iraqi-Soviet relationship was based strictly on the promotion and preservation of their respective national interests and vital needs. Moscow extended support and provided the resources needed to enhance Iraq's interests mainly because they served to achieve Russia's own global ambitions. The Baath Party, on the other hand, was determined to assert its own leadership in the Persian Gulf and was adamant about proving that it had no intention of exchanging Western domination—in the form of colonialism and imperialism—for Soviet domination. Throughout this period, Saddam Hussein pursued an independent foreign policy, remaining defiant, haughty, obstinate, unpredictable, and, often, not a very reliable ally. His self-defeating, counterproductive, and daring policies were already evident at this early stage but did not appear to portend the magnitude of the doom that lay ahead for Iraq and its people.

Baghdad and Moscow cooperated only as long as their interests coincided. One such mutual interest throughout this period continued to be the undermining of the U.S. foothold and obstruction of Western interests in the region and particularly in Iraq. Each had its own agenda, but both agreed that nationalization of Iraq's oil industry and quelling the Kurdish rebellion were indispensable prerequisites to achieving this mutual objective. They did not always agree on the specific tactics to be employed to achieve the main goal. When interests clashed, there was a great strain in the relationship, at times almost to the breaking point, but it was never totally severed. Moscow and Baghdad continued to need each other for different reasons. Ironically, the help that Moscow extended to Iraq so that it could become more self-sufficient was a key factor that enabled Baghdad to progressively disregard its benefactor and to open up to the West. The most dramatic confrontations between the two countries were over Iraq's occupation of Kuwait in 1973—déjà vu!—Saddam's execution of Iraq's Communist Party members, his invasion of Iran, and the Soviet attack on Afghanistan.

Readers of this book who have recently emerged from the traumas or the excitement of the Persian Gulf war and may be searching for conclusive evidence of a would-be Hitler at work will be disappointed. This expert, dispassionate account of Iraq's trials and tribulations and its unflinching resolve to assert its political and economic preponderance contains nothing about sinister, dark forces looming over the horizon. Nor, to their dismay, will such readers detect any tangible evidence of potential psychopathic or intrinsic evil characteristics in Saddam Hussein's persona to presage the human tragedy of Desert Storm. There

are only the usual Arab hang-ups about having been "victimized" by Western colonialist "exploitation" and Saddam's subtle obsession with regaining dignity or saving face in order to redress those perceived wrongs of the past at all costs. This study, whether it intended to or not, puts the subsequent gulf war and its devastating aftermath into a clearer historical perspective.

SHAFIGA DAULET

University of Connecticut
Storrs

TAFT, JOHN. *American Power: The Rise and Decline of U.S. Globalism, 1918-1988.* Pp. xiv, 321. New York: Harper & Row, 1989. $22.50.

In the opening sentence of his preface, John Taft sets the theme of his book with clarity and succinctness. It is "to tell, partly by anecdote and partly by distillation, the story of America as a global power through the lives of its leading protagonists." His theme is the "positive world view," which he defines as " 'internationalist liberalism' " that guided the United States during the decades when it was at the zenith of its power. But his emphasis is less on an analysis of the American population's prevailing intellectual or cultural trends, though this is given due treatment, than on the role played by a series of individuals who inspired, guided, and shaped U.S. policy, while filling "not just a functional but a political and intellectual void." While he carefully weaves social and economic factors into his story, his account is very much in the tradition of the role of the individual in history. There are uniquely American elements here, for probably only under the U.S. political system, with the separation of executive from legislative and with the change of senior administration cadres with the advent of each new presidency, could there emerge the pattern in which key figures were drawn from nongovernmental ranks and installed in powerful positions. Probably, too, only in the United States during the decades from the end of World War I to the catastrophic end of the Vietnam war could such a galaxy of talent be drawn into government service from the ranks of an elite that was cultured and privileged, usually wealthy, and—and this is perhaps the unique feature—possessed of ideas and the enthusiasm to pursue them that at first glance would not seem to spring from their backgrounds.

Taft begins his story with an account of the "impatient purist," William Bullitt, the fervent admirer of Wilsonian internationalism, which found a bipartisan shrine in the Council on Foreign Relations; he ends with the conclusion that this movement had become by the 1970s "an empty intellectual shell, an overall confusion and reaction to defeat." In between, in a series of brilliant portraits, he sketches the rise of the United States' world role to its zenith in a brief period in the aftermath of World War II, when "a cadre . . . took charge at a critical moment" and effected "a great transformation of U.S. foreign policy," not abandoning Wilsonian goals but pursuing them "in a more dynamic way." Its subsequent decline with the Vietnam war, he argues, was "less important in and of itself than for its effects on U.S. policy worldwide." "Nothing fails like failure," he goes on, "and the failure in Vietnam undermined U.S. influence everywhere," tending to discourage moderation abroad, and at home beginning to "destroy internationalist liberalism" and to introduce into the United States what he terms "a new form of isolationism." Taft's book covers the period to 1988 and was published in 1989. Writing on the eve of the dramatic changes in Central and Eastern Europe, he remained skeptical about the outcome of Gorbachev's revolu-

tion. What he would make of the new burst of U.S. globalism as exemplified in the leadership role in checking Iraqi aggression in the Persian Gulf would be an interesting new epilogue to a second edition.

Taft's book is written in a clear, economical style. Over a large canvas he makes many succinct judgments. After 1968, he writes, isolationist liberals argued that "America should withdraw from the world not because of its superior virtue, but because of its unique wickedness." Under Ronald Reagan, "all positive zeal had gone over to Republicans, perhaps they were asserting their own brand of isolationism." Some of his judgments may not please everyone. There are also some questionable points: West Germany hardly achieved "full sovereignty" in 1955; Canadians and Australians may bridle at the suggestion that in early 1941 Great Britain was "the only power then at war with the Nazi Empire." There are no footnote references, but an extensive and thoughtful bibliographical essay reflects Taft's wide reading in the extensive literature as well as his many interviews. Many pages of illustrations add to the attractiveness of this fascinating volume.

ROBERT SPENCER

Trinity College
University of Toronto
Ontario
Canada

AFRICA, ASIA, AND LATIN AMERICA

FORSTER, KEITH. *Rebellion and Factionalism in a Chinese Province: Zhejiang, 1966-1976.* Pp. xiii, 338. Armonk, NY: M. E. Sharpe, 1990. $45.00.

After Keith Forster had taught in China for two long years, Hangzhou City authorities granted him access to local newspapers. So opened the door of the *Hangzhou Daily*, which is mostly unavailable overseas, and the way to our most important province-level case study of politics during the years 1966-76. Forster's reconstruction draws on careful perusal of the *Daily* and corroborating sources.

He cannot fill in all the blanks, but the portion of the Zhejiang story he is able to tell is extremely valuable. Coverage for the later half of the decade is fuller than for the earlier half, partly because informal mass faction publications as well as data on the social backgrounds of Cultural Revolution mass faction activists remain scarce for this province. Over half the book is devoted to 1972-76, when radicalism was renewed in Zhejiang Province after military intervention had put an end to the Cultural Revolution as such.

Forster matches his favored interpretations of individual Zhejiang developments against competing interpretations, mostly casual, found in the literature. This is a nice stylistic feature for readers, including me, who are not closely acquainted with local personalities and events. Zhejiang is a wealthy coastal province immediately south of Shanghai. Its leadership before the Cultural Revolution was stable under Jiang Hua, Party provincial secretary since 1954, who "built up a powerful network of loyal subordinates." Even Jiang's wife was head of the provincial Party's Political and Legal Group and president of the provincial Supreme Court. Powerful protectors at the center included 3rd Field Army senior cadres Tan Zhenlin and Tan Qilong.

On the ever-intriguing subject of center-province relations, Forster finds in the Zhejiang data more support for a "center-held" hypothesis—advanced by Fred Teiwes, Victor Falkenheim, and others—than for a "provinces-empowered" hypothesis, as advanced by Parris Chang, Harry Harding, and others. The differ-

ence is subtle and not well drawn, however, so Forster's argument is a bit forced.

Even less persuasive is a hypothesis that what in essence divided the two contending Cultural Revolution mass faction coalitions in Zhejiang, as nationwide, was "their assessment of the revolutionary credentials of leading cadres" at the center. This flies in the face of major studies by Hong Yung Lee and Stanley Rosen, neither of which are cited.

Forster's analyses of Chairman Mao's indirect interventions in local politics in the form of ambiguous ideological campaigns—such as campaigns to "criticize Lin Biao and Confucius" or to study "bourgeois rights"—are absorbing, the best in the literature.

GORDON BENNETT

University of Texas
Austin

MICHAEL, FRANZ et al. *China and the Crisis of Marxism-Leninism*. Pp. x, 214. Boulder, CO: Westview Press, 1990. $39.50. Paperbound, $18.95.

CHENG, CHU-YUAN. *Behind the Tiananmen Massacre: Social, Political, and Economic Ferment in China*. Pp. xii, 256. Boulder CO: Westview Press, 1990. $29.95.

Conservative critics have long held that the People's Republic of China (PRC) suffers from a tragically inefficient economy and a brutally repressive polity. The two books under review here elaborate on these themes, although they represent different variants of the conservative critique.

China and the Crisis of Marxism-Leninism includes essays by Franz Michael, Carl Linden, Jan Prybyla, and Jurgen Domes. The central focus of the volume is economic and political reform in post-Mao China. Methodologically, the authors proceed deductively, presenting the PRC as a specific manifestation of the general phenomenon of Marxism-Leninism. From this perspective, reform in China is seen as impossible. The fundamental contradictions of a Leninist system cannot be overcome by piecemeal change; the system must be wholly transformed or tenuously continue its wasteful and cruel existence, careening from one crisis to the next.

Although this point is well taken, the chapters on politics and ideology fail to develop the argument persuasively. These essays lack the rigorous analytic framework that their deductive aspiration requires. Marxism-Leninism is described in rather simplistic terms reminiscent of the literature on totalitarianism from the 1950s. The authors do not draw upon more recent and sophisticated analyses of the complex structural dynamics of Leninism found in the work of, among others, Kenneth Jowitt, Andrew Walder, and Barrett McCormick. As a result, the failings of Chinese communism are asserted with little added by way of explanation.

Jan Prybyla's three chapters on economic reform do not suffer from this shortcoming. He eloquently links China's political-economic conundrum to similar, albeit not analogous, experiences in other state socialist countries. His argument draws on extensive reading of Eastern European and Soviet sources, building upon the work of Janos Kornai and others. Key components of PRC domestic economic reform are analyzed with careful attention to Chinese material. Unfortunately, foreign economic policy, the "open door," is virtually ignored. Beyond this omission, Prybyla offers a good systematic critique. His critical eye is somewhat dulled, however, by an economist's abiding faith in neoclassical principles.

Chu-yuan Cheng, also an economist, takes a different analytic tack. He, too, is concerned with the prospects for politi-cal-economic reform in the PRC, but he places the 1989 democracy movement at the center of his book, *Behind the Tiananmen Massacre: Social, Political, and Economic Ferment in China*. His approach differs markedly from the aforementioned volume. Although Cheng states that he is more interested in explanation than description, in fact he moves toward the former by means of the latter, a thick description of sorts. This is a detailed book, seeking a comprehensive account of the many facets of the dramatic events of the 1989 Beijing spring. In a sense, it is an introduction to post-Mao China as seen through the lens of the contemporary crisis.

The first five chapters—which cover economic, political, social, intellectual, and military questions—are most helpful. Cheng demonstrates a wide-ranging knowledge of Chinese affairs. He touches on important questions of economic reform, including the open-door policy, and provides telling bits of insight. Many analysts mention inflation as a background cause of the 1989 demonstrations; Cheng disaggregates the numbers to show the especially large increases in food prices, a politically volatile issue. Although his political analysis suffers from an overly simplistic characterization of factional struggles, Cheng rightly emphasizes the power of the gerontocracy and the prevalence of nepotism. He also provides good overviews on the role of intellectuals and the military in politics. All these chapters are well grounded in Chinese, Hong Kong, and Western sources. In short, the first half of the book does a fine job of describing the context of the 1989 movement.

The last three chapters, which recount the specific events of the democracy movement and its aftermath, are somewhat less successful. This is due, in part, to the passage of time and the appearance of more and better information on the movement, its participants, and its effects. Cheng includes three appendices: a chronology of the key events of 1989 leading up to and immediately following the Beijing massacre; a very useful profile of fifty major figures; and four documents, including the *People's Daily* editorial of 26 April that became a major issue in its own right.

In comparing the two books, it seems that Cheng's historical specificity has produced the better analysis. This is not to say that theory is of no importance to Cheng or to the study of contemporary China. Rather, it may imply a warning to theorists: insufficient grounding in historical circumstance may undermine even the most elegant deductive schemes.

GEORGE T. CRANE

Williams College
Williamstown
Massachusetts

EUROPE

CANNADINE, DAVID. *The Decline and Fall of the British Aristocracy*. Pp. xiv, 813. New Haven, CT: Yale University Press, 1990. $35.00.

No European landed elite held onto wealth, power, and status so tenaciously as did the British, enjoying an unchallenged superiority as late as 1880; no landed elite unraveled so quickly thereafter. It is the latter part of this British singularity that David Cannadine dissects in his long, handsome, sometimes aggravating, stimulating but repetitive, anecdote-packed book. It would have been a better book if Cannadine had connected better the reasons for the landowning classes' durability—on which he himself has written convincingly in the past—to the facts of their downfall.

The British aristocracy hung on so long because it was brilliantly successful at turning to its own purposes the capitalist ethic of its bourgeoisie and even the libertarian traditions of its people. Thus it was an entrepreneurial landlord class that paved the capitalist road in the eighteenth century by developing a high-productivity, labor- and capital-mobile agricultural sector, and it was an almost exclusively landed political elite that ushered in the free-trade, laissez-faire state in the nineteenth century. In return, the landed classes maintained their economic edge over even the most successful merchants and industrialists and were left in relatively uncontested control of the political apparatus. This durable elite remained superior and distinct, yet not apart from society; indeed, there was far more cultural and social overlap between landed and nonlanded elites in Britain than in other countries in the nineteenth century.

But even the highest-tech agriculture could not compete with the economies of scale available on the American plains, and the agricultural depression that swept Europe from the 1870s toppled the British aristocracy from its economic roost. At the same time, another wave of urbanization and industrialization stirred up democratic and social-democratic sentiments that threatened to overwhelm even the middle classes, who tried to respond by directing that hostility against the aristocracy. These dual economic and political blows—nicely explicated by Cannadine in the best, opening chapters of the book—quickly deprived the aristocracy of the superiority on which its distinctiveness had been based. Within a generation—certainly by the end of World War I—the aristocracy had been pushed out of high politics, its fortunes cut down to human size, and its internal cohesiveness fatally weakened.

But precisely because these aristocrats had not been easily distinguishable from their bourgeois brethren in many other ways—they shared schools, universities, faiths, values, investments other than land—many were able to melt quietly and profitably into a compound elite, or establishment. Britain never experienced the violent anti-aristocratic revulsion led by revolutionary and republican movements on the Continent. In consequence, historians and sociologists still debate furiously how much of contemporary British culture is an aristocratic leftover, a debate the French or Germans seem mercifully to have been spared.

This is not the story that David Cannadine has chosen to tell, and he has mostly opted out of that debate. Instead he tends to focus on aristocrats who did not adapt well, who imagined under pressure that they were Junkers or czarist courtiers, who circled the wagons instead of scattering peaceably. Their contortions and rebellions make for interesting reading, and they help Cannadine extend his narrative. Every chapter finds some shadow of an "aristocratic resurgence" or fighting back—in the trenches of World War I, in the Conservative government of the early 1920s, in the colonies, in the military leadership in World War II, in the administrations of Churchill or Eden or Douglas-Home, in the contemporary vogue for English country houses—but each is dispatched in turn as a figment or a fantasy. The aristocracy keeps declining. Cannadine's story is entertaining and in many ways comforting: hubris is punished, the proud peers end up as bus conductors and pornographers. But doubts remain. What happened to all that money, that adaptability, that cultural capital? Did many other aristocrats not disappear safely into the woodwork? What imprint on culture and politics have they left? Finally, doubts are not dispelled by a text marred by too many errors, substantive as well as typographical, despite the beautiful physical presentation, for which full credit goes to both author and press.

PETER MANDLER

Princeton University
New Jersey

NADEAU, REMI. *Stalin, Churchill, and Roosevelt Divide Europe.* Pp. vii, 259. New York: Praeger, 1990. $45.00.

Remi Nadeau states that his purpose is to answer the questions of why and how Europe was divided between the Eastern and Western blocs. He is clearly successful in narrating the history of the war as it pertains to Eastern Europe. The chapters on Polish affairs and Czechoslovakia and appeasements of Eduard Beneš are excellent. We learn about the massacre of Polish officers in Katyn and the promises of the Allies to Stalin about the second front in order to prevent a separate peace between Stalin and Hitler.

Stalin and Churchill were fighting the war as well as thinking about the future of postwar Europe; however, Roosevelt was only thinking about winning the war. Churchill and Eden tried to block the Soviet Union's takeover of Eastern Europe through diplomatic bargaining and military preemption, but Roosevelt failed to understand Stalin's intentions and did not support the British positions. Nadeau blames Roosevelt's shortcomings on his innocence and naïveté. He speculates about the likely outcome of postwar Europe if the Allies had followed what Churchill, who is his hero, wanted to do.

As to the question of why Europe was divided, Stalin's quotation is the best answer. Nadeau quotes Stalin telling Yugoslav official Milovan Djilas, "Everyone imposes his own system as far as his army can reach." Nadeau points out that President Roosevelt, General Marshall, General Eisenhower, and other American officials did not want to confront the Russians for their violations of the Yalta agreement, thereby antagonizing them, because the Americans were anxious to have Russia join the war in the Pacific. This is the reason that Eisenhower did not take Berlin or Prague despite Churchill's pleas. Nadeau then dismisses American worries on the grounds that the

United States had the atomic bomb at the time; therefore, he feels, the United States did not need the Soviets. It would have been naive, however, to rely on a new bomb that was not battle tested. Technological mishaps occur, and the space shuttle *Challenger* is an example.

One can also speculate that the reason Roosevelt seemed to be indifferent to the plight of the East Europeans was that while Churchill was lamenting the loss of Europe to Stalin, the British statesman had no intention of dismantling the British or French colonies all over the world. Roosevelt probably thought, Why not let Uncle Joe have his own empire? This is not naïveté but realism.

A. REZA VAHABZADEH

University of Pennsylvania
Philadelphia

WCISLO, FRANCIS WILLIAM. *Reforming Rural Russia: State, Local Society, and National Politics, 1855-1914.* Pp. xviii, 347. Princeton, NJ: Princeton University Press, 1990. $45.00.

In 1861, the czarist government abolished serfdom, thereby committing itself to a process of modernization. Yet the power of Russia's traditional government rested on traditional classes—nobles and peasants. How could it modernize Russian society without simultaneously destroying its own power? Such puzzles are not of interest just to historians of Russia, of course; they lie behind the whole issue of modernization.

Francis William Wcislo's book explores the attempts of government bureaucrats to reform local government without undermining governmental authority in the years between 1861 and 1914. So what went wrong? Wcislo's carefully researched, and well-organized account concentrates on the problem of bureaucratic "mentalités," that is to say, the attitudes and ideas that bureaucrats brought to the problem of reform. The book belongs, in other words, to the genre of bureaucratic history, which has been taken up enthusiastically by historians of Russia over the last decade or two.

Wcislo finds two distinct traditions among reforming officials: a "generalist" tradition, committed to some form of modernization and willing to incorporate the peasantry within civil society, and a "particularist" tradition, concerned with social order and convinced that the peasantry were not yet ready to participate on equal terms in the work of local government. The distinction is a helpful one, but what struck me was how little even the generalists were prepared, or able, to concede on the broader issue of local participation in decision making. Even the most perceptive of them, such as Sergei Witte, thought of local reform as a way of "co-opting" the support of sections of local society; real devolution of power seems not to have been on anyone's agenda. That is one explanation for the failure of the czarist government to build a viable modern system of local government. The other is that reformers faced the hostility of officials and nobles from the even more conservative particularist tradition, which advocated the defense of autocracy and the traditional estate structure. Wcislo helps us to see such problems from the point of view of his reforming bureaucrats. But what the book shows is the superficiality of even the most intelligent and progressive official analyses of the problems faced by the czarist government, and that makes me wonder how much an analysis of official ideas can really tell us about the deeper problems faced by the czarist government in this period. Still, this volume remains a thorough and well-written contribution to the history of the Russian government and its responses to the profound problems it faced in the half century before 1917.

DAVID CHRISTIAN

Macquarie University
Sydney
New South Wales
Australia

WEBER, EUGEN. *My France: Politics, Culture, Myth.* Pp. 412. Cambridge, MA: Harvard University Press, Belknap Press, 1991. $24.95.

The 15 essays and autobiographical foreword that constitute *My France* represent the unique and important work of Eugen Weber, one of this nation's best French and European cultural historians. Characterized by an incisive and taunting style, this collection of essays on politics, culture, and myth reveals the major themes of Weber's career as a historian.

In essays on the temperaments of Left and Right, national socialism, anti-Semitism, and revolution and counterrevolution, Weber differentiates the French Right as he did in his first book, *The Nationalist Revival* (1959), and subsequent volumes on the Action Française, varieties of fascism, and Maurice Barrès. In the essays, Weber provocatively reiterates his description of communism and fascism as *frères ennemis*, arguing irreverently that not only does fascism have close relatives on the left, but fascism itself is the fruit of the marriage of nationalism and socialism. The marriage between the two largest ideological houses of the late nineteenth and twentieth century, in Weber's opinion, was consecrated by the powerful central state.

Several of the essays in *My France* testify to the frontier that Weber crossed in his move from being a historian of political culture to a historian of culture:

"Nos ancêtres les gaulois"; "In Search of the Hexagon," the hexagon being a recent and fashionable geographic expression for France; "Who Sang the Marseillaise?"; and "Pierre de Coubertin and the Introduction of Organized Sport." These essays fit Weber's general notion that contemporary men and women and the groups that define and represent them increasingly live by ideas alone. These ideas are often half-baked, usually badly served, and seldom well digested.

Nowhere does Weber see the recent and multifaceted making of the modern person more clearly than in the French countryside, in that world that was not Paris. In tune with much contemporary French historiography, Weber finds *la France profonde* ("the France of its provinces") a world far richer and more diverse than was ever acknowledged by high culture or Parisian style. Indeed, the thesis that colors many of these essays and shaped Weber's most important work, *Peasants into Frenchmen*, is that transformation of France's peasants and countryside only occurred irreversibly and overwhelmingly in the second half of the nineteenth century. For peasants to be made into Frenchmen, a whole range of modern economic and government institutions, economic interests and possibilities, and, finally, ideas and sensibilities had to converge in one vast historical transformation. Different facets of this transformation—also partially on display in his recent *Fin de Siècle*—are examined in his fine essays "What is Real in Folk Tales?" and "Religion or Superstition?"

It is in the provinces where Weber found a vantage point on modern history. The diversity and heterogeneity of lives, classes, and ways that shaped France at the turn of the century helped explain the rich and varied forms of life that marked the Romania of his childhood in the 1920s and 1930s. In the provinces, where *systèmes*—theories and abstractions— become men, rather than in Paris, where men become *systèmes*, Weber distinctly grasped the economic, political, ideological, and cultural forces that transformed localities into nations, traditions into folkways, and peasants into citizens. It is in the countryside of the recent past, where Weber, while no sentimentalist for the old order, takes full critical measure of the radical and overwhelming forces that made France a modern nation of citizens and consumers.

As these essays show, France is Weber's workshop. In France, Weber satisfies his boundless curiosity, exercises his passion to find a human explanation for all human things, and plies his trade of pricking the bubbles of the presumptuous. In his essay "About Marc Bloch," Weber contends that the historian must assemble the whole out of its parts—piece by piece, detail by detail, anecdote by anecdote. His pointillism gives precedence to the particular over the general. Weber does not conclude, however, that historians can do without narrative. As bold as Weber is, he does not offer an answer to the question of how these two modes of history can be integrated.

These humane and witty essays are a useful guide for critical thinking about the making of the modern and the contemporary worlds. They are a fine guide to the thinking of one of the better historians of modern France and Europe of the last century and a half.

JOSEPH AMATO

Southwest State University
Marshall
Minnesota

UNITED STATES

CURRIE, DAVID P. *The Constitution in the Supreme Court: The Second Century, 1888-1986.* Pp. xiv, 668. Chicago: University of Chicago Press, 1990. $70.00.

This is David Currie's second volume of a pair of books that encompasses two centuries of decision making on the U.S. Constitution by the Supreme Court. This hugely ambitious work is performed with penetrating insight, balanced evaluation, and graceful expression. It is a challenging book to study because it traverses complicated legal terrain marked by arcane potholes of legal piquancy along with outcroppings of enduring judicial principle. Currie's mastery of that terrain is evident throughout this volume.

The simple organizing principle for this work is to take the eras of the Court, numbering eight in the second century of the Republic, chief justice by chief justice. Part one covers Chief Justice Melville W. Fuller (1888-1910) and the last covers the term of Warren E. Burger (1969-86). For each era, Currie specifies substantive themes that evoke numerous cases and consequential interpretations of law and constitutional meaning. At the turn of the century, the Court's task was to find a balance between the role of government and the rights of firms in an interstate marketplace. Prominent during the Hughes era of the 1930s were the reining in of private economic interests and an increasingly generous interpretation of authority by the federal government while protecting dissident societal voices. The Warren Court is noted for promoting equality, whereas the diverse themes of the Burger Court substantively filled out the meaning of that equality without substantially expanding or reversing it.

Currie characterizes himself as an analyst and critic of the Court "from a lawyer's point of view," in particular as one who thinks that "the Constitution is, as it says, the law of the land, which binds the judges no less than the other officials whose actions they review." His judgments about people and cases are pointed. For example, of Holmes's opinions he says, "Yet for all their stylistic appeal, the constitutional opinions of Holmes' first years are not substantively very satisfying. He was adept enough in putting forth interesting ideas, . . . but he tended to advance them essentially as unsupported conclusions." Of William O. Douglas he says, "Owing in substantial part to his offhand approach to opinion writing, Douglas left behind surprisingly few memorable statements for the Court. . . . His most famous effort . . . *Griswold v. Connecticut* . . . comes across as one of the most hypocritical opinions in the history of the Court." Of *Roe* v. *Wade* he observes, "By all rights the case ought never to have been decided." It was moot on the grounds that when the case reached the Court, Jane Roe was no longer pregnant.

A copiously documented book, it is oblivious to empirical analyses of the Court. Currie takes little cognizance of political jurisprudence and draws upon no behavioral analyses of judicial decision making. He seeks to keep his subjectivity within the bounds of legal logic. He concludes with legal realism, "The key to both the effectiveness of judicial review and control of judges may lie in the fact that the Court's only power is the power to persuade."

The scope and bite of Currie's scholarship adds luster to the outstanding list of legal and constitutional treatises published by the University of Chicago Press.

JACK R. VAN DER SLIK
Sangamon State University
Springfield
Illinois

FABIAN, ANN. *Card Sharps, Dream Books, and Bucket Shops: Gambling in 19th-Century America.* Pp. xi, 250. Ithaca, NY: Cornell University Press, 1990. $24.95.

Americans have always suffered considerable moral confusion about gambling. Today, many people regularly purchase lottery tickets, travel to casinos, and bet on sporting events, even though our society remains somewhat uneasy about these activities. During the eighteenth century, lotteries were popular means to finance public projects, and the slave-owning aristocracy frequently engaged in high-stakes wagering as a way to signify and to solidify their social and economic power. Still, gaming in the eighteenth century was not without its critics.

Ann Fabian identifies the nineteenth century as a crucial period when gambling grew especially "morally troublesome" and when most games of chance eventually were made illegal. Her book succeeds admirably in its purpose: "to follow a history of gambling through the language of those who opposed it, through the actions of those who continued to gamble, and through the metaphors of those who used gambling to comment" about "the new commercial economy." Fabian uses gambling primarily as a window into nineteenth-century economic thinking. Her major argument is that as most Americans came to accept the tenets of capitalism, they redefined gambling as an illogical, selfish practice that transgressed the principles of economic rationality to which the society was becoming increasingly devoted. Most middle-class "reformers" thus accused African Americans and the working class of squandering their money on such games as policy —an early form of the numbers—rather than saving and investing their funds. Not coincidentally, members of the dominant culture frequently condemned gambling at the same time that they condoned "legitimate" speculation in stocks, land, and agricultural commodities.

Fabian's intellectual approach and her decisions both to focus on gambling as a "negative analogue" that helped clarify economic thinking and to rely primarily on the texts of reformers are justifiable. But the effect is to miss much about what gaming might tell us about the subculture of gamblers themselves. Policy players, for example, are presented in an antiseptic fashion: they "carried on a logical revolt against the rampant rationality of nineteenth-century business civilization." While this is a valid and important observation, one wonders how many gamblers actually conceived of their behavior in that fashion. The nitty-gritty world of blacks, immigrants, and working people who often placed bets is left largely unexplored. Still, as Fabian indicates at the outset, her study grew in part from her "perverse reaction" to the categories of social history.

Ann Fabian has written an important and very worthwhile book that uses gambling to examine the evolution of the economic imagination of the dominant culture during the nineteenth century.

BILLY G. SMITH

Montana State University
Bozeman

FOWLER, LINDA C. and ROBERT D. McCLURE. *Political Ambition: Who Decides to Run for Congress.* Pp. xiii, 247. New Haven, CT: Yale University Press, 1990. $27.95. Paperbound, $12.95.

SCHMUHL, ROBERT. *Statecraft and Stagecraft.* Pp. ix, 113. Notre Dame, IN: Notre Dame University Press, 1990. $18.95.

What behind-the-scenes maneuverings take place when a longtime incumbent congressman announces his intention to retire? This is the story Fowler and McClure tell in their meticulously documented study of the battle to succeed New York Congressman Barber Conable in 1984 and 1986. They offer a first-rate microlevel complement to the many macro-analyses of congressional elections as they tell the story of the maneuverings that take place among candidates in one New York congressional district on the occasion of an open seat. Their study is potentially useful not just to students of Congress but also to those interested more generally in elite political behavior and decision making. They tell of opportunities seen by aspirants and those that remained unseen. They tell of realities recognized and those that went unrecognized. They tell of opportunities seized and those ignored. Theirs is the kind of study that serves as a building block upon which other studies can be based.

The authors explain, as have others before them, that political ambition is framed by several factors, including personal costs—to family life or business or both—the financial burden of mounting a successful campaign, and the risk of losing a current elected position. But Fowler and McClure add two additional factors that have traditionally been accorded less recognition: the level of accurate information about the prevailing political environment and the gender of the prospective candidate. Regarding the latter, a potentially strong woman candidate, Democrat Louise Slaughter, hesitated to make the race at a crucial time, thus initially yielding the field to a single-mindedly ambitious—and ultimately successful—candidate, Fred Eckert. Slaughter eventually overcame her hesitation, but only after bypassing the opportunity to seek an open seat in 1984 did she make a bid for the position, unseating Eckert in 1986. To the extent that Slaughter's behavior is indicative of that of women generally, it points to a significant problem in increasing the number of women officeholders at the state and national levels. Certainly women who hesitate and thus miss an opportunity to seek an open seat will have a much more difficult time if they later attempt to unseat an incumbent.

Those who approach Schmuhl's *State-craft and Stagecraft* looking for new information or insights into contemporary American politics and society will undoubtedly come away disappointed. There is, in fact, relatively little new here for those who have closely followed national politics in newspapers and newsmagazines and who have closely observed the media at work, nor will researchers find the kernels of empirically testable hypotheses or revelations derived from new data on the national political scene.

On the other hand, approached from a multidisciplinary perspective, this book offers a brief and accurate portrayal of how and why politicians and the media interact in the process of governing and selecting leaders. The book is filled with accounts of events and anecdotes that trace the interplay of agents of the media and politicians in recent decades. Its brevity makes it thoroughly appropriate as a text for an undergraduate American studies class or perhaps an introductory American government class. The writing is clear and cohesive and the content should not overburden an average undergraduate student. The message should come through loud and clear from this little book that the mass media play a critical role in the political life of Americans today and the better we understand and recognize that role, the more secure we are in our democracy.

TIMOTHY BLEDSOE

Wayne State University
Detroit
Michigan

JOHNSON, HAYNES. *Sleepwalking through History: America in the Reagan Years.* Pp. 524. New York: Norton, 1991. $24.95.

During the decade of the 1980s, Haynes Johnson, one of America's most respected political journalists, was a close and increasingly concerned observer of the American scene, and of the president who dominated the nation's politics and to a large extent its political and social directions for most of the decade. His verdict, on the whole, is a negative one. "It was," he writes in the prologue of this fascinating book, "an age of illusions when America lived on borrowed time and squandered opportunities to put its house in order, . . . a decade that will extract a heavy price from Americans unborn."

The general theme of this volume is the weakening of America and of the American dream. The decade was "a new era of greed," of the lowering of standards in public and private life, of "cynicism and disaffection." Presiding over the nation for most of the decade was "the most conservative administration of the century"—at least once it is called the most "reactionary"—headed by one of the most popular presidents in American history, if the polls and other evidences of popular reactions can be taken at face value.

Johnson, usually an objective reporter, is surprisingly critical of Ronald Reagan. He believes that Reagan's high rating in popular esteem was due more to successful image making than to substantive achievements. "In the myths of the eighties he was the greatest mythmaker of all." He "took a hands-off approach to government. . . . he preferred to reign rather than rule. . . . His was a grandee approach, distant from the daily process of governance. . . . His was a lax and largely inattentive presidency. . . . it was not a generous-spirit presidency. . . . No president since Harding had set so low a standard for public behavior."

And yet, Johnson admits, Ronald Reagan was "a consequential president.

. . . He was among the few who truly altered the condition of the country and affected the way people thought about it. . . . He was a strong president." His irrepressible optimism and positive messages —even his "ebullient brand of no-problems presidential leadership"—gave Americans new pride and confidence. He had a unique ability "to show Americans what they wanted to see." He made them feel good again, even as the nation was declining in so many obvious and less obvious ways. "It was morning again in America."

Most informed Americans will be generally familiar with the highlights of the decade of the 1980s, but all Americans, and many in other countries, may welcome such an interesting and detailed retelling of the major developments of this important decade and especially the analyses of a brilliant observer. Especially interesting are the six chapters on the Iran-contra affair and those on the televangelists, the Wall Street insiders— featuring Ivan Boesky and Michael Milken—the 1988 presidential campaign and election, and the many ethical misconduct cases and scandals that "stained the Reagan record."

For a broader spectrum of views on the Reagan years, one should consult other informed and encyclopedic commentaries, such as Kevin Phillips's *Politics of Rich and Poor: Wealth and the American Electorate in the Reagan Aftermath* (New York: Random House, 1990), which is perhaps more profound, and Lou Cannon's *President Reagan: The Role of a Lifetime* (New York: Simon & Schuster, 1991), which is much more favorable to Reagan. But Johnson's book is perhaps the most readable of any that have yet been written on the subject and will probably be the most widely read.

It should be remembered that in his view the American people, as well as Ronald Reagan, were "sleepwalking

through history" in the 1980s. "All were responsible."

NORMAN D. PALMER

University of Pennsylvania
Philadelphia

NYE, DAVID E. *Electrifying America: Social Meanings of a New Technology.* Pp. xv, 479. Cambridge: MIT Press, 1990. $29.95.

Once upon a time, a history of electrification in the United States would have focused on great inventors, notably Thomas Alva Edison, and great inventions, such as the light bulb. More recently, however, historians of technology have complicated the story by stressing that the crucial electrical inventions were systems, not devices. According to Thomas Parke Hughes, for example, Edison's primary invention was not the incandescent bulb but an integrated system for producing, distributing, and marketing electricity.

David Nye represents a younger generation of historians who have complicated the narrative even further by emphasizing that these systems include social and cultural elements as well as technological ones. "A technology . . . is part of a social world," Nye writes, ". . . an extension of human lives." Or, to use the now-favored terminology, all technologies are socially constructed. Indeed, one of the primary values of *Electrifying America* is the way it summarizes and synthesizes recent scholarship in the history of technology.

Nye's emphasis on the social and cultural dimensions of technological change is evident in the organization of the book. In his first chapter, he introduces not a great inventor but a sort of collective hero —the good people of Muncie, Indiana, whose hometown was studied as "Middle-town" in the 1920s by sociologists Robert and Helen Lynd. Nye gives an overview of the choices made by Muncie citizens as each type of electrification was introduced, beginning with lighting in 1885 and ending with the extension of power lines to surrounding rural areas in the mid-1930s.

Most of the subsequent chapters are organized around the primary social functions that electricity assumed in American life between about 1880 and 1940: outdoor illumination, both for practical street lighting and for more spectacular purposes, such as fairs, advertising, and the like; urban and interurban transportation; factory production; domestic lighting, heating, and cooking; and agricultural production. In all these chapters, Nye stresses the imaginative as well as the utilitarian dimensions of electrification. Two other chapters examine the ideology of electricity, particularly its role as an emblem of modernity.

The main limitation of this book is precisely its ambition. Because Nye is telling such a complicated story—the emergence of multiple electrical systems, each of which is at once social, cultural, and technological—he is bound to displease those who want more detailed treatment of any one element in the narrative. For example, more traditional historians of technology will complain about lack of attention to the hardware. Other historians, more sympathetic to Nye's contextual approach, may wish for more cultural background. For instance, Nye does not always make it clear why he has chosen particular works of art for discussion or how the examples he chooses from high art relate to his examples drawn from popular culture.

But it is the fate of the generalist to hear such complaints from specialists. *Electrifying America* furnishes a splendid overview of a crucial episode in the history of technology. Even more important, this book demonstrates that the history of technology can no longer be regarded as an optional, specialized subdiscipline. By claiming as its domain the study of systems at once technological, social, and cultural, the history of technology has become an integral and necessary part of any American history.

ROSALIND WILLIAMS

Massachusetts Institute
   of Technology
Cambridge

OLSON, WALTER K. *The Litigation Explosion: What Happened When America Unleashed the Lawsuit.* Pp. 388. New York: Penguin Books, 1991. No price.

In order to appreciate Walter Olson's book fully, statistical glimpses at the number and types of cases handled in the court system are helpful. Statistical glimpses are scattered throughout Olson's book. Objective data from another source, the 1988 report of the Conference of State Court Administrators and the National Center for State Courts, confirm the fact that his title is not lightly tossed out merely to sell books. According to this independent report,

More than 98 million new cases were filed in state courts during 1988. Mandatory appeals and discretionary petitions to state appellate courts account for 221,000 cases. The remainder are trial court findings: 16.9 million civil cases, 11.9 million criminal cases, 1.4 million juvenile cases, and 68.2 million traffic or other ordinance violation cases. . . .

. . . By contrast, 45,043 appeals and petitions were filed in federal appellate courts during 1988; 4,775 in the U.S. Supreme Court. There were also 240,232 new civil filings and 44,761 new criminal filings during 1988 in the U.S. District Courts, the main federal trial courts.

Walter Olson's observations aside, it is a fact that almost one in every three citizens will be involved in a legal action in any given year. The statistical argument to justify the claim that we are experiencing a "litigation explosion" could continue. Given that the median duration of U.S. marriages hovers between five and seven years, it is inevitable that the courts are going to spend a lot of time trying divorce cases, dividing property equitably, ascertaining—where required—the validity of grounds for divorce, determining the "best interests of the child," and so on. Olson also notes that "between 70 and 80 percent of obstetricians have been sued, as well as, reportedly, every neurosurgeon in Washington, D.C." But increasing litigation or litigiousness is driven not just by numbers but by a philosophical commitment to the "ideology of litigation," the belief that the most just solution to all social and personal problems can be found through the court system. And as Olson puts it, "A litigation explosion is a civil war in very, very slow motion." It is driven by moral outrage that is "all gas pedal and no brake," by an "immense professional body of lawyers [hired] to stir up grievance for profit."

But lawyers could not "stir up grievance for profit" unless the social-legal system in which they establish their centers of profit allowed this to occur. Most of Olson's book is taken up with tracing the changes in the legal system and our attitudes toward that system, changes that are increasing litigiousness. The book is intended as an extended search for the answer to the question Olson poses at the beginning of his book, "Why do Americans spend so much time and money fighting each other in court?" The answers are quite complicated.

No one whose work I have read has stated the case against using the court system to settle every legal dispute as eloquently as Walter Olson of the Manhattan Institute. One quotable comment:

No philosophy of community and mutual aid should welcome a regime of law that sets people against each other in adversarial bitterness at every turn. No philosophy of utilitarian growth and progress should favor paralyzing productive initiative by strewing the legal environment with concealed land mines of unpredictable jeopardy.

What are some of the things Olson would correct in the legal system to de-escalate litigation? The remedies suggested are numerous; just a few of them include eliminating vague laws, focusing the pleadings of plaintiffs in cases at law and eliminating "shotgunning" defendants with all manner of charges that are unsubstantiated by factual evidence before cases are allowed to go to trial, limiting damage awards, instilling in citizens a respect for alternative methods of resolving disputes, calling attention to the fact that life is pretty miserable in a society in which everyone insists on having his or her rights enforced to the fullest extent, dismantling the litigation industry that has cropped up around the court system—this industry includes, for example, "dial-an-expert testimony mills"—limiting the scope of discovery in civil and criminal cases, holding lawyers strictly liable for frivolous litigation, abolishing contingency-based fees, requiring—as in the English system—losers in legal contests to pay attorneys' fees for parties who prevail, and finding alternative ways of compensating people for harm experienced at the hands of others.

Clearly, however, this is a book with an underlying message. Litigation is not the unalloyed good it was once perceived to be. Litigiousness is exacting a heavy price from American society: the best minds are entering the legal profession, costly product and liability suits are diverting attention from productivity and competitiveness, "public confidence in the legal system" is ebbing away, meritless claims proliferate, and so on. Olson's thesis is supported by the cases he cites. Even if one disagrees with his case approach to examining the "litigation explosion," his book is one of the most thoughtful and provocative treatments of the subjects I have read. It is difficult to see how statistics or other objective data might cause one to reach the conclusion that we are not experiencing a "litigation explosion" fueled by something beyond increasing numbers of people with inevitable disputes to settle.

STEPHEN W. WHITE

Auburn University
Alabama

OWENS, HARRY P. *Steamboats and the Cotton Economy: River Trade in the Yazoo-Mississippi Delta.* Pp. xiii, 255. Jackson: University Press of Mississippi, 1990. $30.00.

This history of steamboats on the Yazoo-Mississippi Delta river system offers a detailed examination of the importance of steamboats for the spread of cotton production in the Southern economy. The Yazoo River, with its tributaries such as the Sunflower, the Tallahatchie, and the Yalobusha rivers, flows into the Mississippi above Vicksburg.

For planters at the landings on these waterways, the steamboat was the only way cotton and other products could be shipped to the New Orleans market and supplies brought back in return. Routes between the landings were known as "trades" as they were served by steamboats, and they were also the routes of passenger travel. Steamboats serving the Yazoo Delta numbered almost 250 before the Civil War, and their golden age was between 1870 and 1890. Harry Owens describes many individual boats and identifies their captains and owners. He focuses on the 45-year steamboating career of Sherman H. Parisot, commodore of the P. Line, which continued beyond the Civil War to 1890. A commanding figure, Parisot achieved a near monopoly of the trade on the Yazoo river system, though he was forced by larger competitors to abandon his intrusion into the New Orleans-Vicksburg trade.

Owens traces the evolution of Yazoo steamboats from sidewheelers to sternwheelers, along with their specialization as cotton gin boats, sawmill boats, ice and mail boats. He describes their shallow hulls and superstructures, which rose three decks to the pilot house. Most post-Civil War boats were between 75 and 150 feet in length, and some reached 200 feet. Parisot's passenger steamers were elegantly furnished and became the "floating palaces" of popular description. Most steamboats were built along the Ohio River, and their life span was shortened by snags, sunken logs, fires, or explosions. Many that sank were raised, were repaired, and ran again. Two chapters in *Steamboats and the Cotton Economy* describe the Yazoo fleet in the Civil War, when "cotton-clad" boats were lined with as many as 2000 bales for protection.

There is more in this volume on steamboats and their role in the cotton trade than on the Southern economy. Four appendices list steamboats, wrecks, river landings, and commercial statistics. The book is marred by excessive, ill-chosen quotations, but the research on individual steamboats and the account of Parisot's steamboating career make this a useful addition to the study of the cotton trade in the Deep South.

RONALD E. SHAW

Miami University
Oxford
Ohio

SMITH, JAMES A. *The Idea Brokers.* Pp. 313. New York: Free Press, 1991. $24.95.

Former Princeton University President Woodrow Wilson, possibly the best-educated president in our history, took little interest in the technical qualifications of members of his cabinet. At a time when social scientists were beginning to take key roles in local and state governments, Wilson as president cautioned against overreliance on experts in national government. Wilson would be dismayed by what has happened in American government in the seventy years since he was in office.

Charging into office on the cry of populism and heralding the good common sense of the American people, Ronald Reagan employed more experts from think tanks than any president before him did. There was good reason for this in that many of these experts were in the vanguard of those who planned his campaign and helped elect him to office.

Reagan, however, was just the most obvious example of a stream of presidents who have come increasingly to rely on the use of technical experts—economists, sociologists, international specialists—to help them run the nation. Franklin Roosevelt had his brain trust—mostly from Columbia University—though he took their advice only when it suited his convenience. John Kennedy, Lyndon Johnson, and Richard Nixon all employed experts in their administrations and also used the talents of staff people from the dozens of think tanks that have developed in Washington since the early years of the century.

The earliest think tanks were staffed by university men—rarely women—who felt that social science could lead to better government. They presumed to offer independent and objective advice to the general public. The newest idea brokers, however, have come to be viewed as scholarly but nevertheless partisan sources of advocacy. The Heritage Foundation, for instance, gained in stature during the Reagan presidency because it presented solidly conservative positions in useful form for legislators and for journalists.

In *The Idea Brokers*, James Smith presents an able account of the growth of the think-tank industry. His analysis is both scholarly and lively and leaves the reader with the impression that ideas coming from think tanks can certainly be useful, but, as Woodrow Wilson might say, care should be taken to use them with caution.

FRED ROTONDARO

Congressional Affairs Press
Alexandria
Virginia

SOCIOLOGY

AMATO, JOSEPH A. *Victims and Values: A History and a Theory of Suffering.* Pp. xxvi, 263. Westport, CT: Greenwood Press, 1990. $45.00. Paperbound, $14.95.

Although this book delivers on both of the promises in its title, its focus is the second of the two: a theory of suffering or, rather, a theory as to why certain privileged claims to having suffered have acquired enormous moral currency in the late twentieth century. Amato is also interested in the degree to which "this immense opening to suffering and victims has the ironic consequence of making us uncertain of how to value our own suffering and that of others." These specific concerns shape the structure of the whole book, but they are particularly emphasized in the last three chapters and the conclusion, and they are Amato's primary concern as a moral philosopher who takes history seriously.

In order to get at his twentieth-century problem, however, Amato has two tasks: he must define suffering and isolate it from such related but separate topics as pain, which he does very well in the first chapter, and he must provide a history of the kind of suffering that has become a moral currency in the late twentieth century in order to explain its present prominence. He does this very efficiently in chapters 2 through 5, sweeping courageously from archaic societies to the twentieth century, focusing, as might be expected from his earlier work, upon the historically Christian tradition of European culture. Eugen Weber's foreword very nicely locates Amato's position as a philosopher and cultural historian.

Amato is a gifted synthesizer of original texts and much secondary scholarship both good and recent. The final two chapters will surely displease a large number of those who currently use the language of victimology, both its moral capital and the status of official victim claimed by some interpreters of the history of blacks, women, and other groups. Amato is certainly not immune to the suffering of official victims, but his concern is for the ways by which some suffering has become privileged to the exclusion of the suffering of others, rather than with the politics of suffering and the division of society into those who suffer or have suffered and those who allegedly did not and do not. Amato sets out to establish a perspective on the modern human condition from which the suffering of some does not negate the value, humanity, and suffering of others or, as he puts it in the conclusion, to restore to everyone their own stories, to value the element of sacrifice in suffering, the risks and gambles about the future that make suffering a common human enterprise, and to expand the dimension of human beyond the narrow discourse of suffering that often inadvertently denies the full humanity of others. Even those who may disagree with Amato ought to read this book. It is uttered by a human voice.

EDWARD PETERS

University of Pennsylvania
Philadelphia

COLEMAN, JAMES S. *Foundations of Social Theory*. Pp. xvi, 993. Cambridge, MA: Harvard University Press, Belknap Press, 1990. $39.50.

It is impossible to do justice to so ambitious a work in so constrained a space as that allowed for this review. We have in *Foundations of Social Theory* an effort to bring coherence to a discipline well known for its sharply divergent traditions. What makes this work notable is its bracing challenge to those who would see sociology differently. Coleman endeavors to set the conceptual tabula rasa for sociology as well as its modus operandi. Along the way, he gives the reader, even the reader who is not persuaded of his larger claims, a wealth of observations about the nature of social interaction, the character of social institutions, and the distinctiveness of modernity that make reading this long book well worth the time.

Organized into five sections—"Elementary Actions and Relations," "Structures of Action," "Corporate Action," "Modern Society," and "The Mathematics of Social Action"—this book is Coleman's endeavor to show how a sociology premised on the assumptions of classical economics can fulfill the ambition of being a science of society. This is no small task, not least because it flies in the face of what most sociologists, including most of sociology's founders, take for granted, namely, that sociology is a necessary corrective to the individualistic rational-actor premises of prevailing economic theory.

There is much to say for the abstract rational actor as a premise, but for all that can be said for this perspective, it precludes very important aspects of social life. One looks in vain for an extended discussion of race and ethnicity, or of love and passion—to name only two factors that have regularly confounded analyses of purposeful interaction. As it happens, much turns on what we take to be purposeful, not to mention who we take to be the "we." Once headed in this direction, hermeneutics is unavoidable and much if not all of the precision and neatness of Coleman's sociology begins to dissolve.

Coleman has given us a foundation for a social theory, not the only foundation of social theory. Though far from the last word, his words will be heeded by sociologists for some time to come.

JAN DIZARD

Amherst College
Massachusetts

DIZARD, JAN E. and HOWARD GADLIN. *The Minimal Family.* Pp. xiii, 285. Amherst: University of Massachusetts Press, 1990. $22.95.

Given the sustained popularity of family studies in the social sciences, it is not surprising that there should be an abundance of interpretive studies of the changing role of the family throughout American history. While any new foray taking this tack runs a risk of being dismissed as one of a flock, *The Minimal Family* has some distinguishing characteristics that will interest both scholars and general readers.

The book is a joint effort by a sociologist and a psychologist who managed to transcend their fundamental disagreements about the family's saliency in contemporary America. In crafting this humanistic study of the changing American family, Dizard and Gadlin employ a wide-ranging interdisciplinary approach in baring and analyzing the structural and functional changes that over time have altered the American family. The historical excursion leads the authors to conclude that the American family of today is in crisis, but this is nothing new, as the American family has never been a steady-state institution.

Much of the current crisis is attributed to external forces like advancing industrialization which in this century drastically altered the work world, stimulated rampant consumerism, and speeded the institutionalization of individualism. Such pressures altered the family and shaped it into what Dizard and Gadlin vaguely call the "minimal family" of today. This pattern is highly diversified and embraces such subforms as the conventional nuclear family with the breadwinning husband and the homemaking wife, the dual-career family, and various "unacknowledged" forms such as cohabiting couples, gay couples, single parents, and never-married adults. And it is through one or more of these forms that Americans seek the comfort of "familism," that constellation of interactive necessities that includes commitment, sharing, sacrifice, and loving intimacy.

For many Americans the quest for "familism" is frustrating and unrewarding, and families, by socializing children for autonomy and individualism, contribute to their own failings by instilling a fear of dependency. Thus Dizard and Gadlin venture the oft-heard suggestion that the burden of "familism" is too much for families to bear, but vouchsafe a less familiar idea that the "familial public" must be encouraged to take up the cause of meeting the familistic needs of Americans. In this "public" expansion of familism, which relies heavily on government programs and employer benefits, America lags behind other industrialized countries. It may not be politic to campaign on the issue of expanding the familial public, but the authors argue that we cannot afford not to do so.

The book is divided into six chapters, with the opening chapters covering the emergence of the modern family and the impact of industrialization and consumerism in shaping the middle-class nuclear family as the "normal" model earlier in this century. The third chapter shows how the forces of autonomy and individualism eroded parental authority by substituting the manipulation of "love" as a means of making children dependent on parents. Such trends account for the "eclipse" of the middle-class nuclear family and the appearance of other family forms such as the dual-career family and other, "unacknowledged" forms. A chapter on rampant individualism as the force that erodes the various family types sets the stage for the final chapter, which enables Dizard and Gadlin to sketch their vision of a "familial public" alternative.

This book is good social history with a challenging "diagnosis of our times" that echoes Karl Mannheim's book with this title. Thoughtful discussions of the impact of work on Americans, of individualization, of manipulative love, and of other topics are appealing. The sources are eclectic, well documented, and critically assayed. One might fault Dizard and Gadlin for failing to include Tocqueville on the impact of equality on American family life, LeMasters on parenting styles, and Jules Henry on the pitfalls of free-enterprise parenting, but there is enough breadth and depth among the sources to satisfy critical readers. Indeed, social scientists and thoughtful general readers are well served by this work.

DAVID Q. VOIGT

Albright College
Reading
Pennsylvania

HOLLAND, DOROTHY C. and MARGARET A. EISENHART. *Educated in Romance: Women, Achievement, and College Culture.* Pp. xiii, 273. Chicago: University of Chicago Press, 1990. $22.95.

PARR, JOY. *The Gender of Breadwinners: Women, Men, and Change in Two Industrial Towns, 1880-1950.* Pp. xiii, 314. Toronto: University of Toronto Press, 1990. No price.

These two excellent books are superficially very different from each other. One, by two anthropologists, is an ethnographic study of women students in two Southern colleges in the 1980s; the other is a historian's study of two industrial towns in southern Ontario between the 1880s and the 1940s. Yet their aims are similar: to explain the production, or reproduction, of gender roles and relations in specified cultural and social contexts. Both deftly use existing social theory to frame their questions, in the process stretching and challenging those theories. Further, these two studies of the textures and constraints of women's lives reach similarly ambivalent conclusions. In *The Gender of Breadwinners*, Joy Parr, working from a post-structuralist feminist stance, insists ultimately on the heterogeneity of women's as well as men's experience when viewed in the multiplicity of their work and family roles. Yet she also highlights the greater, and gender-based, success of men as compared to that of women in influencing and controlling work arrangements and town life. In *Educated in Romance*, Holland and Eisenhart argue that despite the vaunted opportunities for intellectual and professional mobility that college offers American women, female students' educational outcomes are most strongly influenced by the patriarchal system of male privilege reproduced by the peer group. Yet the authors also note that in the face of a virtual imperative that female students participate in that system of gender relations, a number of their subjects actively sought alternatives to, or at least temporary respites from, what the authors call the "sexual auction block."

Joy Parr, a Canadian historian, set out to identify for comparison two towns, one whose labor force was predominantly female, the other predominantly male. She chose Paris, Ontario, for its largely female knit-goods work force, and Hanover, Ontario, as a center of male-dominated furniture manufacture, and analyzed work and domestic culture in the two towns roughly from 1880 to 1950. She paints a richly colored portrait of these two very different villages. Paris was the seat of an important branch of "the largest knit-goods manufacturer in the country," which found itself short of hands in relying on local rural women, and so turned in the early twentieth century to the trained textile labor pool in the British midlands to recruit a female immigrant work force. Parr maintains that the special gendered work culture of this immigrant labor force strongly influenced the mill life of Paris: women who did lifelong wage work were not considered odd, and local commerce and mill rhythms gradually adapted to the special duties and life courses of wives and mothers who were also, most of the time, full-time mill workers.

In the furniture town of Hanover, by contrast, by the early twentieth century the male labor force in the numerous small firms was virtually all local, second- or third-generation German-Canadian, with deep family roots in the surrounding farmlands. Parr persuasively argues that in each community, the construction of gender both drew on broader Western norms and values and responded to the idiosyncratic local combination of ethnicity, economy, and politics. She gives a nice example of this complicated process in comparing the evolution of gendered ideas of knitting—"When is knitting women's work?"—in Ontario and in the English east midlands. Likewise, Parr sensitively analyzes the connections between Hanoverian workers' ideas of "manliness" and several big firms' short-lived attempts to introduce scientific management practices in the 1920s.

While Joy Parr challenges social theories that rest on "binary oppositions" of gender, class, or ethnicity, Dorothy Holland and Margaret Eisenhart use the revisions of social reproduction theory proposed by scholars conscious of class, racial, and gender issues as a grounding for their study of 1980s' college women. Commissioned by the United States National Institute of Education in 1979 to investigate "why so few women were becoming scientists or mathematicians," the authors developed a study that checked longitudinal ethnographic data from 23 women at two universities—one a majority white public school, the other a historically black college—against survey data from 357 respondents from the same institutions.

Holland and Eisenhart's preliminary research revealed an unexpectedly insistent factor in the women's undergraduate careers and educational outcomes: the student culture's "organization around romance and attractiveness." The authors identified an important qualifier, however, and one whose relation to the peer culture of romance they might have clarified earlier in their book: that is, the attitude toward schoolwork each woman student brings to college. Holland and Eisenhart identify three common "interpretations" of schoolwork: "work in exchange for 'getting over' [passing], for 'doing well' [getting high grades in something one was naturally good at], and for 'learning from experts' [acquiring desired skills and knowledge from instructors]." They found in their ethnographic study that there was a staggering discrepancy between the proportion of women in the combined "getting over" and "doing well" categories—18 percent—and the proportion of women in the "learning from experts" category—80 percent—who actually pursued their college interests in their careers. The surprising outcome is, of course, in the "doing well" category.

Most of the women who came to college expecting to do well in their courses, based on their high school performance, fell by the wayside academically after early disappointments, apparently believing that the amount of work they expended on their courses would not significantly affect their grades. These women became just as vulnerable to the peer culture of romance, and its common outcome of early marriage and marginalization of work identity, as the "getting over" group.

Troubling questions arise from this study. It calls out to be replicated in different student populations in different regions of the nation. To what extent was it a product of its historical moment, its region, or its structure? Aside from legitimate questions about the validity and universality of the study's conclusions, university personnel may have profound reasons to resist this portrait of student values without further probing. Holland and Eisenhart have written a persuasive, significant, and rather scary book.

MINA CARSON

Oregon State University
Corvallis

MOWLANA, HAMID and LAURIE J. WILSON. *The Passing of Modernity: Communication and the Transformation of Society.* Pp. xvi, 240. New York: Longman, 1990. No price.

Hamid Mowlana and Laurie J. Wilson have written an important and original contribution to development theory. Since the heyday of development efforts in the years following World War II, at least two major paradigms—modernization, based on liberal/capitalist notions of rationality and individualism, and dependency, based on Marxist/socialist notions of structural inequity—have emerged, neither of which adequately explains the process of social change as it has been variously experienced around the world. Mowlana and Wilson perceive a ground swell of a great human revolution incorporating critiques coming from both liberal/capitalist and Marxist/socialist paradigms that increasingly challenges those dominant traditions. In their place, the authors suggest a new paradigm that defines development not in terms of strategies and plans for solving specific social problems but in terms of culture, worldviews, and the total transformation of human societies. This third approach, which the authors label monistic/emancipatory, emphasizes humanistic, ethical, traditionalist, anti-bloc, and self-reliance theories of social development, and the centrality of communication.

Among its strengths, this book makes accessible Asian perspectives on social change, heretofore not widely included in discussions of development and communication. Islamic notions of dialectical tension between unity (*tawhid*) and fragmentation (*shirk*) and of history as societal rather than national are discussed, as are related Indian—*Brahman* and *atman* —and Chinese—*yin* and *yang*—concepts emphasizing the holistic and dynamic nature of change. By introducing these alternative, historically validated worldviews into the discourse on development, Mowlana and Wilson pave the way to a broader and richer definition of core concepts in the field.

The historical theoretical chapters of the book may be most useful to the majority of readers, especially those with background in the development field. Having grappled with the meaning of development myself and with graduate students for some years now, I found these sections stimulating. However, later chapters that review an admirably wide variety of case studies focusing on everything from folk media to satellite telecommunications are not, in my view, linked directly or clearly enough to the theoretical concerns raised earlier in the book. Sections on space technology do this, perhaps, best. This criticism aside, the book succeeds well at constructing a new, more truly international framework for development theory based on a view of societies as people in communication.

J. DOUGLAS STOREY

University of Texas
Austin

SALTMAN, JULIET. *A Fragile Movement: The Struggle for Neighborhood Stabilization.* Pp. xvii, 453. Westport, CT: Greenwood Press, 1990. $55.00.

WINNICK, LOUIS. *New People in Old Neighborhoods.* Pp. xx, 287. New York: Russell Sage Foundation, 1990. $29.95.

The dynamism of human communities is a virtual truism in sociology. Communities grow, decline, and change in desirable and undesirable ways. Since the founding of modern American sociology, understanding this change, often for the purpose of hastening or redirecting it, has been a core area of interest to social scientists.

New People in Old Neighborhoods focuses on the growth, decline, and renewal of Sunset Park, a neighborhood in Brooklyn, New York. Sunset Park was first settled by European immigrants from Ireland, Norway, and Finland. It was attractive because it was near the waterfront where many of these immigrants worked. These immigrants were later joined by Italians and Poles and by a smaller number of Greeks and Russians, including many Russian Jews who became retailers in the area. The growth of Sunset Park took place over a long period of time, but its decline was precipitous. Winnick blames three disastrous events for undermining the community. The con-

struction of the Gowanus Expressway lacerated and disfigured the neighborhood; suburbanization and declining manufacturing caused the loss of jobs and people; and a City Hall zoning law sacrificed the neighborhood for the sake of industrial development.

These events undermined the desirability of Sunset Park, and the events in subsequent years followed an all too common pattern. Declining housing values and a shrinking tax base made this area even less attractive. This was followed by an influx of absentee landowners seeking to exploit the incoming waves of Puerto Rican immigrants searching for low-cost housing. These immigrants found themselves at the mercy of slumlords and a housing market filled with overpriced substandard units.

The decision to locate a wholesale meat market in Sunset Park precipitated the formation of a neighborhood association dedicated to revitalizing the community. The organization quickly moved to stabilize the local housing market. This was done by salvaging derelict and abandoned structures and by developing programs to make money available for home repairs and purchases by low-income individuals.

Although his analysis focuses intently on the actions of the New York City Hall, neighborhood associations, and other actors in the community, Winnick sometimes hints that other forces played a role in the revitalization of Sunset Park. In fact, reading between the lines, one wonders how much the actions of the aforementioned organizations actually affected the growth, decline, and renewal of the neighborhood. At times, it seems that the fate of Sunset Park has depended more on the irresistible forces of international migration, housing markets, and the changing position of New York City in the world economy. Against such forces, what are the chances that a community can be altered by the actions of its groups or individuals? This is a nagging question that is scarcely addressed.

Juliet Saltman's *Fragile Movement: The Struggle for Neighborhood Stabilization* nicely complements Winnick's volume. While the latter deals with a single community and sometimes seems to gloss over important details, Saltman's work presents an in-depth look at five communities, along with less detailed descriptions of several others.

Saltman begins with a discussion of the theoretical frameworks that motivate her interests in community stabilization movements. Her views are shaped by an eclectic set of ideas taken from the race relations, social movement, and urban sociology literature. Although these ideas undoubtedly inform her discussion, Saltman scarcely mentions them in subsequent chapters.

Saltman is forthright about her biases, and these are reflected in her choice of case studies. Out of the five in-depth portraits, three are successes, one is an outright failure, and another shows mixed results. One may wonder how well these cases represent the actual distribution of successes and failures.

Indianapolis, Milwaukee, and Rochester are cities with neighborhoods cited as successful cases. In this instance, success is defined as the preservation of neighborhood integration and the maintenance of a neighborhood organization committed to that cause. The lone failure in this collection was Hartford, Connecticut, where segregation and white flight increased and the local neighborhood association faltered and went out of business. A neighborhood in Akron, Ohio, is designated a conditional case because, while racial integration declined, the neighborhood association devoted to combating this problem has survived into the present.

The events and circumstances affecting these communities are presented in exacting and sometimes excruciating detail. Included is information about staffing, funding levels, organizational structure, and often such minutiae as details about the publication of newsletters. Organizational documents are an important source of data for Saltman's analysis, and she omits few details about the subjects of her study.

In the last chapter, Saltman brings some order to the volume of information she presents, and she makes a credible case for her hypotheses about why some neighborhoods succeed in maintaining a racial balance while others cannot. Her list of factors contributing to neighborhood stabilization is fairly lengthy. Among these factors, however, she includes an effective fair-housing program, dispersal of public housing, and a supportive city. Saltman recognizes but pays little attention to large-scale factors such as the regional economy and the role of state government. Yet in a book already so rich in detail, this is perhaps an unfair criticism.

I would not hesitate to recommend either of these books to colleagues or students, though for very different reasons. I would recommend Saltman's book to professionals, graduate students, and advanced undergraduates needing a good source of secondary material about neighborhood organizations. For such persons and purposes, densely packaged information is a virtue. The Winnick book would appeal to undergraduates and others interested in a scholarly yet highly readable discussion of community change.

C. MATTHEW SNIPP

University of Wisconsin
Madison

SHANNON, GARY W., GERALD F. PYLE, and RASHID L. BASHSHUR. *The Geography of AIDS.* Pp. vii, 192. New York: Guilford Press, 1991. $30.00.

Shannon, Pyle, and Bashshur have produced a descriptive yet complex view of the epidemic of acquired immune deficiency syndrome (AIDS). The perspective presented most clearly is the geographic pattern of the epidemic. The sprinklings of virology, animal reservoirs, and social and behavioral science are more obtuse. One is tempted to be less critical of these latter shortcomings because of the authors' own self-effacing disclaimers. The fact remains, however, that the most useful parts of the book are concentrated in two chapters, 6 and 7. These are the chapters written most clearly, with the best understanding of the AIDS epidemic. These chapters deal with the AIDS epidemic as it is experienced in the United States, and the authors write best about this experience because it is in the United States that the epidemic is best understood.

The book begins with an overview and then follows with two more chapters about virology and possible origins of the virus. These three chapters flow easily but answer few pertinent questions about the epidemic. The authors present a variety of theories without clearly indicating which are false. The danger is that some readers may choose to believe the most incredible of these stories. If readers choose to believe that the virus is extraterrestrial, the material presented does little to dissuade them. Readers could as easily believe that the virus comes from sheep in European mountains or monkeys in Africa.

The fourth chapter begins to delineate the African experience with the AIDS epidemic. The geographic descriptions are weakest here, and the authors acknowledge the dearth of reliable statistical studies in the area. The social, political, and economic renditions are, on the other hand, quite fantastic. Descriptions of cultural practices including the levirate, exotic fertility rituals, and sexual mutilations are part of the narrative. Other discussions focus on social problems including prostitution, lack of preventive health care, and lack of hygiene. All these factors are held partially responsible for the unique pattern of AIDS in Africa. The possible influences of each of these social and cultural factors are speculative as well; the validity of explanations based on these social and cultural factors, however, cannot be greater than the reliability of the statistics used to measure them. Thus the authors may be right about only one thing in this chapter: that the persistent interest in Africa is driven by the unique distribution of AIDS on this continent—a 1:1 ratio of males to females—and, by extension, the implications this has for AIDS as a heterosexual threat in the Western world.

The sixth chapter marks the beginning of the usefulness of this book for understanding reliably the geography of the AIDS epidemic. The pages in chapter 5 describe the pattern of AIDS, its diffusion across the face of the United States, reliable state-to-state comparisons, unique regional aspects of the epidemic, and urban characteristics of the disease pattern. Chapter 7 discusses and documents briefly the cost and range of care for people with AIDS, ethical and legal issues, and policy implications for the U.S. public health care system.

The eighth and final chapter is in sharp contrast to the preceding pages. The methods are for a specialized audience, although the conclusions are stated simply enough for anyone to understand. The projections here concerning the expanding numbers of AIDS cases add to the admitted hundreds of expert projections already extant but introduce a spatial element.

In many ways, this book fails where the authors concede it fails and succeeds only partly where the authors attempt to succeed. The book is useful for a broad range of readers who have little expertise in any of the areas that it treats. There is a risk, though, that such unsophisticated readers may take for fact what is presented as speculation.

ROBERT J. JOHNSON

Kent State University
Ohio

STEIN, HOWARD F. *American Medicine as Culture*. Pp. xxii, 281. Boulder, CO: Westview Press, 1989. $29.95.

Howard F. Stein has written a fascinating and informative account of contemporary American medicine. Using what he refers to as a "psychoanalytically sensitive ethnographic method," he shows that there is far more to contemporary medicine than the science of maintaining and restoring bodily health. Like any ongoing collective human enterprise, medicine has its own complex culture. Understanding modern health care requires understanding that culture—how it shapes and is shaped by its participants as well as how it interacts with the culture of the society of which it is a part.

For Stein, this primarily means understanding the psychological nature of physicians, nurses, medical students, health care educators, medical institutions, and the like. It means understanding the largely unconscious, hence unacknowledged, motives and values that animate modern medical practice. If Stein is correct, and he does make a plausible case, modern medicine is not only about control and conquest of disease and illness. It is also about control and conquest of patients, control and conquest of vexing social problems, and, perhaps most important, control and conquest of the medical professional's own repressed fears and anxieties.

Stein seeks to provide readers with more than an outsider's understanding of medical practice while also penetrating beneath medicine's own self-image. In both these regards, he is largely successful. By taking us inside the practice of medicine and the psyche of the medical professional, Stein humanizes medicine. Behind the apparent scientific objectivity and neutrality of medicine we find human beings, under great stress, attempting to cope with their own psychic and cultural dilemmas while also struggling to provide the kind and the quality of health care that we demand.

American Medicine as Culture is a valuable resource for scholars of contemporary medicine and should also interest general readers. Unfortunately, readers who are dubious about the validity of psychoanalytic approaches will find little here to reduce their qualms since Stein often writes as if his psychoanalytic interpretations are self-evidently true. Fortunately, for me anyway, he usually translates his psychoanalytic jargon into more accessible language. The merits of his descriptions and analyses can therefore be appreciated even in the face of such skepticism. Furthermore, Stein makes extensive use of case studies, again and again allowing his subjects to speak for themselves. This, too, does much to mitigate the skeptical reactions bound to be provoked by his reliance upon psychoanalytic tenets.

MAURICE L. WADE

Trinity College
Hartford
Connecticut

WOLFE, ALAN. *Whose Keeper? Social Science and Moral Obligation*. Pp. xvii, 371. Berkeley: University of California Press, 1989. $25.00.

Sociological studies of the problems of postindustrial societies are numerous, but studies that combine theory and empirical research, detailed case studies and comparative analysis, and a moral imperative are rare. This important volume does a solid job in all these dimensions. It demonstrates that sociology can focus on the big picture as well as churn out detailed empirical case studies.

Wolfe joins the argument of how "modernity"—the life and values of advanced industrial societies—can maintain and expand social services while maintaining economic functions that provide the material basis of modern society. In keeping with the recent tradition of the social sciences, Wolfe reviews the roles of the state and the market. He does this in pursuit of three hypotheses: first, "neither the market nor the state was ever expected to operate without the moral ties of civil society"; second, society's increased reliance on either the market or the state for moral guidance will present increased tensions—contradictions; third, it is sociology's task among the social sciences to "recover the moral tradition" of the enlightenment.

The core of the book investigates how well contemporary society can be understood by using the market and the state as frameworks for analysis. The market is currently in great vogue, but Wolfe notes that contemporary advocates of market theories have ventured quite far from Adam Smith and the Scottish Enlightenment. Not least of the limitations on the market approach is a rigid and "imperialistic" economic determinism, which, ironically, closely resembles Marxist approaches. The more totally social relationships are perceived as forms of market transactions, the greater the damage to essential social institutions such as family and community. Wolfe does a solid job of tying these theoretical considerations to empirical evidence. While such aggregate socioeconomic data—for example, family income, home ownership, school attendance—are never unambiguous, they do place his arguments in a tangible context.

Wolfe's analysis of the role of the state looks carefully at American political science and political philosophy. He sees surprising similarities in the expectations of rationality and public interest in both the "rational choice"—Buchanan and Tullock—and moralist schools—Rawls. He makes these issues tangible in a concise and balanced review of the development of the Scandinavian welfare states since 1945. These experiences collectively represent the most sustained effort by democratic states to combine full social citizenship with democratic governance. The older welfare state based on transfer payments and social insurance has been increasingly supplemented with a new pattern in which the state strongly promotes "moral obligations in civil society." The most striking consequence of recent family policies is the "public family," with the state providing many services traditionally the responsibility of the private family.

Wolfe's description of both the accomplishments and the shortcomings of the Scandinavian experiments are comprehensive and fair. He is well tuned to the problems and anxieties that such efforts face. He does not fully anticipate or note the capping of social expenditures and the limitations in resources that have dominated Scandinavian policies in the past decade. Nor does he detect the accelerating shift toward privatization that was appearing by the mid-1980s. These changes were at first very limited indeed, but it will be interesting to see whether privatization in the Scandinavian context will combine universal and adequate programs with innovative and more efficient means of delivery.

In the concluding section Wolfe masterfully brings society back into the picture and with it the case of sociology. It may be as populist as ideal markets—

based on how large numbers of people choose to act—and as authoritative as the state, aggregating the dynamic rules by which people live and act. Sociology continues to provide both empirical data and provocative theories that can shape the public discourse. Wolfe's tour de force of the discipline, especially its comparative dimensions, and its potential moral contributions are inspiring and encouraging.

ERIC S. EINHORN

University of Massachusetts
Amherst

ECONOMICS

COHN, THEODORE H. *The International Politics of Agricultural Trade: Canadian-American Relations in a Global Agricultural Context.* Pp. x, 267. Vancouver, Canada: University of British Columbia Press, 1990. $36.95.

Agriculture has two major characteristics that complicate trade in farm products: first, many industrial countries encourage agricultural output—generate surpluses—through subsidies, price supports, or other government policies; second, agricultural trade is not covered by the General Agreement on Tariffs and Trade (GATT) or any other global convention. Indeed, one of the chief U.S. goals in the current, Uruguay round of GATT trade negotiations has been to extend the GATT to agricultural goods. In *The International Politics of Agricultural Trade*, Theodore H. Cohn examines the interplay between the political and economic factors, both domestic and international, that have affected U.S.-Canadian agricultural exports to third countries.

Cohn's model encompasses four dependent variables: the level of conflict in the bilateral U.S.-Canadian relationship; the amount of cooperation in bilateral

relations; the choice of strategies to achieve agricultural trade objectives; and the ability of each country to achieve its objectives.

Focusing on the period between 1950 and the late 1980s, he examines eight independent variables. These include four "environmental" variables: the U.S. balance of payments; political/security objectives—for example, who is willing to sell to which Communist nations and on what terms; the relative economic sizes of the two countries; and the degree of interdependence between the two nations. There are also four agriculture-specific variables: the state of supply relative to demand in world markets; the relative sizes of the two nations' agricultural economies; competition in agricultural trade; and the strength or weakness of the international agriculture-trade regime.

These North American nations are two of the world's largest agricultural exporters. Since wheat is a major product and export of both nations and is important in international trade, Cohn uses the history of the two countries' policies relating to the domestic production and export of this grain to illustrate his arguments. During crop year 1984-85, the United States and Canada, respectively, accounted for 13.7 and 4.1 percent of world wheat output and—again respectively—36.6 and 16.8 percent of international wheat exports.

From an economic perspective, Cohn's conclusions—for instance, that with a far-larger agricultural economy, unilateral U.S. actions have more impact on international wheat trade than do Canadian actions—are not surprising. In the context of international relations, however, his findings are both important and reassuring. Cohn finds that except for a few years in the 1970s and the early 1980s, the two nations have generally sought to resolve trade frictions through consultation; that conflicts have often encouraged new forms of cooperation between the two nations; and that competition for markets has often given rise to new forms of Canadian-U.S. cooperation.

Theodore Cohn has produced a well-written volume on the political economy of trade in farm products. *The International Politics of Agricultural Trade* provides the wherewithal to understand the domestic and international political and economic dynamics underlying the ongoing efforts to achieve freer markets—both domestic and international—for agricultural products.

MICHAEL ULAN

U.S. Department of State
Washington, D.C.

DiFILIPPO, ANTHONY. *From Industry to Arms: The Political Economy of High Technology.* Pp. ix, 204. Westport, CT: Greenwood Press, 1990. $42.95.

The central theme of this book is that the military dimension of U.S. policy concerns has absorbed the nation's technological development to such an extent that the American industrial economy has seriously suffered. There is a declining quality of life, DiFilippo asserts, as measured, for example, by falling or stagnant real median family income in the past twenty years, by the collapse of employment in once-prosperous basic industries like steel and the concomitant rapid rise of "low paying service jobs," and by a swiftly decaying national infrastructure —roads, bridges, harbor facilities, sewage systems—and related public services.

At the same time, the essential thrust provided to technological development by research and development (R&D), whether financed by government or private corporations, has had a decided bias favoring the military sector, not least because of the huge R&D component—in 1987 over $48 billion—in the U.S. mili-

tary budget and the profitable prospects provided by defense contracts. The spin-off effect of all this military-oriented R&D for nonmilitary productive uses "is minimal at best," DiFilippo argues. For example, the advanced technological research developed to free U.S. submarines from detection by enemy sonar is said to have "no practical application." What is needed, therefore, is a new "industrial policy" for the United States justified by new, post-Cold War realities and lowered threat perception. There should be a "conversion process" in the American economy, which, according to DiFilippo, in one year alone could divert as much as $150 billion from military uses to an upgrading of productivity and competitiveness in the nonmilitary sector.

DiFilippo is not an economist but an associate professor of sociology at Lincoln University in Pennsylvania and the author of other works on political economy, including a 1986 case study of the declining American machine tool industry and its relation to the military focus of U.S. technological development. His new book, fact-packed and laden with statistics, in successive chapters deals with the criteria and the "conventional explanations" for the decline of the American "post-Industrial" economy. It then takes up the primary defense concerns of U.S. government policy and the resulting "resource drain" in competitive innovation and nonmilitary R&D, and then it examines the elements needed for a new "reindustrialization" of the U.S. political economy. Such a new industrial policy, DiFilippo concludes, "unburdened by military expenditures," not only would open the way to a more effective use of the nation's resources but, at the same time, could give workers "progressively more participatory power" in the shaping of production policies that directly affect them.

Each chapter is well annotated and there is an excellent and comprehensive bibliography, which demonstrates the author's wide-ranging and interdisciplinary approach to technology and industrial policy. Because the book has avoided the more arcane analytical equipment of the economist, it is of value also to, among others, the general reader seeking an understanding of some of the current problems bedeviling the American economy and its competitive position in the world.

The main thesis of this book, however, hardly is new. Not only has it been a staple of the Left for decades, but in the past four years discussion has abounded concerning what to do with a presumed peace dividend and how to make the U.S. economy more competitive. DiFilippo's suggested prescriptions, in his concluding chapter, are much too categorical and pat. He is not aware of how difficult it is to bring about deep economic change in a modern industrial democracy.

More fundamentally, if the current national U.S. debate over a new industrial policy in the United States has suggested anything, it is that the extent of global interdependence today, whether in technological innovation or in the procurement of the resources of production and marketing of goods and services, requires a much broader policy scope than is provided in these pages. It is no longer a question of exploring "the transition to a civilian economy" in the United States but of relating that transition to the changing and ever more sharply competitive economics of Western and Eastern Europe and Japan and to the persistent and catastrophic lag in many parts of the Third World. Insightful as DiFilippo's book often is, it is being overtaken by the speed with which the problems of an international economy—resource allocation, stabilization of commodity prices, currency control, trade and investment restriction and liberalization, social conditions and human rights—are pressing upon American industrial policymaking.

A global analysis also helps to put the ailments of the U.S. economy in a proper perspective. In 1989, the total value of all goods and services produced by the world was $24 trillion. The U.S. economy alone accounted for more than 15 percent of this, and no other national economy is even close. Nonetheless, there is no room for complacency, to be sure, and DiFilippo's contribution is a valuable diagnosis of where improvements may be made.

JUSTUS M. VAN DER KROEF

University of Bridgeport
Connecticut

KELLER, MORTON. *Regulating a New Economy: Public Policy and Economic Change in America, 1900-1933.* Pp. x, 300. Cambridge, MA: Harvard University Press, 1990. $27.50.

BEST, GARY DEAN. *Pride, Prejudice, and Politics: Roosevelt versus Recovery, 1933-1938.* Pp. xvii, 267. New York, Praeger, 1991. $45.00.

Although examining different chronological periods, both books under review offer revisionist interpretations of federal regulatory policies and their legacies. Owing to methodological deficiencies, both fail to substantiate their interpretations.

Keller's monograph is the more sophisticated and comprehensive of the two. Primarily a derivative work based on an extensive and often insightful reading of the secondary literature, Keller's study chronicles the disruptive changes wrought by the rise of big business, technology, and the emergence of a more consumer-oriented economy during the first three decades of the twentieth century. He then analyzes how these changes both precipitated and defined federal regulatory policy. In the process, he offers to the nonspecialist an impressive overview of Progressive Era and New Era economic policy. Keller's purpose, however, is not simply to synthesize earlier scholarship but to offer an original interpretation subsumed in what he claims are two guiding themes of "persistence" and "pluralism": "the importance of institutional and ideological *persistence* in the regulation of the economy" and that "*pluralism* best describes the configuration of early twentieth-century public policymaking." Keller does not convincingly document this thesis of persistence and pluralism, having based this interpretation on a review of selected contemporary periodicals. His research sample is both incomplete and unrepresentative in that the consulted periodicals document the priorities of elite opinion alone. That the elite shared a narrow consensus and sought to accommodate demands for change within established institutions and without repudiating the conventional wisdom is not evidence of the forces shaping and defining popular and congressional regulatory policy. In addition, Keller tends to compress time periods and thereby to minimize the impact of the events and the underlying assumptions that distinguished Progressive Era and New Era politics.

Best's approach differs markedly, and his research methodology is neither rigorous nor well conceived. Harshly critical of the Roosevelt New Deal, Best contends that Roosevelt and New Deal economic policy decisions failed to address realistically the crisis of the Great Depression and that this failure stemmed from Roosevelt's pride, prejudice, and politics. To Best, not only did Roosevelt fail to grasp reality, but his refusal to follow the advice of his critics, and his adherence instead to the "nonsense" offered by advisers such as Felix Frankfurter, stemmed from deficiencies of his "mind and character" and his "pathological" aversion to his critics in the business and journalist communities. Yet, Best does not document these harsh criticisms by researching records relating to Roosevelt's decisions and underlying philosophy. His research centers instead on contemporary criticisms of the Roosevelt New Deal, most notably by conservative columnists and newspapers—H. L. Mencken; *Chicago Tribune*—or business publications and representatives, such as the *Wall Street Journal* and the National Association of Manufacturers. These sources do not offer insights into Roosevelt's priorities and decision making but rather into the politics and priorities governing the responses of formerly powerful public opinion leaders whose advice no longer shaped national policy during the 1930s. From unquestioned dominance during the New Era, economic leaders in the academic, journalist, and business communities experienced a striking loss of influence with the adoption of the New Deal. Not surprisingly, then, they became strident critics of the New Deal. Best's work, however, suffers less from a questionable methodology than from an underlying ideological bias. For when he assesses Roosevelt's lack of "realism," he does so based on particular conceptions, stated in his prefatory comments: "A wise president, entering the White House in the midst of a crippling depression, should do everything possible to stimulate enterprise. . . . and will consult with competent business and financial leaders, as well as economists, to determine the best policies to follow." That apparently simple statement is based on very specific value and ideological assumptions as to what constitutes both competence and consultation. Identifying uncritically with Roosevelt's contemporary critics, Best in essence reaffirms the criticisms that former Republican President Herbert Hoover affirmed throughout the 1930s and after 1945. The resulting tendentious monograph, more a polemical tract than serious historical inquiry, says more about Best's politics and prejudices than about the philosophy and assumptions governing New Deal regulatory policy during the 1930s.

ATHAN THEOHARIS
Marquette University
Milwaukee
Wisconsin

OTHER BOOKS

AKAHA, TSUNEO, ed. *International Handbook of Transportation Policy.* Pp. 408. Westport, CT: Greenwood Press, 1990. $65.00.

ALLEN, JOHN and LINDA McDOWELL. *Landlords and Property: Social Relations in the Private Rented Sector.* Pp. viii, 209. New York: Cambridge University Press, 1989. No price.

ANSARI, MAHFOOZ A. *Managing People at Work: Leadership Styles and Influence Strategies.* Pp. 218. Newbury Park, CA: Sage, 1990. $26.00.

BARROW, DEBORAH J. and THOMAS G. WALKER. *A Court Divided: The Fifth Circuit Court of Appeals and the Politics of Judicial Reform.* Pp. xiv, 274. New Haven, CT: Yale University Press, 1990. Paperbound, $13.95.

BARRY, JOHN M. *The Ambition and the Power: A True Story of Washington.* Pp. 788. New York: Penguin Books, 1990. Paperbound, $12.95.

BEAN, FRANK D., GEORGES VERNEZ, and CHARLES B. KEELY. *Opening and Closing the Doors: Evaluating Immigration Reform and Control.* Pp. 156. Lanham, MD: RAND/Urban Institute Press, 1989. $23.75. Paperbound, $9.25.

BENTON, LAUREN et al. *Employee Training and U.S. Competitiveness: Lessons for the 1990s.* Pp. vii, 115. Boulder, CO: Westview Press, 1991. $34.50.

BERKOWITZ, BRUCE D. and ALLAN E. GOODMAN. *Strategic Intelligence for American National Security.* Pp. xiii, 232. Princeton, NJ: Princeton University Press, 1989. $19.95.

BROMLEY, SIMON. *American Hegemony and World Oil.* Pp. viii, 316. University Park: Penn State Press, 1991. $39.50.

BURCH, MARTIN and BRUCE WOOD. *Public Policy in Britain.* 2d ed. Pp. viii, 251. Cambridge, MA: Basil Blackwell, 1990. Paperbound, $21.95.

CAMPBELL, WALLACE J. *The History of Care: A Personal Account.* Pp. 256. New York: Praeger, 1990. $42.95.

CARLSON, JERRY S., BARBARA B. BURN, JOHN USEEM, and DAVID YACHIMOWICZ. *Study Abroad: The Experience of American Undergraduates.* Pp. 264. Westport, CT: Greenwood Press, 1990. $42.95.

CHAPPELL, PHILIP, JOHN KAY, and BILL ROBINSON. *Which Road to Fiscal Neutrality?* Pp. xi, 56. London: Institute of Economic Affairs, 1990. Paperbound, no price.

CLATTERBAUGH, KENNETH. *Contemporary Perspectives on Masculinity: Men, Women and Politics in Modern Society.* Pp. ix, 182. Boulder, CO: Westview Press, 1990. $39.95. Paperbound, $14.95.

CRESPI, IRVING. *Public Opinion, Polls, and Democracy.* Pp. xii, 148. Boulder, CO: Westview Press, 1989. $39.95. Paperbound, $15.95.

DARNTON, ROBERT. *Berlin Journal 1989-1990.* Pp. 352. New York: Norton, 1991. $22.95.

DEIGHTON, ANNE. *The Impossible Peace: Britain, the Division of Germany, and the Origins of the Cold War.* Pp. x, 283. New York: Oxford University Press, 1990. No price.

DiIULIO, JOHN J., Jr., ed. *Courts, Corrections, and the Constitution: The Impact of Judicial Intervention on Prisons and Jails.* Pp. 338. New York: Oxford University Press, 1990. No price.

DUNN, JOHN. *Interpreting Political Responsibility.* Pp. viii, 274. Princeton, NJ: Princeton University Press, 1990. $49.50. Paperbound, $16.95.

EDWARDS, GEORGE C., III. *At the Margins: Presidential Leadership of Con-*

gress. Pp. xiv, 233. New Haven, CT: Yale University Press, 1990. $27.50. Paperbound, $12.95.

EDWARDS, GEORGE C., III with ALEC M. GALLUP. *Presidential Approval: A Sourcebook.* Pp. vix, 214. Baltimore, MD: Johns Hopkins University Press, 1990. $35.00.

ERRINGTON, ELIZABETH JANE and B.J.C. McKERCHER, eds. *The Vietnam War as History.* Pp. 216. New York: Praeger, 1990. $42.95.

FEATHERSTONE, MIKE, ed. *Global Culture: Nationalism, Globalization and Modernity.* Pp. 411. Newbury Park, CA: Sage, 1990. $47.50. Paperbound, $19.95.

FEHRENBACHER, DON E. *Constitutions and Constitutionalism in the Slaveholding South.* Pp. xiv, 115. Atlanta: University of Georgia Press, 1989. $16.00.

FELDMAN, MARTHA S. *Order without Design: Information Production and Policy Making.* Pp. xii, 201. Stanford, CA: Stanford University Press, 1989. $29.50. Paperbound, $9.95.

FITZGERALD, FRANK T. *Managing Socialism: From Old Cadres to New Professionals in Revolutionary Cuba.* Pp. xiv, 162. New York: Praeger, 1990. $39.95.

FONTANA, BIANCAMARIA. *Benjamin Constant and the Post-Revolutionary Mind.* Pp. xvii, 165. New Haven, CT: Yale University Press, 1991. $25.00.

FOREMAN, CHRISTOPHER H., Jr. *Signals from the Hill: Congressional Oversight and the Challenge of Social Regulation.* Pp. x, 214. New Haven, CT: Yale University Press, 1990. $30.00. Paperbound, $11.95.

FORMAINI, ROBERT. *The Myth of Scientific Public Policy.* Pp. 160. New Brunswick, NJ: Transaction, 1990. $24.95. Paperbound, $14.95.

FRIEDLAND, ROGER and A. F. ROBERTSON, eds. *Beyond the Marketplace: Rethinking Economy and Society.* Pp. 365. New York: Aldine de Gruyter, 1990. $52.95. Paperbound, $25.95.

FRIEND, JULIUS. *Seven Years in France: Francois Mitterrand and the Unintended Revolution, 1981-1988.* Pp. xiv, 249. Boulder, CO: Westview Press, 1989. $34.95.

GILBERT, ALAN. *Democratic Individuality.* Pp. xv, 510. New York: Cambridge University Press, 1990. $59.50. Paperbound, $19.95.

GLOSS, MOLLY. *The Jump-Off Creek.* Pp. 186. Boston: Houghton Mifflin, 1990. Paperbound, $8.95.

GOLLIN, ALFRED. *The Impact of Air Power on the British People and Their Government, 1909-14.* Pp. xii, 354. Stanford, CA: Stanford University Press, 1989. $39.50.

GREELEY, ANDREW M. *Religious Change in America.* Pp. vi, 137. Cambridge, MA: Harvard University Press, 1989. $25.00.

GREEN, CHARLES and BASIL WILSON. *The Struggle for Black Empowerment in New York City: Beyond the Politics of Pigmentation.* Pp. xvi, 183. New York: Praeger, 1989. No price.

GUDMUNDSSON, BRUCE I. *Stormtroop Tactics: Innovation in the Germany Army, 1914-1918.* Pp. xvii, 210. New York: Praeger, 1989. $39.95.

GURTOV, MEL, ed. *The Transformation of Socialism: Perestroika and Reform in the Soviet Union and in China.* Pp. x, 258. Boulder, CO: Westview Press, 1990. $36.50.

HECHTER, MICHAEL, KARL-DIETER OPP, and REINHARD WIPPLER, eds. *Social Institutions: Their Emergence, Maintenance, and Effects.* Pp. vi, 342. New York: Aldine de Gruyter, 1990. $49.95.

HEINEMAN, ROBERT A., WILLIAM T. BLUHM, STEVEN A. PETERSON, and EDWARD N. KEARNY. *The World of the Policy Analyst: Rationality, Values, and Politics.* Pp. 192. Chatham,

NJ: Chatham House, 1990. Paperbound, $14.95.

HELLER, AGNES. *Can Modernity Survive?* Pp. vii, 177. Berkeley: University of California Press, 1990. $25.00.

HIGGS, ROBERT, ed. *Arms, Politics, and the Economy: Historical and Contemporary Perspectives.* Pp. 380. New York: Holmes & Meier, 1990. $45.00. Paperbound, $19.95.

HSÜ, IMMANUEL C. Y. *China without Mao: The Search for a New Order.* 2d ed. Pp. xviii, 324. New York: Oxford University Press, 1990. No price.

HUFF, C. RONALD, ed. *Gangs in America.* Pp. 351. Newbury Park, CA: Sage, 1990. $36.00. Paperbound, $17.95.

KAISER, DAVID. *Politics and War: European Conflict from Philip II to Hitler.* Pp. 435. Cambridge, MA: Harvard University Press, 1990. $29.95.

KAPLAN, JACOB J. and GUNTHER SCHLEIMINGER. *The European Payments Union: Financial Diplomacy in the 1950s.* Pp. xx, 396. New York: Oxford University Press, 1990. $72.00.

KELLEY, DONALD R. and HOYT PURVIS, eds. *Old Myths and New Realities in United States-Soviet Relations.* Pp. 192. Westport, CT: Greenwood Press, 1990. $39.95.

KENNEDY, MALCOLM J. and MICHAEL J. O'CONNOR. *Safely by Sea.* Pp. 346. Lanham, MD: University Press of America, 1990. $40.25.

KRYDER-COE, JULEE H. et al., eds. *Homeless Children and Youth: A New American Dilemma.* Pp. xviii, 323. New Brunswick, NJ: Transaction, 1991. $34.95.

LANDGREN, SIGNE. *Embargo Disimplemented: South Africa's Military Industry.* Pp. xv, 276. New York: Oxford University Press, 1989. $65.00.

LEE, LAI TO. *The Reunification of China: PRC-Taiwan Relations in Flux.* Pp. xviii, 179. New York: Praeger, 1991. $39.95.

LEIGHTON, MARIAN. *Soviet Propaganda: As a Foreign Policy Tool.* Pp. 190. Lanham, MD: Freedom House, 1991. $19.95.

LODGE, JULIET, ed. *The 1989 Election of the European Parliament.* Pp. xviii, 249. New York: St. Martin's Press, 1990. No price.

LOWENTHAL, ABRAHAM F., ed. *Exporting Democracy: The United States and Latin America.* Pp. x, 422. Baltimore, MD: Johns Hopkins University Press, 1991. $55.00.

MAGAT, RICHARD, ed. *Philanthropic Giving: Studies in Varieties and Goals.* Pp. xv, 360. New York: Oxford University Press, 1989. $49.95.

MAISEL, L. SANDY, ed. *The Parties Respond: Changes in the American Party System.* Pp. xviii, 363. Boulder, CO: Westview Press, 1990. $50.00. Paperbound, $19.95.

MANVILLE, PHILIP BROOK. *The Origins of Citizenship in Ancient Athens.* Pp. xiv, 265. Princeton, NJ: Princeton University Press, 1990. $35.00.

MASTNY, VOJTECH and JAN ZIELONKA, eds. *Human Rights and Security: Europe on the Eve of a New Era.* Pp. viii, 274. Boulder, CO: Westview Press, 1991. $45.00.

MELLER, PATRICIO, ed. *The Latin American Development Debate: Neostructuralism, Neomonetarism, and Adjustment Processes.* Pp. xiii, 220. Boulder, CO: Westview Press, 1991. $37.50.

MELMAN, YOSSI and DAN RAVIV. *Behind the Uprising: Israelis, Jordanians, and Palestinians.* Pp. 255. Westport, CT: Greenwood Press, 1989. $39.95.

MELVILLE, ANDREI and GAIL W. LAPIDUS, eds. *The Glasnost Papers: Voices on Reform from Moscow.* Pp. vii, 359. Boulder, CO: Westview Press, 1990. $42.50. Paperbound, $18.95.

MERQUIOR, J. G. *Liberalism Old and New.* Pp. xiv, 180. Boston: G. K. Hall, 1991. $24.95. Paperbound, $11.95.

MEZEY, SUSAN GLUCK. *No Longer Disabled: The Federal Courts and the Politics of Social Security Disability.* Pp. xiii, 195. New York: Greenwood Press, 1988. No price.

MIDDLE EAST WATCH. *Human Rights in Iraq.* Pp. xiv, 164. New Haven, CT: Yale University Press, 1990. $19.95.

MILNER, HENRY. *Sweden: Social Democracy in Practice.* Pp. xx, 260. New York: Oxford University Press, 1989. $39.95.

MORGAN, WILLIAM D. and CHARLES STUART KENNEDY. *The U.S. Consul at Work.* Pp. x, 260. Westport, CT: Greenwood Press, 1991. $45.00.

MORONEY, ROBERT M. *Social Policy and Social Work: Critical Essays on the Welfare State.* Pp. xiii, 257. Hawthorne, NY: Aldine de Gruyter, 1991. $41.95. Paperbound, $21.95.

NATION, R. CRAIG. *War on War: Lenin, the Zimmerwald Left, and the Origins of Communist Internationalism.* Pp. xviii, 313. Durham, NC: Duke University Press, 1990. $45.00.

NEHER, PHILIP A. *Natural Resource Economics: Conservation and Exploitation.* Pp. ix, 360. New York: Cambridge University Press, 1990. No price.

NOCK, ALBERT JAY. *The State of the Union: Essays in Social Criticism.* Pp. xxx, 340. Indianapolis, IN: Liberty Press, 1991. $20.00. Paperbound, $7.50.

PACEY, ARNOLD. *Technology in World Civilization.* Pp. 225. Cambridge: MIT Press, 1990. $19.95.

PERROW, CHARLES and MAURO F. GUILLEN. *The AIDS Disaster: The Failure of Organizations in New York and the Nation.* Pp. xii, 206. New Haven, CT: Yale University Press, 1990. $25.00. Paperbound, $9.95.

PLUCKNETT, DONALD L., NIGEL J. H. SMITH, and SELCUK OZGEDIZ. *Networking in International Agricultural Research.* Pp. xiii, 224. Ithaca, NY: Cornell University Press, 1990. $28.95.

RHOADS, JOHN K. *Critical Issues in Social Theory.* Pp. x, 374. University Park: Penn State Press, 1991. $45.00. Paperbound, $14.95.

RIPP, VICTOR. *Pizza in Pushkin Square: What Russians Think about Americans and the American Way of Life.* Pp. 224. New York: Simon & Schuster, 1990. $18.95.

ROSS, JOHN F. L. *Neutrality and International Sanctions: Sweden, Switzerland and Collective Security.* Pp. xiv, 248. New York: Praeger, 1989. $42.95.

RUSSELL, LOUISE. *Medicare's New Hospital Payment System: Is It Working?* Pp. xi, 114. Washington, DC: Brookings Institution, 1989. $22.95. Paperbound, $8.95.

SCHIEFFER, BOB and GARY PAUL GATES. *The Acting President.* Pp. xii, 397. New York: E. P. Dutton, 1989. Paperbound, $9.95.

SCOTT, JOHN. *A Matter of Record: Documentary Sources in Social Research.* Pp. x, 233. Cambridge, MA: Basil Blackwell, 1990. $49.95. Paperbound, $17.95.

SIVAN, EMMANUEL. *Radical Islam: Medieval Theology and Modern Politics.* Enlarged ed. Pp. xi, 238. New Haven, CT: Yale University Press, 1990. $27.50. Paperbound, $11.95.

SMITH, JOHN W. and JOHN S. KLEMANSKI. *The Urban Politics Dictionary.* Pp. xv, 613. Santa Barbara, CA: ABC-Clio, 1990. No price.

SOREL, GEORGES. *From Georges Sorel.* Vol. 2, *Hermeneutics and the Sciences.* Edited by John L. Stanley. Translated by John and Charlotte Stanley. Pp. 219. New Brunswick, NJ: Transaction, 1989. $44.95.

SPECTOR, LEONARD S. with JACQUELINE R. SMITH. *Nuclear Ambitions: The Spread of Nuclear Weapons 1989-1990.* Pp. xii, 450. Boulder, CO: Westview Press, 1990. $54.00. Paperbound, $12.95.

STEINBERG, SHELDON S. and DAVID T. AUSTERN. *Government, Eth-*

ics, and Managers: A Guide to Solving Ethical Dilemmas in the Public Sector. Pp. 184. Westport, CT: Quorum Books, 1990. $35.00. Paperbound, $12.95.

STILLMAN, RICHARD J., II. Preface to Public Administration: A Search for Themes and Direction. Pp. ix, 242. New York: St. Martin's Press, 1991. No price.

SUNDIATA, IBRAHIM K. Equatorial Guinea: Colonialism, State Terror, and the Search for Stability. Pp. x, 179. Boulder, CO: Westview Press, 1990. $34.95.

SWENSON, PETER. Fair Shares: Unions, Pay, and Politics in Sweden and West Germany. Pp. x, 260. Ithaca, NY: Cornell University Press, 1989. $29.95.

THAYSEN, UWE, ROGER H. DAVIDSON, and ROBERT GERALD LIVINGSTON, eds. The U.S. Congress and the German Bundestag: Comparisons of Democratic Processes. Pp. xxi, 582. Boulder, CO: Westview Press, 1990. Paperbound, $42.50.

TIBI, BASSAM. Islam and the Cultural Accommodation of Social Change. Translated by Clare Krojzl. Pp. xiv, 272. Boulder, CO: Westview Press, 1990. $37.00.

TODD, OLIVIER. Cruel April: The Fall of Saigon. Pp. viii, 470. New York: Norton, 1990. $24.95.

TUNANDER, OLA. Cold Water Politics: The Maritime Strategy and Geopolitics of the Northern Frontier. Pp. 194. Newbury Park, CA: Sage, 1989. $35.00.

UNITED NATIONS DEVELOPMENT PROGRAMME. Human Development Report 1990. Pp. x, 189. New York: Oxford University Press, 1990. No price.

WACHTER, KENNETH W. and MIRON L. STRAF, eds. The Future of Meta-Analysis. Pp. 238. New York: Russell Sage Foundation, 1990. $29.95.

WHITE, LUISE. The Comforts of Home: Prostitution in Colonial Nairobi. Pp. xiii, 285. Chicago: University of Chicago Press, 1990. Paperbound, $14.95.

WIARDA, HOWARD J., ed. New Directions in Comparative Politics. Pp. xiv, 274. Boulder, CO: Westview Press, 1991. $54.95. Paperbound, $18.95.

WILLBORN, STEVEN L. A Secretary and a Cook. Pp. viii, 214. Ithaca, NY: Cornell University, 1989. $32.00. Paperbound, $14.95.

WILLIAMS, PHILIP J. The Catholic Church and Politics in Nicaragua and Costa Rica. Pp. xvi, 228. Pittsburgh, PA: University of Pittsburgh Press, 1989. $34.95.

WILLIAMS, ROBERT F. The New Jersey State Constitution: A Reference Guide. Pp. 192. Westport, CT: Greenwood Press, 1990. $49.50.

WILLIAMSON, OLIVER E., ed. Organization Theory: From Chester Barnard to the Present and Beyond. Pp. vi, 214. New York: Oxford University Press, 1990. No price.

WILLMOTT, H. P. The Great Crusade: A New Complete History of the Second World War. Pp. xii, 500. New York: Free Press, 1990. $24.95.

WOOD, ALLEN W. Hegel's Ethical Thought. Pp. xxi, 293. New York: Cambridge University Press, 1990. $49.50.

ZOPF, PAUL E., Jr. American Women in Poverty. Pp. xviii, 211. Westport, CT: Greenwood Press, 1989. No price.

INDEX

227

The ANNALS of the American Academy of Political and Social Science

ELECTRONIC LINKS FOR LEARNING

Special Editors: Vivian M. Horner and Linda G. Roberts

The remarkable technological advances of the electronics and telecommunications revolution have affected the personal and professional lives of millions, both in America and abroad. Television, radio, and video entertain, while computers, copiers, and fax machines propel business toward the twenty-first century. Technology has entered the classroom too: students and teachers are facing new challenges to the current system of print-oriented, classroom-based instruction.

Until recently, there's been no clear consensus on how to employ these powerful technological resources to meet the critical needs of the educational process. **ELECTRONIC LINKS FOR LEARNING** examines today's learning environment and the unique ways of bringing information to new audiences.

From foreign language instruction in American high schools to skill improvement for teachers in Indonesia, **ELECTRONIC LINKS FOR LEARNING** presents cutting-edge articles and a series of evaluative case studies in the use of new technologies.

Educators, policymakers, social and behavioral scientists, and human resource professionals will find this volume of **THE ANNALS** an invaluable guide for exploring the possibilities and effects of this rapidly expanding field.

The ANNALS, Volume 514, March 1991

Softcover	*Hardcover*
$15.95 individual	$25.00 individual
$23.00 institution	$28.00 institution

SAGE PUBLICATIONS. INC.
2455 Teller Road
Newbury Park. CA 91320

SAGE PUBLICATIONS LTD
6 Bonhill Street
London EC2A 4PU. England

SAGE PUBLICATIONS INDIA PVT LTD
M-32 Market. Greater Kailash I
New Delhi 110 048 India

Was This The Last Time You Bought Insurance?

Face it — it's been a long time. A lot has changed since then. Your family. Maybe your job. And more than likely, the amount and types of coverage you need from your insurance program. That's why you need insurance that can easily adapt to the way your life changes — AAPSS Group Insurance Program.

We Understand You.

Finding an insurance program that's right for you isn't easy. But as a member of AAPSS, you don't have to go through the difficult and time consuming task of looking for the right plans — we've done that work for you. What's more, you can be sure the program is constantly being evaluated to better meet the needs of our members.

We're Flexible.

Updating your insurance doesn't have to be a hassle. With our plans, as your needs change, so can your coverage. Insurance through your association is designed to grow with you — it even moves with you when you change jobs.

We're Affordable.

What good would all these benefits be if no one could afford them? That's why we offer our members the additional benefit of reasonable rates, negotiated using our group purchasing power. Call 1 800 424-9883 (in Washington, D.C., (202) 457-6820) between 8:30 a.m. and 5:30 p.m. Eastern Time for more information about these insurance plans offered through AAPSS:

Term Life • Excess Major Medical • In-Hospital • High Limit Accident • Medicare Supplement

AAPSS Insurance

Designed for the way you live today. And tomorrow.

STATEMENT OF OWNERSHIP, MANAGEMENT, AND CIRCULATION (See also attached P.S. Form 3526). 1A. TITLE: THE ANNALS OF THE AMERICAN ACADEMY OF POLITICAL AND SOCIAL SCIENCE. 1B. PUB. # 00027162. 2. DATE OF FILING: October 1, 1991. 3. FREQUENCY OF ISSUE: Bimonthly. 3A. # ISSUES ANNUALLY: 6. 3B. ANNUAL SUB. PRICE: Paper-inst. $120.00; Cloth-inst. $144.00; Paper-indiv. $39.00; Cloth-indiv. $54.00. 4. PUB. ADDRESS: 2455 Teller Road, Newbury Park (Thousand Oaks), CA 91320. 5. HDQTRS. ADDRESS: 3937 Chestnut Street, Philadelphia, PA 19104. 6. PUBLISHER: Sara Miller McCune, 689 Kenwood Ct, Thousand Oaks, CA 91360. EDITOR: Richard Lambert, The American Academy of Political and Social Science, 3937 Chestnut St., Philadelphia, PA 19104. MNG'NG EDITOR: Erica Ginsburg (same as editor). 7. OWNER: The American Academy of Political and Social Science, 3937 Chestnut Street, Philadelphia, PA 19104. 8. KNOWN BONDHOLDERS, ETC.: None. 9. NONPROFIT PURPOSE, FUNCTION, STATUS: Has not changed in preceding 12 months.

	Avg. No. Copies of Each Issue During Preceding 12 Months	Act. No. Copies of Single Issue Published Nearest to Filing Date
10. Extent & Nature of Circulation		
A. Total no. copies	6443	5826
B. Paid circulation		
1. Sales through dealers, etc.	787	255
2. Mail subscription	4403	4393
C. Total paid circulation	5189	4648
D. Free distribution/free copies	141	141
E. Total distribution	5330	4789
F. Copies not distributed		
1. Office use, etc.	1113	1037
2. Return from news agents	0	0
G. Total	6443	5826

11. I certify that the statements made by me above are correct and complete.
Nancy Hammerman, Acting Director, Sage Periodicals Press